HELL
ABOVE
EARTH

HELL
ABOVE
EARTH

The Incredible True Story of an American
WWII Bomber Commander
and the Copilot Ordered to Kill Him

STEPHEN
FRATER

St. Martin's Press ✿ New York

HELL ABOVE EARTH: THE INCREDIBLE TRUE STORY OF AN AMERICAN WWII BOMBER COMMANDER AND THE COPILOT ORDERED TO KILL HIM. Copyright © 2012 by Stephen Frater. All rights reserved. Printed in the United States of America. For information, address St. Martin's Press, 175 Fifth Avenue, New York, N.Y. 10010.

www.stmartins.com

Library of Congress Cataloging-in-Publication Data

Frater, Stephen.
    Hell above earth : the incredible true story of an American WWII bomber commander and the copilot ordered to kill him / Stephen Frater. — 1st ed.
        p. cm.
    ISBN 978-0-312-61792-9 (hardcover)
    ISBN 978-1-4299-5682-6 (e-book)
    1. Goering, Werner, 1924– 2. United States. Army Air Forces. Bomb Group, 303rd—Biography. 3. Bomber pilots—United States—Biography. 4. Göring, Hermann, 1893–1946—Family. 5. Rencher, Jack P., 1921– 6. B-17 bomber—History—20th century. 7. World War, 1939–1945—Aerial operations, American. 8. World War, 1939–1945—Campaigns—Europe. 9. World War, 1939–1945—German Americans— Biography. 10. World War, 1939–1945—Participation, German American. 11. German American soldiers—Biography. I. Title.
    D790.253303rd.F74 2012
    940.54'4973092—dc23
    [B]
                                                                            2011041352

First Edition: March 2012

10 9 8 7 6 5 4 3 2 1

For Dr. and Mrs. Stephan I. Frater

CONTENTS

AUTHOR'S NOTE

Goering in German is spelled using the umlaut: Göring. For clarity's sake I have used "Goering" to refer to Werner and members of his family in the United States and "Göring" to refer to Hermann Göring and his ancestors in Europe. Karl F. Goering's name, as recorded by U.S. Immigration, the passenger list of German ocean liner *Bayern,* and the U.S. Census Bureau is spelled with a *K.* At some point, Karl switched to the more anglicized spelling, "Carl." I have used the former throughout.

Dialogue in certain chapters has been reconstructed from firsthand source interviews, mission group reports, post-incident reports, airmen's private journals, and wartime letters home.

Personal interviews were conducted with all Goering crewmen then alive: pilot Werner Goering; copilot Jack Rencher; top-turret gunner Orall Gustafson, and also with wing commander William Heller. The passage of sixty-seven years has no doubt left room for omission, error, or lapses. Dialogue is therefore not a verbatim transcript, but it is the way these aviators all seem to remember the war—as if it happened yesterday.

Any errors, which I'm sure exist, are strictly my own.

ACKNOWLEDGMENTS

"Writing history, A.J.P. Taylor used to say, was like W. C. Fields juggling: it looks easy until you try to do it yourself," is the way distinguished historian Andrew Roberts introduced his latest book. Truer words have never been written.

This book would have never started without the help, kindness, and encouragement of Michael Korda, to whom I owe a debt I can never repay. My agent, Michael Carlisle, and his talented colleague Lauren Smythe at Inkwell Management, were always there for me with wise, patient, and confident counsel. My editors at St. Martin's Press, Marc Resnick and Sarah Johnson, waded through ever-shifting drafts and shaped the book in too many ways to describe. Werner and June Goering opened their home, scrapbooks, and a lifetime of memories to a total stranger. Their children, Scott Goering and Carlinda Dirks, have been stalwart supporters since the very beginning and I thank them and Werner's granddaughter Zoe Dirks, for their tireless efforts. The late great Jack Rencher, his son Brian, and daughter-in-law Monica, all devoted innumerable hours to help me. It is a personal regret that Jack did not live to see his story in print. Jack's sister, Gladys Ashton, was kind enough to always make herself available, as did Jack's niece and Gladys' daughter, Kay Johansen. Gary Moncur spent hours helping me with everything from fact-checking to finding photos; his dedication to the 303rd BG, as historian, is a tribute to his late father, Vern, and all Hell's Angel airmen. Mark Forlow, and Mike Faley, the historian for the 100th Bomb Group and the 13th Combat Wing and board member of the Eighth Air Force

Museum and Roger A. Freeman Eighth Air Force Research Center pointed me in the right direction on more than one occasion. Baerbel Johnson, German genealogy specialist at the Family Library Division of The Church of Jesus Christ of Latter-Day Saints undertook an incredible research effort in pinning down the Goering family tree back to 1601. Dresden historian Marshall De Bruhl provided me with tremendous insight into the horrors and conflicting rationale surrounding the subject matter I was about to tackle. George Hoidra, public affairs director of the Eighth Air Force Historical Society and Dr. John Q. Smith of the Air Force Historical Studies Office at the Pentagon both made generous contributions and suggestions. My good friends John and Marjorie Meyer helped make this book a reality by providing encouragement and support which I appreciate beyond words. Dr. Ivan Harangozo always helped at critical junctures, no matter at what hour. Connie Konsler spent untold, mind-numbing hours sorting through various drafts and was an indispensible and talented editorial assistant. Joni Adno, the daughter of John Pyram King, a WWII copilot made stylish and wise suggestions and graciously introduced me to her father. Talented editor Hilary Hinzmann provided generous detailed editorial guidance at an early stage without which this book could not have been completed. John Flicker also provided crucial editorial assistance. Thanks as well to Sally Sheets Wiggins, Elizabeth Curione, Mark Lerner, Fred Preller, Douglas Keeney, Phyllis A. Blackwell, C. Douglas Sterner, Mike Connelly, Jan Gehle, and last but never least, my brother, Thomas, my sister, Dr. Susan Stephens, and my nephew, James Christopher Stephen, who all provided me with periodic morale boosts and a belly laugh whenever the road seemed too steep.

Heartfelt thanks to all.

PREFACE

While writing a nonfiction book review about the Battle of Britain, I stumbled across newspaper articles, books, and military Web sites that categorically stated that Nazi Luftwaffe head Hermann W. Göring, Adolf Hitler's legal successor, had American relatives including a nephew, Werner G. Goering, who was a WWII bomber pilot in the European theater.

Army records confirmed that Werner, a twenty-one-year-old "Mighty Eighth" army air force captain in early 1945, commanded forty-nine "Flying Fortress" combat missions over Nazi-occupied Europe, well beyond the thirty sorties that then constituted a lead pilot's tour of duty. He could have gone home by Christmas 1944 as most of his original crewmates did, but at the peak of the bloody air war, Werner signed on for a second tour with the British-based 303rd Bombardment Group, famed as the Hell's Angels, one of America's most storied warrior fraternities and the single most active bomber group in the army air force. He fought until the bitter end—the Nazi surrender on May 8, 1945. Among a fistful of other medals, he received the Distinguished Flying Cross, one of the nation's highest military decorations.

Gary Moncur, the 303rd Bombardment Group's historian and son of Captain Vern Moncur, a WWII Hell's Angels pilot, features Werner's story on the unit's Web site, where a page is devoted to the irony of the Goering crew fighting against the Luftwaffe led by Werner's infamous uncle, Hermann Göring. When I contacted him for information about Werner, Gary's reply was: "Good luck. I've never met, corresponded, nor spoken with him." Werner would have been eighty-five and Gary thought he was still alive.

During the sixty-five years following the Nazi capitulation, Werner attended only one annual reunion of the Hell's Angels, in 1992 in Boise, Idaho—the hometown of his copilot, Lt. Jack Rencher. Goering's appearance was a singular tribute to his lifelong friend and copilot. He is the unit's reclusive, legendary specter and prodigal son who served his country well beyond a full measure and then seemed to vanish. It took months to reach Werner for a brief phone call. Taciturn and wary—he hated reporters—he didn't want to talk about the war or his family with a stranger, yet consented to meet if I was willing to come to Tucson. But, he warned, "It will be a waste of your time and money, since I didn't do anything special and left the war behind a long time ago." Days later, while flying to meet the reclusive Goering, who avoided the spotlight for nearly seven decades, it hit me that it was the chronological equivalent of meeting a Civil War veteran in 1930. He is among the very last of his peers—a man who saw and did things the world had never previously experienced and never will again. He quietly carried the burden of his blood-soaked surname throughout the war and beyond; battled the Nazi war machine in the war's longest and deadliest battle for Americans; and was nearly assassinated by a suspicious U.S. government even as the Luftwaffe was killing his comrades by the tens of thousands. Being an aloof, quiet loner and nondrinker didn't help. He avoided the officer's club, the center of WWII military social life, which just heightened the mystery surrounding the "damn reservist" American pilot with the infamous surname. "What the hell was Werner Goering doing piloting an American heavy bomber over Germany?" It was a question military and civilian intelligence had struggled with and prepared for, with extreme prejudice, if and when the need arose.

Stephen Frater
Narragansett, Rhode Island
June 24, 2011

Is not God in the height of heaven? And behold the height of the stars, how high they are! And thou sayest, How doth God know? Can he judge through the dark cloud? Thick clouds are a covering to him, that he seeth not; and he walketh in the circuit of heaven.   —Job 22:12

For a long time we hated the idea of the heavy bomber. . . . We now know that the champion, that the backbone of air power is the heavy bomber.
                                        —*Bombs Away*, John Steinbeck, 1942

HELL
ABOVE
EARTH

PROLOGUE

1943. Werner has the world by the tail, or perhaps vice versa.

As a new pilot, he has one of the most dangerous training assignments in the army. Fifteen thousand fellow aviators, kids mostly, will die in stateside accidents without ever seeing combat, but somehow he's sure that won't happen to him. He is a Goering, born to command men in the air as his uncle Hermann did in WWI. But now, Hermann Göring is Werner's personal enemy.

The army has just tossed the nineteen-year-old former slacker, who barely graduated at the bottom of his high school class, the keys to a new 4800-horsepower warplane that tops out at 302 miles per hour and can obliterate an entire postal code. His B-17 heavy bomber carries two and a half tons of explosives and cruises at altitudes three times higher than a man can breathe at—almost a mile higher than the tip of Mount Everest—where wisps of clouds form pearly shrouds that will permanently envelop 120,000 Allied airmen in the European theater during this war.

He is responsible for the lives of ten highly trained youngsters, a ton of intelligence and signals data, a top-secret Norden bombsight, and a hell of a lot of firepower. A winged, righteous avenging angel with a personal grudge, commanding the world's most sophisticated weapons system: for the tall, handsome, squeaky-clean, blond, blue-eyed Mormon son of German immigrants, this is as good as it gets. His faith and the military have imbued him with ideals delivered in familiar noble words: sacred glory, salvation, duty, sacrifice, war against evil, peace on earth.

Less clear are images of insanity, drowning, burning, freezing, dismemberment, or quietly spiraling from the heavens, like Icarus, into an inferno he has ignited. For Werner, it's not just good versus evil; it's about a young kid reclaiming the family name and fighting an evil warlord in his own arena—the skies over Germany. Werner, on the side of light, proudly wears hard-earned silver wings on his puffed-out chest. He is going to war, the biggest, bloodiest war humanity has ever fought, a war in which strategic airpower—his chosen specialty, his only art—is the key factor.

The world is tearing itself apart, yet Werner fears no evil since he believes, beyond any shadow of a doubt, that his Lord and Savior cradles him in the hollows of his bloody hands.

Given the odds he faced, Werner needed divine protection. He was about to join "the war's longest continual battle." Army-issued Colt .45 pistols held seven rounds. If a man were to play Russian roulette with one round in the magazine, he'd have about a 14 percent chance of dying—almost the same odds as a Mighty Eighth WWII-era bomber crewman had on any given day. On some days in some units, more than 40 percent were lost; on others, none, yet of those who flew in the Mighty Eighth, more than 12 percent died in ways too varied and horrible to imagine.

The Luftwaffe captured, repaired, studied, and flew dozens of B-17s, and their fighter command quickly discovered its Achilles' heel; early Flying Fortress models lacked adequate forward-firing capability. Despite having a dozen .50 caliber Browning machine guns, none could be pointed dead ahead, so German pilots simply engaged them head-on at closing velocities that approached the speed of sound.

Commanding *Ruthie II* in 1943, en route to bomb Hanover, pilot Robert L. Campbell, Ruthie's husband, and copilot John C. Morgan had just made landfall over the continent when they were attacked head-on by a BMW-powered 1700-horsepower Focke-Wulf 190 fighter, described by its designer as a "cavalry horse as opposed to a racehorse." A machine-gun burst from the fighter blasted through Campbell's windshield, "splitting his skull," but not killing him instantly. Campbell "collapsed forward over the control column" and clasped "his arms tightly around it so the copilot, Morgan, had to use brute force to work the controls on his side" to keep the bomber under control. The "striking six-footer Morgan needed all of his 200 pounds to overcome the crazed strength of the dying pilot," as Campbell, out of his mind, attacked his friend Morgan and tried to wrest the controls away. The dying pilot, streaming blood, punched the copilot in the face, knocked some teeth loose, and blackened both eyes as Morgan fended off the blows with his left fist while keeping his roundhouse right firmly on the yoke. The shock of the awful injury and unexpected life-or-death struggle in the cockpit went unnoticed by the eight other men whose lives depended on the outcome. Morgan hollered for help over the plane's interphone but got no reply. "The same burst of fire that mortally wounded Campbell also struck the top turret gunner, severing Sgt. Tyre C. Weaver's left arm just below the shoulder." During a cockpit emergency, it was usually the navigator or the top gunner—the men closest to the cockpit—who came to assist. Weaver "slid down into the rear of the nose compartment and slumped onto the floor behind the navigator, Lt. Keith J. Koske, who immediately went to his aid." Since the interphone was inoperable, the horrific drama under way in the cockpit continued for more than an hour, unknown to the other crewmen, who were initially fighting off waves of Luftwaffe fighters.

In the rear of the plane, the waist gunners, radio operator, and tail gunner had all fallen unconscious from lack of oxygen since the plane's onboard oxygen system had been knocked out. They were in mortal danger. Koske, wearing a portable oxygen unit, tried to tie off Weaver's arm with a tourniquet, but there was not enough of a stump left. He also tried to give the turret gunner a shot of morphine, but the syrette, likely frozen, malfunctioned. Realizing Weaver would never survive the four-hour return flight, Koske strapped a parachute onto Weaver and was dragging him to the escape hatch when Weaver, in shock, jerked the chute open with his remaining hand while still inside the howling cabin. Koske bundled the billowing silk under Weaver's sole arm and shoved him into space. Unaware of the gruesome struggle under way in the cockpit, he then went aft to find out why the guns were silent and rendered aid to the unconscious and badly frostbitten gunners. Almost two hours had passed since Campbell had been shot in the head when Koske finally moved forward to find Morgan still "flying with one hand while keeping the still-struggling Campbell off the controls." Morgan, not hearing his plane's guns firing, assumed that most of his crew had bailed out. And, despite his ordeal, had continued on and completed his Hanover bombing run. With Koske's help, they were finally able slide the pilot out of the cockpit, where the navigator "held him to prevent him from slipping through the open hatch." After the successful bombing run, Morgan returned to England and landed at the first RAF station he saw and became a Medal of Honor recipient. Weaver, the one-armed turret gunner, survived his ordeal as a POW. The army memorialized the incident for propaganda purposes in a heroic cartoon that can be seen on YouTube, at "Medal of Honor—with One Hand."

Soon, a new Fortress model was introduced, the B-17G, which featured forward-firing machine guns mounted in a Plexiglas "chin turret" that the bombardier operated.

Another 1943 mission gained the dubious distinction of "the biggest fiasco" of the year. As 338 B-17s rumbled toward Stuttgart, cloud cover was heavy and fighter opposition was scarce. In the opinion of historian Roger Freeman, both were indicators that the attack should have been called off. The Germans, using cloud-penetrating radar, had figured out the target and were marshaling their forces over Stuttgart. As the bombers reached their target, several fighter groups approached the formation from the eleven o'clock and twelve o'clock positions. At twenty-second intervals, entire squads of fighters attacked the formation and rolled out for another pass; thirty-one Fortresses and 310 men were lost in short order. "The 563rd bomb squadron . . . was completely wiped out."

And again, on the afternoon of October 14, 1943, remembered today as "Black Thursday," before long-range P-51 Mustangs were available to escort the bombers, the Mighty Eighth lost sixty Flying Fortresses: 600 men were missing or dead, and another 47 dead or wounded were unloaded from the "lucky" stragglers that managed to return from an attack on Schweinfurt's ball-bearing production center. "The loss incurred . . . amounted to more than double the ten percent of force figure that the Eighth Air Force considered prohibitive. . . . Morale at bomber bases was at a low ebb and . . . the Fortress crews were . . . incurring a casualty rate higher than any other branch of the U.S. Forces."

1

"NOW TERROR, TRULY"

The thundering ships took off one behind the other. At 5,000 feet they made their formation. The men sat quietly at their stations, their eyes fixed. And the deep growl of the engines shook the air, shook the world and shook the future.

—John Steinbeck, 1942

Perhaps it was the scale, as well as the horror of it all, that still boggles the mind. Before WWII no one had seen anything like the terrifying spectacle of hundred-mile-long armadas of 2,000-plus bombers and fighters regularly and methodically razing the continent. Day after day, night after night, airmen took flight over Europe, bombing and strafing factories, ports, and cities, killing hundreds of thousands of civilians in the process.

Between 1940 and 1945, the United States, with the help of more than 3 million workers hustled onto assembly lines, produced 296,000 airplanes at a cost of $44 billion—more than a quarter of the war's $180 billion munitions bill. The gross national product soared 60 percent from 1938 to 1942. Five million new jobs were created. GM employed half a million persons and accounted for a tenth of all wartime production. At the peak, Boeing was making sixteen new Flying Fortresses a day, and its 40,000 employees literally worked around the clock. Boeing lost $3 million in the five years before 1941 but enjoyed net wartime profits of $27.6 million. "Ford alone produced more military equipment . . . than Italy."

Across Nazi-occupied Europe, a calculated mixture of incendiary and high-explosive bombs obliterated buildings that had stood for centuries. Fire-driven, oxygen-sucking winds whipped flames into pyres of biblical proportions; some were hundreds of feet high and as wide as city blocks—convenient homing beacons for subsequent waves of bombers. Automobiles and streetcars melted in temperatures above 1,000 degrees Fahrenheit. Asphalt ignited and flowed like lava. People who sought safety in water towers, ponds, and fountains were trapped and "boiled alive." Others, who sought safety belowground, suffocated from a lack of oxygen.

In 1945, *Newsweek*, referring to civilian bombing, published an article entitled "Now Terror, Truly." Dresden historian Marshall De Bruhl wrote that "in less than fourteen hours, the work of centuries had been undone." The scene was similar in all major German cities. Most of Berlin was demolished. Toward the end, it was ceaseless: almost three-quarters of all the Allied bombs dropped on Europe fell during the final twelve months of the war. By May 1945, up to 80 percent of most of Germany's urban centers were wiped out and up to 650,000 civilians lay dead, 16 percent of them children. Another 800,000 were wounded. In France, 70,000 civilians died, in Italy another 50,000. England, by comparison, suffered 60,000 civilian deaths at the hands of the Luftwaffe. During the war, the Allies killed "two or three German civilians by bombing for every German soldier they killed on the battlefield." It was literally hell on earth.

The air battle over Nazi-occupied Europe was a different kind of fresh hell. It lasted about three years for the Americans and about double that for the English. It was the longest battle of the war, during which an average of about 115 Allied airmen died daily, as did about 650 civilians, including women, children, pensioners, and slave laborers, most of who died following the United States' entry into the war.

In his 1942 book, *Bombs Away*, Stanford University dropout John Steinbeck neatly summed up the challenge facing bomber crews and their commanders.

> Of all branches . . . the Air Force must act with the least precedent, the least tradition. Nearly all tactics and formations of infantry have been tested over ten thousand years. . . . But the

7

Air Force has no centuries of trial and error to study; it must
feel its way, making its errors and correcting them.

The errors and corrections were recorded in blood. About 26,000
men and women died in aircraft accidents during the war. In the British-
based U.S. Army's Eighth Air Force alone, another 26,000 Americans, or
12.3 percent of the third of a million men who flew, were killed in
action—more than the total U.S. Marines death count for the entire war.
Only the United States' Pacific submariners suffered higher fatality
rates—more than 20 percent. Yet in total numbers, the Eighth Air Force
alone lost more than seven times the global number of U.S. submariner
fatalities. The Mighty Eighth suffered 26,000 combat deaths out of its
350,000 officers and men who flew. By comparison, the U.S. Navy suffered 37,000 deaths out of the 4.1 million who served in the WWII Navy.
The battle also cost the British Royal Air Force 56,000 dead. If wounded
and captured airmen totals are included, the Eighth Air Force had "the
highest casualty rate in the American Armed Forces in WWII."

Allied saturation bombing shattered not only Nazi Germany's industrial spine but also American notions of isolationalism in a rabid war.
It washed away all naivety regarding the human and moral costs of industrial war in which the cogs of the machine are not only soldiers but
also the civilians supplying their material needs. Air war was, in large
part, about the substitution of capital for labor—of machinery for men. A
single crew of trained fliers could hope to kill a very large number of Germans even if they flew only twenty successful missions before being
killed or captured themselves.

The men who devastated Nazi Germany from the air are dying daily.
With them dies the personal experience of setting a continent aflame. Few
other men in history have deployed such devastating force for as long as
the crews of the U.S. Army Air Force did over Europe: 1,042 days, from
1942 to 1945. The air battle over Europe, one of the longest and costliest
of any war, heralded not only the nearly complete devastation of the
world's cultural cradle but also the controversial decision by Western democracies to engage in industrial-scale terror bombing on civilian populations. It neatly ushered in atomic-age rationale for a new corps of battle
planners, such as Maj. Curtis E. "Old Iron Ass" LeMay, to whom the
wholesale destruction of cities was a near-daily personal routine.

The men and boys, like Werner and Jack, who carried out these attacks, almost on a daily basis, weather permitting, were truly a unique breed of highly trained specialists utilizing the world's most sophisticated weapons platforms of the era. To combat the terror in the skies they faced, and Nazi terror on the ground, they were ordered to create a literal hell on earth for enemy military, industrial and, ultimately, civilian targets.

Although they slept in clean sheets and ate hot meals every day bomber crews flew, even while training, was like D-day, exacting tremendous amounts of emotional uncertainty and trauma. Some men, like Werner, accepted this, even thrived on and welcomed the adrenaline rush. Werner knew death could come in a variety of ways: an unlucky flak burst, Luftwaffe fighters that could appear anywhere at any time, pilot error while flying less than fifteen feet apart. Even the air they breathed four miles above the earth was deadly. Others suffered more as their mission totals mounted; the risks of air combat harrowed them fiercely as they neared the magic number that would allow them to return home, duty done.

Werner was an exceptional pilot. Gifted. His nerves of steel, combined with his unwavering ability to make split-second decisions, saw his crew safely home, mission after grueling mission. But for Werner, there was an added danger: he didn't realize that at any moment his family name could cost him his life.

2

THE BOTTOM RUNG

With the exception of the Civil War, the two greatest existential threats to the United States were the Great Depression and WWII, the latter being the greatest man-made catastrophe in human history. Hitting back-to-back as they did, anyone coming of age between 1930 and 1945 was exposed to the political equivalent of crippling childhood diseases: economic collapse and the rise of virulent, fascist militarism. The adolescent body politic, weakened by the first, was more vulnerable to the second. Like a teenager, America was headstrong, naïve, self-absorbed, increasingly muscular yet unsure, untested, and often unwise. Before heavy bombers and atomic weapons debuted in WWII, the rest of the world seemed distant, uninteresting, and dangerous to most Americans.

Even after the European war broke out in September 1939, for the first two years, most Americans had no clear picture of, and often little interest in, their nation's unique and vital role in the preservation of democratic freedom as a political system. "Let them fight their own wars," was a common sentiment promoted by those prepared to find accommodation with Hitler. The isolationists included the U.S. ambassador to Britain, Joseph P. Kennedy; Nazi sympathizer and Fascist anti-semitic Charles Coughlin, who had an audience of up to 30 million listeners, about a fifth of the country; Senator Alf Landon; and, most notably for air-war planners, aviator Charles Lindbergh, who before Pearl Harbor was the influential face of nearly 1 million members of the America First Committee, probably "the foremost non-interventionist [and] anti-war organization in American history." President Franklin

Delano Roosevelt (FDR) was privately convinced that Lindbergh was a Nazi. "If I should die tomorrow, I want you to know this," Roosevelt exploded to Secretary Henry Morgenthau in May 1940, "I am absolutely convinced that Lindbergh is a Nazi."

Polls taken in July 1940, ten months after the European war started, showed only eight percent of Americans supported war against Germany; immediately prior to Pearl Harbor, another poll confirmed what Franklin Roosevelt already knew: more than three-quarters of Americans remained opposed to another war with Germany. The nation of immigrants, with German Americans representing a fifth of the population, hoped and prayed they'd left thorny Old World rivalries and grudges behind, and focused on securing their personal patch of grass in the vast fields of opportunity that America offered. Roosevelt was forced to resort to blatant yet, in retrospect, forgivable and essential lies about the United States' likely entry into the war so as to secure his third term in 1940. During the run-up to the war and the all-important and unprecedented third-term 1940 elections, FDR's ability to juggle the fears and outright opposition of isolationists, his own military, the industrialists, and his Republican opponents in Congress—all simultaneously—surely ranks among the greatest of all of the master's political conjuring feats.

The large industrialists, almost all Republicans, who ran the companies FDR needed to kick-start the enormous military production runs were wary. The men running U.S. Steel, General Electric, General Motors, and Ford distrusted Roosevelt and saw an enormous one-customer arms market as both a danger to the profits that they enjoyed in making refrigerators, toasters, and automobiles; as well as a possible Trojan horse for a creeping form of socialism in which the government dictated both production and profit. His 47 percent to 42 percent win over Wendell Willkie, the isolationist Republican candidate, confirmed that FDR's sly, misleading, and cynical pragmatism trumped truth as total war loomed. He was the genial aristocrat with the common touch, the Hudson Valley gentleman farmer, the Wall Street lawyer, and the stamp collector who knew his country's industrial capacities were all that stood between freedom and global tyranny. This president, at this time, saw the future as few others could and did what was needed to save the world from a form of tyranny that could well have snuffed out the torch of liberty across the globe.

·　·　·

New immigrants always faced the hardest challenges, and so it was for the family of Karl Frederich Goering in Salt Lake City, Utah, during the Roaring Twenties and Great Depression. Karl's second son, Werner, was born eleven months after his family emigrated from Germany. In 1914, when WWI broke out in Europe, Karl Goering was a thirty-nine-year-old, balding, overweight bank accountant who spoke passable English. He had not served in the military as a youth and seemed destined for a respectable, humdrum petit bourgeois existence. Lacking any semblance of martial bearing, Karl was assigned safe, boring garrison duty in Cologne, a heavily fortified supply and transportation hub close to the Western Front where Germany was entangled in meat-grinding trench warfare with the Allies.

Cologne was targeted for some of the first Allied aerial bombings during WWI, but it never amounted to much since even the largest English biplane biplane bomber, the Handley Page 0/400, introduced in 1918, only carried about a dozen inaccurate two-hundred-pound bombs. Yet the experience profoundly affected Karl. Facing a scarlet sunset one evening atop a hill overlooking the city, he had a vision of Cologne consumed in flames. Werner recalled hearing his father tell the story in 1932 when he was eight years old. A dozen years later, Werner led bombing raids on Cologne that turned his father's apocalyptic premonition into a smoldering reality. His grandmother still lived in Cologne.

After WWI ended, in 1918, Karl worked in a Cologne-based bank for five years, as did Joseph Goebbels, an embittered young man with a Ph.D. in German literature from the prestigious University of Heidelberg. Goebbels, despite his sterling academic credentials, had failed completely as an author and was forced to take a job as a lowly bank clerk. (He developed his thesis, eighth-century romantic drama, under Professor Friedrich Gundolf, a noted Jewish literary historian.) In a few years he would become the best-educated top Nazi in the Reich.

Karl was enticed to the New Zion at Salt Lake by Mormon missionaries in Germany, yet as a banker and an accountant, he could not have missed the unmistakable implications of the postwar economic collapse of Germany triggered by the massive financial reparations demanded by the Allies in the Treaty of Versailles. The Allies initially demanded, in

1921, that Germany pay $31.5 billion. The final adjusted installment was only settled by Germany in 2010, nearly a century after the war started.

John Maynard Keynes, a British Treasury delegate at Versailles, published *The Economic Consequences of the Peace* in 1919, in which he argued for a more generous peace. The harsh reparations, to be paid to the Allies in gold, coal, and steel, engendered the widely held belief in Germany that the treaty was in fact a Carthaginian peace. Compared with the $13 billion Marshall Plan, which the victorious United States instituted in more than a dozen European countries after WWII, for enemies and allies alike, Versailles proved to be a shortsighted and ineffective devil's bargain.

Field Marshal Ferdinand Foch of France, who felt the restrictions on Germany were too lenient, declared, "This is not Peace. It is an Armistice for twenty years." He proved to be off by "only 65 days." The reparations undermined Germany's postwar economy, the Weimar Republic, and added fuel to the spark lit by nascent fascist movements that arose immediately after Versailles and culminated in Adolf Hitler's ascension to power fourteen years after the treaty was signed.

Karl, his wife, Adele, and their ten-year-old son, Karl Jr., sailed from Hamburg to the United States on the German ocean liner *Bayern,* and were processed at Ellis Island on April 19, 1923. In the 1930 U.S. Census they were registered as residents of Salt Lake City.

When Karl and his family left Germany, they joined the tail end of the largest wave of immigrants in U.S. history up to that time. From 1820 to 1920, 5.5 million Germans immigrated to the United States, more than from any other country, including 4.4 million Irish, 4.1 million Italians, and 3.7 million Austro-Hungarians—including their minorities of Slavs, Poles, Czechs, and a half dozen other, smaller ethnic groups.

Arriving in Salt Lake City in 1923, Karl Goering found menial work as an employee of the Mormon Church. At first, he worked as a common laborer, landscaping church property. For the nearly fifty-year-old overweight former bank clerk, pulling weeds and cutting lawns in Utah's blazing summer desert was a rude awakening to the reality of being an immigrant. As Karl's family settled into the large German American community in Salt Lake City, he let it be known that his younger brother Hermann, a famously decorated WWI fighter ace and successor to the Red Baron, was a close adviser to the strongman then rising in the fatherland, Nazi

13

Party leader Adolf Hitler. The Goerings took special pride in the eminence of Werner's famous uncle, Hermann.

For nearly two decades, from 1923 to 1939, the Utah Goerings, like many other German Americans, believed the Nazis were good for Germany. Werner read about Hermann's rise as Hitler's right-hand man when the world press ran articles about the handsome, aristocratic, and heroic former fighter commander and ace who had risen above all competitors in the führer's favor. When Hitler became chancellor of Germany in 1933, Reichstag president Hermann Göring was featured in a January 30 Associated Press article and accompanying photograph published worldwide. In the picture, Göring, Hitler, and Vice Chancellor Franz von Papen are all seated. Göring is on Hitler's right and is the first name mentioned in the photo caption. About a half dozen other long-forgotten members of Hitler's newly appointed cabinet stand in a semicircle behind the three leaders.

Compared to the economic chaos of the Depression, Germany's resurgence and low unemployment during the 1930s was envied worldwide. Fascist economies in Germany and Italy weathered the Depression better than democracies did. There was no avoiding the fact that a significant number of German Americans applauded Hitler and the Nazis for their economic policies. Karl felt a vicarious pride, and possibly a bit of envy. He sent congratulatory letters to Hermann and received replies. Werner recalled that the German community in Salt Lake City was "ecstatic" about the fatherland's accomplishments during the Depression.

Despite his menial job, Karl was fortunate to have been employed by the Mormon Church, the strongest and most stable financial and political entity in Utah. His work was tough but steady, and eventually Karl got an office job: he became both an accountant and a translator for the church. "We lived in a neighborhood full of immigrants; Swedes, English, Irish, Dutch, and we were all poor," Werner recalled. "Hell, three-fourths of the city was poor, but I don't ever remember going hungry." That was not the case for many dust bowl drifters and immigrants: Utah was among the hardest hit states, with an unemployment rate that topped out at 36 percent. In November 1930, police rounded up hundreds of indigent men who had followed the rails to Salt Lake and forcibly sent them packing. As elsewhere, credit and jobs evaporated. Banks suddenly imploded, along with the deposits of their customers, triggering runs on other financial institutions. During one of several runs on his Utah bank, Mariner Eccles—later Federal Reserve Board chairman for fourteen years, "managed to keep his institution open through an agonizing day of massive withdrawals . . . only by instructing his tellers to work in slow motion, deliberately counting out sums in small-denomination bills" and then counting them again. Hundreds of families lost their homes and lived in makeshift cardboard and tin hovels on vacant lots all over Salt Lake City. The city handed out free vegetable seeds until the money ran out.

The Goerings, although poor, benefited from Karl's steady employment during the Depression and, as it turned out, until his death in 1950. In 1936, the Mormon Church established the Church Welfare Plan. The local relief effort amounted to about 10 percent of the total federal expenditures in the state between 1936 and 1940, years when Utah received $7 in federal aid for every dollar sent to Washington in taxes. The level of per capita federal aid in Utah was among the highest in the nation.

For the Goerings, struggling through the Great Depression in Utah along with everyone else, Hermann's sudden and ostentatious displays of wealth and power were a stark contrast to their humble existence. When it came to graft and gluttony, the most notorious Nazi of all was Hermann Göring. According to Burleigh:

> The annual running costs of Goering's magnificent hunting lodge Carinhall [in Prussia] . . . were nearly half a million RM, on top of the RM 15 million the complex had already cost the taxpayer. Göring had another hunting establishment, Rominten, a villa in the Air Ministry complex in Berlin, an alpine residence on the Obersalzberg, a castle and five more hunting lodges scattered across Pomerania . . . then there was the special train with its bakery and wagons for 10 luxury automobiles. The two residential carriages alone cost the taxpayers RM 1.32 million per annum. The German car industry threw in a yacht called *Carin II* to complement Carinhall. named after his [first] wife worth another RM 750,000. His personal art collection, mostly stolen from Jews and others, had 1,375 paintings [Hitler owned 5,000], 250 sculptures, and

168 tapestries worth a total of several hundred million marks. His declared taxable income was RM 15,795, on which he paid RM 190 tax.

Karl gained status from his increasingly famous last name, and the family proudly spoke German at home and with their German neighbors.

When Karl and his family visited Salt Lake's movie palaces in the 1930s, the newsreels often included segments about Nazi Germany that featured the flamboyant Hermann Göring, either at Adolf Hitler's side or occupying the center of attention on his own. Among his multiple positions of authority, Hermann was the Nazis' aviation minister. In this role, he directed the buildup of German plane production, at first ostensibly for civilian purposes and then, in open defiance of Versailles, for the Luftwaffe, which Hitler unveiled in 1935.

It was a reflex action for the newsreels and other news media of those years to note the imposing, charismatic, and—before he ballooned in weight—even handsome figure presiding at flyovers of powerful new planes and similar events. As a German pilot in WWI, Hermann Göring had twenty-two "kills" of enemy aircraft, well more than the ten needed to qualify as an ace, and almost died after being shot in the thigh by a British Sopwith Camel biplane. He not only won the Iron Cross First Class and the Blue Max, Germany's highest military decoration, equivalent to the Medal of Honor; he was also chosen as the last commander of the Flying Circus, the world-famous fighter squadron originally led by Count Manfred von Richthofen, the famed Red Baron.

With no expectation that the United States and Germany would ever again be at war, why should Karl and his family not be proud of his heritage? Certainly there was no harm in enjoying vicarious glory within Salt Lake's German American community. Nor could there be any harm in Karl's instilling a spirit of emulation in Werner, who showed signs of possessing some of Hermann Göring's soldierly qualities.

Karl's dreams of a better life for his family gradually focused on Werner because of the boy's forceful personality and, at least to some extent, because of his appearance. If Werner physically resembled any male Goering, it was not his father or his older brother, but rather the young Hermann Göring. Throughout his boyhood and teenage years, Werner developed an ambition, encouraged by Karl, to distinguish himself as an officer in the U.S. military, possibly even as a pilot, like his uncle Hermann.

Despite his histrionics and increasingly ominous and bellicose prognostication, Hitler and his vision for Nazi Germany found admirers in such prominent observers and personalities as Charles Lindbergh, Henry Ford, former British prime minister David Lloyd George, and the soon to be former king of England, Edward VIII.

Lindbergh was one of the world's most respected heroes, an aviation expert and probably the world's foremost media sensation after his son's infamous 1932 kidnapping and murder in the "crime of the century." In 1936, Lindbergh "made a much-publicized visit to Nazi Germany . . . as the guest of Hermann Goering . . . [who] thoroughly brainwashed [him]." In Utah, twelve-year-old Werner saw newspaper features about Lucky Lindy's German adventures with Uncle Hermann.

In 1937, Werner entered South High School, where he proved to be an indifferent student. He "hated school," played no sports, joined no clubs, and barely graduated at the bottom of his class. He worked as both a paperboy and a uniformed Western Union telegram delivery boy. He often skipped school, stole hubcaps, and rode his bike down to the city's vast rail yards. "We were a bunch of no-good kids. My friend Guy Metnick, a Jewish kid, and I would hang around in pool halls."

Although Utah's Wasatch Mountains offered some of the best skiing in the world, "that was for rich kids," and Werner never tried it. The only place Werner stood out was in the high school's ROTC program, where, despite his low grades and insularity, a self-confident Werner became the student cadet commander.

In 1938, a month before *Kristallnacht,* the widespread Nazi rampage against Jews that resulted in numerous murders and $400 million worth of destruction to Jewish-owned businesses, Lindbergh was again fêted by Göring at the American embassy in Berlin. Göring awarded the politically hapless Lindbergh Germany's highest decoration for noncitizens: the bejeweled Grand Cross of the German Eagle. Lindbergh came away believing German aircraft production was at a level of 40,000 planes annually, more than four times Germany's actual capacity at that time. Ironically, Lindbergh's over-the-top production figures, fed to him by Göring, may well have had the opposite effect he intended in the White House.

Airpower was the key to everything, and although Roosevelt was physically immobilized by polio and nearly politically immobilized by widespread isolationist tendencies compounded by economic malaise at home, he was never paralyzed, blinkered, or buffered by Hitler. Although a self-confessed "navy man," and former assistant secretary of the navy during the Great War, Roosevelt spent far more on air armament than on any other single instrument of war, to the consternation of both the army and the navy.

Although the U.S. air corps budget nearly doubled from 1935 to 1938, FDR knew it wasn't enough. On October 16, 1938, the president approved a secret plan largely funded in a politically risky move, by the Works Progress Administration, the New Deal jobs program that chief aide Harry Hopkins oversaw, for the production of 15,000 warplanes annually.

Joseph Maiolo describes how FDR ordered Army Chief of Staff General Malin Craig to prepare personnel and facilities for the first of many increases in annual bomber production, the weapon Roosevelt knew would be critical in deterring or fighting the war he saw looming between the great powers.

A "flabbergasted" Craig, who desired traditional munitions expenditure increases instead, demanded, "What are we going to do with fifteen thousand planes? Who [are] you going to fight, what are you going to do with three thousand miles of ocean?" Roosevelt eventually needed and got almost 300,000.

Waving aside the chief's shortsighted concerns, Roosevelt approved the procurement of fighters, medium bombers, transport planes, naval aircraft and, above all, the "heavies," the B-17 Flying Fortress, the B-24 Liberator and, finally, and only at the very end of the war in the Pacific, the much-delayed and initially accident-prone "super-heavy" B-29 Super Fortress.

Right after *Kristallnacht,* on November 14, 1938, Roosevelt again called in his military advisers and demanded a "huge air force so we do not need to have a huge army to follow that air force." Deputy Army Chief of Staff George C. Marshall "stewed," while Air Force Chief "General Henry 'Hap' Arnold, the only aviator in the room, could barely contain his glee." FDR anted up the aviation arms race to a level his own military chiefs opposed, American industrialists feared, and his political opponents would have salivated over had the true numbers been common knowledge.

As the 1930s drew to a close, newsreels about Germany took on a darker tone. The signs of another war, and of Germany's central involvement in it, were unmistakable. For Americans, the big question was whether the United States could avoid being drawn into the approaching conflict. When the Nazis invaded Poland in September 1939, breaking the Munich agreement signed a year earlier with England and France, newsreel footage brought home the fact that Hermann Göring's Luftwaffe had been conceived and developed not to defend Germany but as the leading element of overwhelming offensive tactics against other countries.

The newsreels now included another kind of footage that could not fail to concern Karl Goering, his family, and their German American neighbors. In the equivalent of today's media "perp walks," the newsreels showed FBI agents sweeping up suspected German and German American members of Nazi spy rings.

Karl Goering was not alone in his increasing criticisms of Hermann Göring and the rest of the Nazi leadership after September 1939. Werner shared his father's anger, shame, embarrassment, and wounded pride. Hermann Göring had betrayed not only England, Poland, and France; he had also betrayed the Salt Lake City Goerings, shaming them in front of their friends and neighbors, and potentially implicating them in the eyes of U.S. authorities. When, just months after Pearl Harbor, the United States began interning German Americans suspected of disloyalty, they housed some of them in the Salt Lake City jail, a fact that every German American in town knew.

Karl cut correspondence with Hermann after war broke out, and the former pride in their family name turned to ash. Even worse, Werner wasn't the only one to take note of his father's ties to, and decade-long correspondence with, Hermann Göring. The letters most likely also caught the attention of the army, the FBI, and, most assuredly, the Abwehr, German military intelligence.

The situation changed dramatically in two stages for the Salt Lake Goerings, as it did for most Americans of German ancestry not already opposed to the Nazis. First was the German invasion of Poland in 1939, which Werner, then fifteen years old, remembered stunned his father. Not only had the Nazis brazenly lied, but also Göring's Luftwaffe had bombed civilians in Warsaw, making Germany an international pariah yet again. Second was the Japanese attack on Pearl Harbor on December 7, 1941, and the U.S. entry into war against Japan, Germany, and Italy.

From 1939 on, Karl Goering condemned the Nazis as fools leading Germany to ruin. Werner remembered that until the invasion of Poland, Hermann Göring remained a widely admired figure. The early letters that went back and forth between Berlin and Salt Lake City ceased when war engulfed Europe.

Hermann, obese, morphine-addicted, and happy with the status quo, was "skeptical" about the planned attack on Poland. Hermann worked furiously but unsuccessfully behind the scenes contacting English acquaintances, trying to prevent a widening of the war. He was preparing to visit England personally when Hitler announced the German-Soviet nonaggression pact, the news of which scuttled Göring's visit.

As the likelihood of U.S. participation in the war increased, Werner talked with his father about his options. His father never experienced WWI trench warfare, but he had seen its results in the endless flow of disfigured German youth through Cologne's rail hub. Expecting a similar bloody slog in the coming war, Karl discouraged Werner from the infantry.

When war broke out, Werner went to the recruiter to apply as an air cadet. He was told that with his lousy academic record and absence of college credits, he could only qualify by taking a special test the army offered to kids without two years of college, an expensive luxury during the Depression. Poorly educated kids from the lower social strata, like Werner, were not considered pilot material. The air force was still an elite branch of the military, populated with upper-class kids, West Pointers, and college graduates. Three days after Pearl Harbor, and a day before Hitler declared war on the United States, the army substituted the test for the college requirement; the next year it lowered the minimum age from twenty to eighteen and admitted married men for the first time, all to meet the quota. The qualifying test for kids like Werner was extremely tough, and the vast majority of those who took it never became pilots.

For the first time in his life, Werner was highly motivated and finally buckled down and studied furiously to prepare for the test, his only route to wings. "Something impressed itself on me that I had to pass this test. Had to. I read up on all the math, engineering, physics, mechanics, and hydraulics. I thought 'I'll never make it,' but was determined to try; and miracle of miracles, I passed." He "was tickled shitless." Had he known how deadly cadet training was, he might have been scared shitless instead. WWII-era U.S. aviation-related training and noncombat accidental deaths amounted to about eight times the combined fatalities of Pearl Harbor and D-day. For good reason the shocking statistics were kept secret during the war. Laura Hillenbrand notes:

> Pilot and navigator error, mechanical failure, and bad luck were killing trainees at a stunning rate. In the Army Air Forces . . . there were 52,651 stateside aircraft accidents over the course of the war, killing 14,903 personnel. . . . In August, 1943, 590 airmen would die stateside, 19 per day.

Werner wanted nothing more than to enter the war and fight the Nazis. He was determined to distinguish himself in combat and hoped to become a pilot. He entered what historian Stephen Ambrose called the army air force's "largest single educational organization in existence." In 1942, the army "determined that it needed one million air cadets," and it paid the price in lives and dollars. By 1944, more than a third of the army was in its air force. Colleges and universities across the land accelerated graduation schedules to meet military personnel requirements.

In November of 1942, Werner went to Santa Ana, California, for flight training. Having been an ROTC cadet commander served well; he already knew the parade ground inspections, drills, and marching instructions, which he had perfected in crisp, drill-master detail. He was appointed to a similar cadet commander role in the training corps, which gave him a leg up in the military hierarchy and likely contributed to his selection as a heavy-bomber commander.

He completed preflight studies, but during basic flight training he almost washed out when he turned in a shaky performance with an officer on board checking him out prior to his solo flight. The officer, contrary to the usual practice, gave Werner a miraculous second-chance "washout" flight during which his nerves calmed down, and he "flew like a bird."

Following advanced flight training, Werner chose to enter the multi-engine bomber program since he "figured bombers were the cutting edge of aviation technology." Through "sheer dumb luck at age nineteen," Werner became a heavy-bomber commander and trained at New Mexico's Roswell Field, where a school for specialized four-engine pilot and bombardier training had been established in 1941.

After completing a 100-hour B-17 training course as commander, Werner was sent to the Eighth Replacement Wing in Salt Lake City for crew assignment, when his military career suddenly and inexplicably stalled. Pilots and crew were being formed up and shipped out daily; Werner languished in limbo for months. The American intelligence services had tumbled to the implications of having a Goering in command of one of the air force's best and biggest bombers.

3

GERMAN AMERICANS IN WWII

An often overlooked aspect of the era is the suspicion directed at German Americans. The internment orders that President Franklin D. Roosevelt signed on February 19, 1942—a little more than two months after the Japanese attack on Pearl Harbor and declarations of war between the United States and the Axis powers of Japan, Germany, and Italy—applied to people of German and Italian, as well as Japanese, descent and nationality.

Not that the numbers of people interned were comparable. Some 110,000 Japanese Americans and Japanese residents of the West Coast were interned during WWII. By contrast, the FBI arrested 1,500 Italian aliens at the beginning of the war; 250 of them were interned for two years, until Italy's surrender in 1943. And a total of 11,507 German Americans and German aliens were interned for the duration of the war in locations throughout the country, including military bases and local jails. Another 4,500 people of German descent were extradited from fifteen Latin American countries.

The War Department drafted plans for mass expulsions of German Americans and German aliens from coastal areas but had to abandon them on practical grounds: German Americans were the most populous immigrant group in the country. Even compared to recent Hispanic immigration, German Americans remain the largest of all immigrant groups, although these demographics will change in the coming decades. Today's 51 million German Americans represent about 17 percent of the U.S. population.

Precise figures are not available because the Census Bureau did not keep the same categories of records then, but there is no question that German Americans formed an even larger percentage of the WWII-era population. Taking 20 percent as a conservative estimate, this would mean that more than 26 million of a total population then numbering 133.4 million people were of recent or distant German descent. The federal government did not have the resources to intern even a fraction of these 26 million men, women, and children.

As many commentators of the day pointed out, there was no rational basis for doing so. Most German Americans were fervent patriots and assimilationists, a tendency that greatly accelerated because of anti-German feeling during WWI. German Americans were prominent in every field, not least in the military. Several WWII military commanders, including Dwight D. Eisenhower and Chester W. Nimitz, had German ancestors. "Two Americans of German . . . ancestry were prominent in the USAAF campaign in Europe, along with Ira Eaker, the second head of the Eighth Air Force. The USAAF commanding general, Henry 'Hap' Arnold, and the commander of the Eighth Air Force, Carl 'Tooey' Spaatz, were both from a background in which a paternal grandparent still spoke German." Probably 2 million men and women of German descent served in the U.S. military during WWII, but relatively few of them spoke, read, and wrote fluent German, although Werner did. And none of them were related to Germany's highest-ranking military officer, the Reich Marshal, Hermann Göring.

Even if the vast majority of German Americans were loyal to the United States, as was most certainly the case, there was still concern that the country's vibrant German American communities could provide recruits or cover for Nazi spies and saboteurs. In the mid-1930s the German American Bund was a Nazi clone that attracted as many as 200,000 supporters nationwide:

> Reliable estimates place membership at 25,000 dues-paying members, including some 8,000 uniformed Sturmabteilungen (SA), more commonly known as Storm Troopers. The German American Bund carried out active propaganda for its causes, published magazines and brochures, organized demonstrations, and maintained a number of youth camps run like Hitler Youth camps. German American Bund activities often led

to clashes—even street battles—with other groups, most notably with Jewish veterans of World War I. A February 1939 rally was held on George Washington's birthday to proclaim the rights of white gentiles, the "true patriots." This Madison Square Garden rally drew a crowd of 20,000 who consistently booed President Franklin D. Roosevelt and chanted the Nazi salutation "Heil Hitler."

The German American Bund cooperated with the Christian Front, which was organized by the anti-Semitic, isolationist, and hugely popular radio priest Father Charles Coughlin. The Bund's activities led both Jewish and non-Jewish congressional representatives to demand that it be investigated by the House Un-American Activities Committee, chaired by Martin Dies. The committee hearings, held in 1939, showed clear evidence of German American Bund ties to the Nazi government as well as likely financial support for Father Coughlin.

In October 1940, even *after* the invasion of Poland and the outbreak of the war, the Bund was able to organize a sizable parade in New York City's gilded Upper East Side.

In the spring of 1941, the FBI arrested thirty-three members of the Duquesne spy ring, headquartered in the Yorkville neighborhood of Manhattan. Ringleader Frederick Duquesne and all but two of the others were either German Americans who became U.S. citizens between 1913 and 1940 or German nationals residing in the United States. The hero of the case was also a German American, an airplane plant worker who served in the German army during WWI. Pressured to join the spy ring while he was visiting his mother in Germany, he reported the contact at an American consulate and became a double agent for the United States.

Such events made their way into popular culture and films, with the enthusiastic assistance of J. Edgar Hoover's FBI. The films were part of the American propaganda effort, much like many films made in Germany during the war.

On December 2, 1941, five days before Pearl Harbor, Warner Bros. released *All Through the Night,* starring Humphrey Bogart as "Gloves" Donahue, a gambler with a heart of gold who helps a beautiful nightclub singer escape the clutches of a German American spy ring. Fans of docudrama-style film noir will also remember *The House on 92nd Street,* made with the cooperation of the FBI and based closely on the events of the Duquesne spy ring. Among the many films with similar plot elements are Alfred Hitchcock's *Saboteur* (1942) and *Notorious* (1946). In *Notorious,* Ingrid Bergman, playing the loyal-to-America daughter of a German American spy for the Nazis, infiltrated a neo-Nazi conspiracy by marrying its leader, played by Claude Rains, and passed information to an American intelligence agent, played by Cary Grant.

With the changing political climate, the Utah Goerings' pride in their famous German relative turned to ashes.

4

J. EDGAR HOOVER

On September 4, 1943, a "confidential letter of transmittal" attached to a fat intelligence file regarding Werner George Goering landed with a thump on J. Edgar Hoover's desk at the FBI. The top-secret file, from Col. L. R. Forney, assistant executive director of the War Department's Military Intelligence Service and a member of the U.S. Army's General Staff Corps, would determine Werner's fate.

The file, classified until October 7, 2009, when it was released under the Freedom of Information Act, details how both the FBI and G-2, the War Department's intelligence division, thoroughly investigated Werner and his family because of his relationship to Hermann Göring. Werner was placed under surveillance at the request of Maj. Lawrence B. Rhodes, the intelligence officer at Werner's air cadet training base in Santa Ana, California. Rhodes recommended that "the subject's personal background and his family background be thoroughly investigated to determine whether the subject is disaffected and . . . if such investigation establishes the subject is disaffected, the subject be transferred out of the Army Air Force."

J. Edgar Hoover was born on New Year's Day, 1895, in Washington, D.C. He was the son of Dickerson Naylor Hoover, who spent much of his life in and out of mental institutions. As a teenager J. Edgar was forced to get a job to support his mother. Just out of high school, Hoover was hired as a messenger and clerk in the Library of Congress. At night he studied law at George Washington University. When he died in his sleep sixty-two years later, still on the job in 1972, at the age of seventy-seven, Hoover had been on the federal payroll for almost a third of the nation's existence.

Harold "Bruno" Mangum holds the record as the longest-serving federal employee. He worked for the U.S. Department of Agriculture's Farm Service Agency and served in the navy for a total of seventy-one years, from 1936 to 2007. Lillie Steinhorn retired from the Social Security Administration in 2000 after a sixty-five-year career; and Virginia Saunders, who started at the FBI in 1945, finished a sixty-four-year federal career at the Government Printing Office.

Hoover was among the handful of long-serving federal employees and certainly was by far the longest-serving major department head in American history, the military included. By comparison, even counting his West Point education, General Douglas MacArthur served the nation for only fifty-one years.

After Hoover graduated from law school in 1917, his uncle, a judge, got him a job in the Justice Department as an assistant to Woodrow Wilson's attorney general, Alexander M. Palmer. The ruthlessly ambitious and efficient Hoover was quickly noticed; he was tapped to head a new division whose mission was to gather evidence about, arrest, prosecute, and deport foreign-born subversives. Hoover targeted Emma Goldman, a vocal Russian-born leftist who had been implicated and briefly arrested in connection with the 1901 assassination of President William McKinley by Leon Czolgosz; before being executed, Czolgosz had mentioned Goldman's name during a protracted and rough interrogation.

After the United States entered WWI and Congress passed the Selective Service Act of 1917, Goldman was one of the most visible opponents of the draft and the war against Germany. Hoover had her arrested and imprisoned for two years. Hoover, then only twenty-two and single, prime draftee material, never explained how he personally avoided military service.

As head of Justice's General Intelligence Division, Hoover was intent on enforcing the Anarchist Exclusion Act of 1918 by deporting any foreign-born residents or naturalized citizens he could identify as threats. Leveraging his training as an archivist at the Library of Congress, Hoover created a massive index file of those he considered subversive, one that he expanded and maintained for the next half century, until his death near the end of the Vietnam War.

On the second anniversary of the Russian Revolution in 1919, Hoover approved the investigation of thousands of suspected communists in twenty-three different cities. Most were innocent and released. But Goldman, along with 247 others, was deported to Russia, even though she was a U.S. citizen and had lived in America for thirty-four years.

Following the sweep, Hoover recorded the names of hundreds of lawyers nationwide willing to represent "subversives." The lawyers' names, along with those of their clients, were added to the burgeoning secret index file. In 1924, President Calvin Coolidge named Hoover head of the Bureau of Investigation, the precursor to the Federal Bureau of Investigation, which was created in the mid-1930s by Franklin Roosevelt.

Hoover, who served nine U.S. presidents from Wilson to Nixon, ran the FBI from Washington's Department of Justice headquarters at 950 Pennsylvania Avenue, built in 1935 and arguably the most ornate and lavish structure ever built by the government. Richly accented with art deco flourishes, the 1-million-square-foot building—eventually and ironically named for former Attorney General Robert F. Kennedy, Hoover's greatest nemesis—contains the largest historic art collection of any General Services Administration facility. "All entrances to the building feature twenty-foot-high aluminum doors that slide into recessed pockets. Interior stair railings, grillwork, and door trim are aluminum, as are torches and doors for the building's 25 elevators, and more than 10,000 light fixtures."

Whenever Hoover strode across the towering Great Hall to announce to reporters some gangster's death or the capture of a spy ring, he could not miss the twelve-and-a-half-foot-tall, bare-breasted statue *Spirit of Justice,* which, unlike almost all other depictions of Lady Justice, wears no blindfold symbolizing judicial impartiality.

During the Spanish civil war (1936–39), Hoover spied on Americans who fought with the Fifteenth International Battalion (more commonly known now as the Abraham Lincoln Brigade). Most were volunteers who wanted to fight the fascist general Francisco Franco. Göring used the civil war to perfect his Condor Legions tactics, most famously at Guernica, immortalized by Picasso's painting of the same name. On a well-known market day in 1937, for more than three hours, Germany's most sophisticated bombers dumped thousands of pounds of high-explosive and incendiary bombs onto the village while Messerschmitt and Fiat fighters strafed the town. The town burned for days, and up to 70 percent of it was destroyed. Unknown hundreds of civilians died. It was probably the deadliest single civilian aerial bombing in the history of Europe to that date, including the WWI Zeppelin raids on England in which about 550 people died, and a taste of things to come. But it was not unique in the world. "As Secretary of State for War and Air, [Winston] Churchill used air power without compunction to help quell the Iraqi revolt of 1920. The world was more shocked when the Germans used bombers against Guernica; Mesopotamian villages were seen as fair game, European cities not so. Japanese air strikes against China after 1937 only seemed to confirm the adage that 'the bomber would always get through,' and with devastating results." In the 1930s, the Japanese did the same in China, as did the Italians in Ethiopia, with conventional bombs as well as outlawed gas-filled bombs. Fascism and airpower were on the march worldwide, arm in arm, and even the colonists had shown a willingness to employ airpower on distant primitive subjects.

Although FDR personally but silently preferred the Republican (antifascist) side in the Spanish civil war, the Republicans had engaged in attacks on the Catholic clergy, and Roosevelt wouldn't risk the alienation of 30 million American Catholics. Eleanor Roosevelt, "as she was wont to do, complicated her husband's life by militating in favor of the Spanish Republicans."

As late as 1937, fascists concerned Hoover less than did leftists, labor movements, socialists, and communists. Although some Americans who fought in the Spanish civil war against Franco's Nationalists were indeed communists, many liberals and artists instinctively supported the Republican side out of disgust with Hitler, Mussolini, and Franco. Prominent antifascists included, in addition to Eleanor Roosevelt, Paul Robeson,

Dashiell Hammett, Lillian Hellman, Dorothy Parker, Pablo Picasso, Sam Yorty, Helen Keller, Woody Guthrie, and Ernest Hemingway, who covered the war as a correspondent. In 1940, Hemingway published *For Whom the Bell Tolls,* the story of Robert Jordan, a noble American attached to a Spanish Republican unit. The novel is widely regarded as one of Hemingway's greatest works. The 1943 film adaptation, starring Gary Cooper and Ingrid Bergman, was nominated for nine Academy Awards, including Best Picture; it became the top box-office hit of 1943 and served as potent antifascist propaganda.

During WWII, Hoover ensured that former international brigade members were ineligible to become officers in the U.S. military, even though Soviet dictator "Uncle Joe" Stalin, as FDR called him, was the Allies' most indispensable ally in crushing the Nazis. Hoover, obsessed with power, public relations, alien spies, and subversives, exaggerated the extent of Nazi subversion and often overstepped legal bounds in his pursuit of perceived enemies of the state. He was an admirer of Anthony Comstock, an efficient World War I-era U.S. postal inspector, and soon monitoring domestic mail to and from potential enemies became standard operating procedure. The inspectors could not have missed the elegantly embossed envelopes that arrived from Berlin's W8 ministry district with the address of Leipzinger Strasse 3, from Hermann W. Göring, *Der Reichminister der Luftfahrt und Oberbefehlshaber der Luftwaffe.* Not only head of the Luftwaffe, Göring was also prime minister of Prussia, head of the Gestapo, and minister of the Interior.

The letters from Germany's second most powerful man were addressed to Werner's father, Karl Frederick Goering, at 347 Lucy Street, Salt Lake City, Utah, which is two and a half miles south of the Mormon Temple, on the good side of the rails, in what was then the heart of Salt Lake's burgeoning immigrant community.

Postal inspectors alerted the FBI, who took a closer look at the Utah Goerings. The FBI already had a file on one of Karl's American relatives, Chicago-based engineer and steel industrialist Herman A. Brassert, variously described as Göring's cousin or in-law. H. G Brassert & Company contracted with Nazi Germany during the 1930s to build steel blast furnaces for the Hermann Göring Works, which became one of Europe's largest industrial conglomerates in the 1940s.

Although he had traded with the Nazis in a critical war material before the war, Brassert wouldn't be piloting the world's most sophisticated bomber over the fatherland, as Werner Goering was about to do.

5

A MATTER OF NATIONAL SECURITY

German intelligence regularly scoured the foreign press for information about military officers, especially pilots, and, most particularly, anyone connected to top Nazis. Diplomatic cables show that in 1939, Joseph Goebbels, the Nazi minister of propaganda, boasted about the existence of Nazi third-columnists inside the United States. He told Cornelius Vanderbilt Jr., the seven-times married heir and sometime journalist, " 'When we get good and ready, we will take your impertinent nation from within.' . . . This . . . was Nazi bravura. . . . Hoover . . . had done a very thorough job of infiltrating American Axis-sympathetic organizations."

Four days after Pearl Harbor, Hitler needlessly and foolishly declared war against the United States. Soon afterward, in early 1942, German U-boats sent two small groups of Nazi agents ashore in Jacksonville, Florida, and Long Island, New York, equipped with explosives for sabotage. The two four-man teams were quickly apprehended when one of the would-be saboteurs, after going on a bender in New York City, got cold feet and ratted his comrades out to the FBI. The eight hapless German spies were arrested, tried, and convicted by a military tribunal, and six were quickly frog-marched to the electric chair. The other two were given thirty-year prison sentences but were released in 1948 and deported to Germany. Hoover, basking in unearned glory, intensified his hunt for potential German spies and plants within the German American community and enlisted Hollywood to enlighten the nation about the dangers afoot in the homeland.

Hoover made the first arrests of German agents in 1938, before the war even started. By then, the Salt Lake City Goerings had come to the attention of the nation's top G-man. When authorities realized Werner was on track to become a bomber commander in late 1942, something had to be done. Hoover wasted no time ordering a thorough investigation and full surveillance of Werner. Attached to the file on Hoover's desk was a surprisingly deferential top-secret cover note to a civilian during wartime. Colonel L. R. Forney, writing on behalf of the chief of military intelligence, wrote Hoover: "The attached communications are forwarded for your information and such action as you consider advisable."

The file included the following "adverse information":

1. Subject's father was born in Germany.
2. Subject's mother was born in Germany.
3. Subject is reported to be hotheaded, bullheaded, and a cutup.
4. Subject is reported to be related to Marshal Hermann Göring of the German Luftwaffe.
5. Subject is reported to have stated that he was investigated by the FBI at Salt Lake City, Utah.

The file on Werner contained requests for an "investigation in detail for pro-German background," associations, and leads from G-2, Western Defense Command, including surveillance and mail coverage. The request also went to the Salt Lake City branch of the FBI, calling for a "neighborhood check regarding subject's family and background with particular attention being paid to the fact that the subject's parents are German-born; a high school check at South High School regarding subject's activity in this school during the years 1939 to 1941; a junior high school check at Horace Mann Junior High School; a check at Bamberger Railroad regarding subject being employed as a clerk; a check at Ogden General Depot regarding subject's being employed as a laborer by said depot; a check at Radio Station KSL regarding subject's being employed as a receptionist, with particular attention being paid to subject's possible pro-Nazi sympathy; a check at the Western Union Telegraph Company, and the *Deseret News*," both also former employers of Werner. The Salt Lake City Police Department was also consulted and their files reviewed.

In short, every single employer, neighbor, and teacher Werner had ever had since the sixth grade was interviewed by the FBI, as were officials of the Mormon Church, where his father was employed, and all his known associates. After the exhaustive surveillance and widespread federal and local investigations began, Karl Goering and everybody the Goerings had ever known in the United States knew something serious was up. In a case of closing the barn door after the horses were out, as soon as Karl heard whispers that the feds were looking into his family, it is likely he took his correspondence with Hermann and burned it all in a steel drum behind the house. The letters were now clearly liabilities that could adversely affect Werner's career and life. Werner was never directly approached during the investigation.

Paralleling the Salt Lake investigations, the case moved forward in Santa Ana, California, at Werner's air cadet base. One item contained in the file came from the Office of Naval Intelligence, which had not even been mentioned as a cooperating agency by Forney. "Their records indicated that the Subject was mentioned in an article quoted from *Collier's National Magazine*," which then had a million-copy circulation, "on the Week of 14 June to 20 June 1942":

> Fort Douglas, Salt Lake City. Eighteen-year-old Werner George GOERING, former errand boy at a local radio station, hopes to drop an egg on his Nazi relative's fat neck. Werner is a nephew or a cousin—he isn't sure which—of Barrelhouse Hermann, Germany's air chief; and as a prospective cadet, prays that his future relationship with Hermann will be closer than in the past. Just once.

The file confirmed that military intelligence and the FBI investigated Werner because of his relationship to Hermann Göring; dozens of pages are totally illegible and stamped "Best Copy Available." Yet seven decades after the fact, the government released Werner's "Army-originated records" only under the Freedom of Information Act. Werner's FBI file and perhaps other documents remain classified on the grounds that "release of some of the information would result in an unwarranted invasion of the privacy rights of the individual concerned." An appeal of the decision to withhold "some of the information" made directly to the secretary of the army in late 2009 was ignored without further explanation, a circumstance that at the very least indicates that the still-classified documents may contain information of considerable potential embarrassment to the FBI and the U.S. military.

After interviewing dozens of people, the government's conclusion was that there was no concrete evidence that Werner or his family were anything but loyal Americans, although Werner was described as "bullheaded as hell; literal to the point of annoyance; a cut-up; snotty; difficult to handle; slow; and keeps to himself." Yet the report also describes Werner almost as another person: "a good soldier; neat; excellent military bearing, willing worker; studious; self-sufficient; more or less of a young kid."

What was Hoover to make of all this, especially since Hermann Göring had "dreamed audibly about developing bombers that could attack New York"? The "kid," who spoke perfect German and looked like he was sent from central casting for the part of Aryan air commander, was a cipher. If he ever did develop misguided dreams of ancestral glory and voluntarily defected to Uncle Hermann's Luftwaffe, he would probably be given a parade, a promotion, a decoration, and a German crew to command. Goebbels would have had a field day, and the Luftwaffe would have another interned American flight crew in their stalag luft camps and an intact Flying Fortress to cover with swastikas and use in both training and combat, as Germany had already done with earlier captured American bombers.

If Werner defected, the Luftwaffe would also gain access to the latest U.S. technology, including an intact and top-secret Norden bomb-targeting system that was being installed in Allied bombers in large numbers by 1943. During the war, approximately forty B-17s did fall into German hands and were flown either with Nazi markings or, for intelligence and infiltration purposes, in Allied colors. The captured B-17s were used to determine the airplane's vulnerabilities and to train German interceptor pilots in antibomber tactics. Others, with the cover designation Dornier Do 200, were used in a long-range transport "special-duties" unit to carry out agent drops and supply secret airstrips in the Middle East and North Africa. They were chosen for these missions since it was thought they were more suitable than available German aircraft, not always in an attempt to deceive the Allies, and were operated in full Luftwaffe markings. One such B-17 was interned for the rest of the war by Spain when it unexpectedly landed at Valencia on June 27, 1944. Some B-17s kept their Allied markings and were used by the Luftwaffe to infiltrate bomber formations and report on their position and altitude. The practice was initially successful, but the army air force crews quickly established standard procedures, first to warn off and then to fire upon any "strangers" trying to join a group's formation.

Hoover would not risk it all on the nineteen-year-old, "bull-headed, difficult, loner" Werner Goering. It would be a huge coup for the Nazis and a great embarrassment to Hoover and the army if the Nazis got hold of Werner, even if he remained a loyal American officer as a prisoner of war. And if he didn't remain loyal, it would be even worse. On the other hand, if Werner completed a European combat tour successfully or died fighting the Nazi war machine, there would be a useful German American victory for the Allied cause.

So the top-secret order went out from the director of the FBI: find someone to place in the copilot's seat next to Werner with orders to shoot to kill if for any reason—a treasonous decision on Werner's part, enemy fire, or even mechanical failure—their plane can't get back its base or to another Allied airfield. Hoover was taking no chances and ensured that if Werner's Flying Fortress was downed over Nazi-occupied Europe, someone would be in the cockpit to eliminate the problem. Military intelligence and the FBI decided they'd never let Göring get his chubby, jewel-encrusted hands on his nephew. Werner Goering would never land alive in Nazi-occupied Europe; if the Germans didn't kill him, the Americans certainly would.

The FBI and the army would not prevent Werner from serving his American homeland in war, but neither would they risk the propaganda coup that his desertion, or even his live capture, would represent for Nazi Germany.

In early 1943, FBI agents fanned out across the United States to find a man capable of and willing to shoot Werner dead in the cockpit: someone who could get the plane back home.

They found Jack Rencher, twenty-three, a tough, insular, B-17 instructor in Yuma, Arizona, who also happened to be one of the army's best shots. He was the eldest son of a hard-drinking, no-nonsense, old-school World War I infantry veteran and Arizona sheriff named Guy

Rencher, who wore a six-shooter until the day he died. Jack grew up "with a pistol in his hand." Even better, from the FBI's perspective, Jack was half-Jewish on his mother's side and considered Nazis beneath contempt. He was the right man, with the right skills, in the right place, at the right time.

6

JACK "POVERTY-STRICKEN" RENCHER

Against all odds, high school dropout, teetotaler, and Depression-era vagabond Jack P. Rencher succeeded: not only did he become an officer in an elite, class-conscious aviation culture, where college education and drinking in the officers' club were almost prerequisites; he also became one of the best and most experienced bomber instructors the army produced, and a dead shot with a pistol.

He was one of the hard, unsentimental flight instructors the army kept home to train tens of thousands of men to fly and fix bombers, knowing full well many of their charges would die. For a Depression-era kid from the wilds of Arizona, it was important and steady yet dangerous work.

Jack joked that his middle initial stood for "poverty-stricken," but it actually stood for Preston, his paternal grandfather's middle name. Rencher's mother, Irene Ramona Eigholz, born in Los Angeles on March 12, 1896, was the daughter of Pasadena newspaper editor Julius Eigholz and his wife, Jennie. Julius was Christian and Jennie (née Bernard) was Jewish. They were American-born children of German immigrants who had arrived in the United States during the great nineteenth-century exodus to America.

The family surname Eigholz was originally von Eigholz, the "von" signifying membership in at least the lower orders of German aristocracy. Jennie Bernard was born into a middle-class German Jewish family.

German Jews immigrated to the United States in significant numbers from the mid–nineteenth century on, and no account of German American contributions to America would be complete without acknowledging the achievements of persons of German Jewish descent. This multicultural irony of German American immigrants and their first- and second-generation descendants during WWII highlighted the fates of Jack and Werner.

Jack knew his maternal grandparents well and understood that his mother and all her children were considered Jewish under Hebraic religious law. That fact seemed quite remote from his rural Arizona upbringing, however, and Jack never thought of himself as being either German or Jewish in any way. Guy Rencher had fought the Germans as an American soldier in World War I; the Renchers had been Mormons for generations, and Irene raised her children as Mormons.

After earning teaching degrees in Los Angeles during WWI, Irene and a girlfriend applied for grade school teaching positions in a small desert town called Eagar, Arizona, located in the middle of the state, fifteen miles west of the New Mexico border. It was as far from Los Angeles as the moon. For the two teenage girls, the move to Eagar was a radical and foolhardy adventure into the unknown.

Jack's grandfather, Peter Preston Rencher, had moved to Eagar from Blanco, Texas, a few years earlier and built a large home in the remote town. Although it was one of the most imposing homes in Eagar, it lacked both electricity and plumbing.

Peter Rencher's two sons were fighting in France during WWI, and their rooms on the second floor were available for rent. Irene and her friend were hired to teach at the Eagar Grammar School, and Peter Rencher rented the rooms to the girls, with board. When Peter's son Guy sent letters home, Peter would read them aloud at the dinner table, where the displaced and lonely Irene heard dramatic war tales set in faraway, exotic France.

Irene was fascinated by Guy's letters and began to put small notes for him in the replies Peter sent. Guy, equally lonely, responded to her unexpected notes, and a pen-pal romance developed. When Guy returned from the war, he courted Irene and married her on June 6, 1920. Guy, despite having seen the lights and sights of "gay Paree," was at heart a cowboy who, with several rodeo-circuit drinking buddies, would drink and shoot guns all day long. The liquored-up cowboys "would put a cigarette on a fence post and bet a dollar on who could shoot it off." Guy first worked as an Arizona lawman, but then got hired, for more money, by the U.S. Forest Service.

The Forest Service furnished the newlyweds with a house in the wilderness at a desolate location called Reynolds Creek, fifty miles north of Globe, on State Highway 288, which was then and is today still largely unpaved. It took an entire day to get there from Globe in an old Model T Ford. The road was often muddy or washed out; the car broke down all the time and regularly got flats.

Before Jack was born, Irene took the Santa Fe Railroad from Phoenix to Los Angeles to be with her parents for the March 25, 1921, delivery. It was a trip she made on two other occasions: when her other son, Frank, and her daughter, Gladys, were born.

Irene returned to Reynolds Creek with baby Jack and a puppy named Powell, born on the same day and given to him by his maternal grandfather. Reynolds Creek was a place of near total isolation. "We had two neighbors, one lived three and a half miles in one direction and had six dogs, the other lived three and a half miles in the other direction and had a billy goat," said Jack. There were no other kids around during Jack's early years.

Jack and Powell did everything together and spent their days in the woods alone, usually chasing skunks. When his parents would yell for Jack to return, he stayed silent, but Powell always barked a reply and his parents would find them. Powell never left Jack's side. By age five, Jack "learned how to bark pretty well, but I could not talk in a way people could understand me and my parents thought I might be tongue-tied, so they took me to a doctor." The doctor said, "He's not tongue-tied," but needed socialization among other children in a proper school setting. So when Jack was about six years old, his paternal grandfather, Peter, gave Guy and Irene a house on five acres in Eagar, and the family moved there so that Jack, a badly introverted and insular child, could go to school.

When he started first grade, teachers and the other kids couldn't understand a word he said; only his mother really could. The lonely childhood spent in the wilderness and the experience of not being able to communicate and of having other kids make fun of him caused Jack to withdraw further into himself. "I've always been a loner," he recalled. Jack learned to shoot when he was a kid, and he eventually learned to speak properly; as a Preadolescent during Prohibition he would hang around with his father's shooting and drinking buddies.

He learned to weld metal as a youngster and made galvanized iron stills. "The galvanizing was done with zinc, to keep the still from rusting, but if the zinc leaked through and you drank the whiskey, it could kill you or make you blind. We had quite a few blind people around there, quite a few dead ones, too, come to think about it," Jack recalled years later. To his dying day, Jack never tasted a drop of alcohol or touched a cigarette.

Later, Jack's family moved to Phoenix, where his mother continued her teaching education and Jack finished grammar school and entered Phoenix Union High School. Like Werner a few years later, Jack landed a paper route in the afternoon, saved up, and bought a bicycle. With the bike, he got a job as a uniformed Western Union delivery boy in the evenings, and for the first time, he made a little money.

Guy Rencher, however, wasn't made for city life, and when he was offered another remote posting with the Fish and Game Service, he moved back to the wilderness with Irene and their two smaller children, Gladys and Frank. Jack, dreading the isolation, decided to stay in Phoenix, continue in high school, and support himself with his two jobs. He lived mostly with friends, sometimes sleeping on back porches or in garages.

During the Depression the overcrowded Union High School enrolled 5,000 students in two staggered shifts, one at 8:00 A.M. and the other at 9:00 A.M. In his freshman year, Jack was in the nine o'clock shift and did well. He worked his two jobs after school, often riding his bike fifty miles a day delivering papers and telegrams until midnight, and developed into an unusually fit teenager. In his sophomore year, Jack was assigned to the early shift, which cut into his sleep, so he simply continued to show up at nine o'clock, accumulating late demerits until he was called in to see the vice principal. Jack explained his problem with the early shift, given his jobs and need to rest. He pointed out that there were "rich kids getting dropped off in limousines at 9:00 A.M." and asked to be returned to that shift. The administrator peremptorily, and in Jack's view rudely, dismissed the request from a good student who simply needed to work late hours in order to remain in school.

He called himself "Doctor something or other and had a sign on his desk with his name and title on it," said Jack, who thought of a doctor as a medical doctor. The vice principal got nasty and hollered, "What do you want to be when you grow up, a bum?" Jack snapped back that he "certainly didn't want to be a lousy schoolteacher who calls himself a doctor." With that, the vice principal got up, came around his desk, grabbed Jack by the collar, and yelled, "You can't talk to me like that." Jack said, "Turn me loose, you old goat," and then "slugged him in the side of the head. He went flat onto the floor, crawled on his hands and knees to the door, and ran." Jack went back to class as if nothing had happened.

The next day the principal called Jack in and suspended him for a week and said he had to continue with the 8:00 A.M. session. Jack said he was not coming back. Thus ended his formal education, in the tenth grade, at the height of the Depression.

Homeless for the next several years, Jack worked and slept anywhere he could. In addition to his paper route and telegram job, Jack worked on farms during harvest and on fire crews when forest fires erupted. He worked road construction, chopped wood, welded stills, and played poker with the road crews. He lived alone in a tent in the mountains north of Scottsdale, bought a .22 rifle, and ate whatever he could. Although he'd learned to shoot as a kid, hunger focused his marksman's eye. He shot birds, jackrabbits, squirrels, and deer, fished mountain streams, and stealthily avoided authorities so as not to become a ward of the state as a minor or as a poacher. He had become a tough, lonely, yet independent teen.

7

BOOTLEGGERS, BODYGUARDS, AND BANK ROBBERS

One day, Lionel Bert "Breezy" Cox, a heavyset, middle-aged former rodeo champ and sometime bootlegger, contacted Jack and arranged to meet him at a remote abandoned barn. Breezy showed up with a big pile of copper sheets four feet by eight feet and left them with Jack to weld into a still. He would come back for them, he said.

Breezy then went to Silver City, New Mexico, to rob a bank. His otherwise successful getaway was complicated when he left his Stetson behind with his name printed on the sweatband. Breezy knew a posse would be coming and fled into the mountains near Glenwood, New Mexico. He hid both his loot and his pistol in the wilderness. The posse soon arrested Breezy, and he was sentenced, in the days before bank robbery was a federal crime, to two years in a New Mexico state prison.

Breezy knew Jack's dad, Guy Rencher. As it happened, Guy had served with the warden, Tom Summers, in France during WWI. He went to see Summers, and by hook, crook, or cash, he was able to spring Breezy. Summers made Breezy promise "to stay out of sight for two years, not to pack a pistol, not to rob any more banks, and not to make any more moonshine."

Breezy, as a thief and a well-known man of his word who had an aversion to jail, agreed and instantly made himself scarce in the remote Blue River Valley region of Arizona's White Mountains in the eastern part of the state. He worked on a ranch and stayed out of sight for two years as promised. When he resurfaced, Breezy told Jack to keep the still. He also told Jack exactly where he had hidden his pistol. If Jack wanted it, he could have it. Jack knew the region well and found the pistol, which he kept for the rest of his life. No mention of the cash, but it had probably helped grease Breezy's "early" parole.

Fats Wadsworth, a professional gambler who ran floating poker games, hired Jack as a bodyguard. The plump older man knew when payday fell for big employers across Arizona and New Mexico, and Fats went to the town, bribed the local sheriff, and made deals with saloon owners to rent a back room. He provided cards and poker chips; all he needed was a table and Jack. Fats gave Jack a $10 chip and a borrowed deputy sheriff's badge. Jack sat at the table, ostensibly as a player, and when some drunken loser got aggressive, he came to Fats's rescue. When the inevitable problems arose, Jack got up, pulled out his deputy's badge, and told the victim, "I'm a deputy sheriff in this county, and if you want to get to Fats, it will be after you get past me." Usually they left quietly after eyeballing Jack's barrel chest, rough hands, and arms corded with muscle. Jack "learned the odds; learned to take a man's measure, and became something a card shark." When Jack won, he repaid Fats $10 and kept the change. Fats covered Jack's room and board. During the Great Depression many rural counties were poor because nobody paid taxes. A little grease went a long way with sheriffs and wardens.

Jack hitchhiked everywhere looking for work, and at sixteen, he got a job sweeping out airplane hangars. Because of its great weather, Phoenix had been an aviation mecca ever since Charles F. Willard flew a Glenn Curtiss Golden Flyer to the city in the first years after the Wright brothers flew at Kitty Hawk. Willard's plane is thought to have been the first to fly in many parts of the American West, including California. In 1909, before Arizona was a state, Phoenix's city fathers organized an aerial exhibition for the following year and attracted pilots from all over the country. "Arizona City Plans to Have Sky Pilots Cavort in Atmosphere and Raises the Cash," the *Los Angeles Times* editorial headline announced jealously on January 21, 1910. Only three days later, the *Times* ran another story headlined: "Three Days with Curtiss as Star Actor; Guaranty of $12,000 All Raised and $50,000 Aero Club

Organized—Territorial Fair Grounds Make Ideal Field for Flights—Will Advertise All Over the Southwest."

By 1937, when Jack got the job, flying schools and airfields dotted the state. He wanted to get as close to the airplanes as possible and graduated from sweeping out hangars to washing off dusty biplanes. He swapped wages for flight time and, over two years, learned to fly, getting "fifteen minutes here and there" in the air.

In 1939, Jack volunteered for the Citizens Military Training Corps (CMTC), a program authorized by the National Defense Act of 1920 that provided young volunteers with four weeks of military training in summer camp each year from 1921 to 1941. Approximately 30,000 trainees participated each year. Those who voluntarily completed four summers of training became eligible for reserve commissions. The camps differed from National Guard and reserve training in that the program allowed male citizens to obtain basic military training without an obligation to call up for active duty.

The program didn't pay anything, but it reimbursed Jack five cents a mile round-trip from Phoenix to Fort Bliss, Texas, where the training was held. That added up to about $50 for travel, and since he hitchhiked both ways, Jack pocketed the cash. He also got a free uniform and food for a month each summer for the next few summers. At Fort Bliss, attached to the Seventh Cavalry, Jack trained as a cavalryman; not much had changed in the six decades since George Armstrong Custer had commanded the unit at the Little Big Horn. For a poor ranch kid, riding around the desert shooting off guns "was a paid vacation."

In January 1941, Jack talked his way into his first steady job at the notorious Phelps Dodge open-pit copper mine in Morenci, Arizona, located on U.S. 666, an offshoot of the famous Route 66. The road, just over one hundred miles long, crosses the Apache National Forest and ranges in altitude from 2,900 feet to over 11,000 feet. Historian Jonathan D. Rosenblum records that the road contains hundreds of switchbacks where countless drivers have crashed to their deaths off its steep cliffs.

> From the time it was numbered, people who lived along the road worried about a possible connection between ancient symbolism and their modern fate. For those nearest the Phelps

Dodge copper mines in Morenci, the allusion was obvious. the beast in the Book of Revelation rose from a pit with the marking "666" to signal the apocalypse. At the road's dedication in the 1920s, local Apaches . . . performed a ceremony called "the Devil's Dance." Residents regularly wrote the highway department and their congresspeople to change the highway number. After all, an Arizona car owner cannot even purchase a vanity plate with the number 666 on it—the state won't permit it.

By 1900, 20 percent of Arizona's men were employed in mining-related jobs. The Morenci mine in southeastern Arizona covered approximately 60,000 acres and had five pits, three of them still in operation in the first decade of the twenty-first century. It was the largest copper mine in North America and one of the largest open-pit mines in the world. As recently as 2005, Morenci had a workforce of 2,000 employees and produced 840 million pounds of copper annually. Morenci began operations in 1872 as an underground mine and moved to open-pit mining in 1937. Rosenblum noted that the "unincorporated" corporate town "sold the ice for the icebox and bread for the breadbox. (Each loaf came in a Wonder Bread–like plastic bag with the insignia 'Phelps Dodge.') Everything from electric power to police services to the dirt under residents' feet was either owned or administered by Phelps Dodge." Management of the mines was exclusively Anglo and lived on the highest hilltops in town, overlooking the meaner dwellings of the half-Mexican labor force. The town's Anglo mayor was the pit boss.

Jack, as an Anglo, got a relatively high starting wage of $4.13 a day to grease and refuel the mine's heavy trucks and machinery. Many less-skilled employees, mostly Mexican or Mexican American, worked the mine's smelters in 130-degree temperatures and were exposed daily to hazardous levels of arsenic, lead, cadmium, and other heavy elements, all of which damaged their livers, kidneys, lungs, nervous systems, and brains.

For nine millennia, copper has been an essential military material. Before WWI, the Wilson administration sent future Supreme Court Justice Felix Frankfurter to Morenci to settle a brutal strike in which several workers were killed fighting scabs and company thugs brought in by

Phelps Dodge. In WWII, the Roosevelt administration likewise moved to ensure that the mine's long, bitter history of labor strife would not interfere with war production.

Jack quickly qualified as a master mechanic; he was a natural. He bought his own tools and soon was earning $6 a day. He was, as always, a hard worker, and was quickly promoted by Caterpillar foreman Jimmy Fernandez to drive the service truck and fix broken forty-ton-plus D8 Caterpillar bulldozers, which were introduced in 1937 and are still made today.

Rencher became one of Fernandez's top bulldozer drivers and mechanics and eventually made $15 a day, a fortune. His mechanic's skills paid off handsomely during the war, when he regularly worked voluntarily with ground crews at night to ensure bombers were airworthy. Jack was literally a jack-of-all-trades.

8

OFFICER, GENTLEMAN, AND PILOT

After Pearl Harbor, despite the CMTC's promise of not creating an obligation for active duty, the military had Jack's number, and he was soon drafted. "I never got the telegram they sent," Jack fibbed. Leaving Phelps Dodge in February 1942, he rushed to a Phoenix army recruitment station and inquired about volunteering for the air corps. He faced a gruff recruitment sergeant, who told him flatly, "You'll enlist, but no way will you get into the air corps because first, you have an overbite and the army doesn't want officers with bad teeth, and second, you have to have two years of college or you need take the test." Jack insisted on taking the test but knew it would be a long shot for a kid who hadn't even completed his second year of high school.

Jack took the same test as Werner. For kids like them, with no college education, it was the only path to becoming a pilot, and it was notoriously difficult.

Jack heard that the army air corps didn't want kids with civilian flight experience. It preferred to train them from scratch "the army way," so when asked if he had any flight training, Jack lied and said no. It was the correct answer.

The recruiter spent half an hour explaining to him all the reasons he'd flunk the test, but Jack stuck to his guns, and two weeks later, after boning up on math, physics, and current events, he was one of only two boys to pass, out of 140 who took the test. He was admitted to the army's air cadet program—provided he passed the physical. The physical alone washed out about a fifth of cadets. Lots of disappointed boys went on to become successful bombardiers, navigators, radiomen, and even enlisted gunners; what mattered most was that they were all airmen, wearing wings of varying types.

Jack, five-foot-ten, with blue eyes and brown hair, weighing 185 pounds, stood stark naked in an examination room with a hundred other teens. Doctors checked them from head to toe, with particular emphasis on their middle parts. Physicians and dentists ruthlessly culled the group. "The Great Depression had taken a physical toll on American manhood; even though the Army would accept just about anyone sane over five feet tall, 105 pounds in weight, possessing twelve or more of his own teeth, and free of flat feet, venereal disease and hernias, no fewer than forty percent of citizens failed these basic criteria." For an aspiring air corps officer, it was even tougher.

Jack saw several cadets staring at him and talking among themselves. He was shy and felt insecure surrounded by naked cadets from higher socioeconomic levels, many of who were older, with two years of college to their credit.

"What's wrong with those guys?" Jack asked Dwight, his new pal. "I'll go over and slug them if they don't stop it pretty soon," he said. "Easy, Jack, they're just admiring your muscles," said Dwight with a grin. From years of toil in 100-degree heat, working construction, mining, bicycling, horseback riding, and military calisthenics, Jack had developed an intimidating physique and an easily misunderstood blunt mien. After working as a bootlegger and an armed faux–deputy sheriff bodyguard in saloons all over the Depression-era Southwest, during the days of Dillinger, who was arrested in Arizona, Jack had pretty much seen it all. He was rawhide-tough and it showed, but he was just a big, strong, very clever kid.

Army shrinks not so obliquely asked the boys if they were gay, "Do you like girls?" Jack did. After what the recruiter had told him, what he dreaded most was the dental exam. The dentist approached him and Jack fearfully opened his mouth. After shining a light around, the dentist stopped and called to a colleague, another dentist. "Hey, Harry, you've got to see this." Harry came over and took a look, and Jack was sure he was headed to the infantry. "I've never seen a kid his age without a single cavity or filling." Jack had vaulted another hurdle, overbite and all.

* * *

Before the flight training began, the air cadets were required to take a series of aptitude, vision, and reflex tests. The first was a primitive stress test in which the students were told to hold a stick attached to a box through a very narrow hole. Every time the stick touched the side of the hole, a shrill electronic beep sounded. A drill sergeant shouted into the candidate's faces as they held the long, wobbly stick, and nervous, jittery kids would shake, causing the beeper to go off. Jack was rock-steady.

The next exam was designed to test the speed of their reflexes. The kids were told to look at a red light on a display with two foot pedals at their feet. When the light turned from red to green they were told to take their foot off the right pedal and depress the left. Jack carefully watched the student in front of him and noticed the apparatus was connected to a stopwatch that was engaged by a small lever that hit the watch, timed the reaction, and tripped the green light switch.

"When I took the test, I ignored the lights completely and just focused on that lever above the stopwatch, and as soon as that thing moved, wham, I slammed on the brake."

The instructor said, "Holy shit, that's impossible, the kid did it in one-tenth of a second. Nobody has ever done it that fast." Jack was told to do it again, and with similar results he set a new record.

Finally, depth perception was tested. There was a narrow darkened box about twenty feet long with two ropes connected to markers inside that the candidates had to align perfectly through a small peephole. He again studied the apparatus and noticed that the ropes had dark smudges on them from the hundreds of sweaty palms that had preceded his. Jack ignored the markers in the dim box and immediately aligned the two darkened sections of rope. He passed, again in record time. By the time the physical and aptitude tests were finished, half the cadets were gone. Another 20 percent would wash out or die during flight training, and of those who survived most became navigators, bombardiers, or machine gunners.

The lucky minority of boys who passed and qualified to train as pilot cadets were sent to, among others, California's Santa Ana Air Base to take a ten-week pilot preflight course that included twenty-four hours of physics, twenty hours of math, twenty hours of map reading, eighteen hours of aircraft recognition, and the killer, forty-eight hours of Morse code. The cadets had daily physical and military training. As officer trainees, they were supposedly exempt from more menial tasks, but when the mess hall was shorthanded, the cadets inevitably pulled KP duty. They also stood guard, carrying WWI rifles without ammunition.

The army, as always, took guard duty, KP, and shooting seriously. During training, Jack was tested for firearms proficiency. The range master asked him if he knew how to shoot a .45 pistol. He said he did. The drill sergeant began to ridicule Jack in front of his mates, even though on his military record he had listed his only active hobbies as "hunting, rifle and pistol shooting, and collecting old guns and ammunition." Jack said, "If you give me one practice shot, I'll put the next six into the center of that bull's-eye." The gunny, wearing a broad smile, handed him the pistol and said, "Let's see you do it, boy." Jack took the practice shot to gauge the wind and smoothly pumped six consecutive rounds into the bull's-eye, gaining him an almost unheard of Excellent rating with a 96 score on his first attempt. Werner scored 77.

Jack also became an expert with the Tommy gun, the .45 caliber Thompson submachine gun. He played softball, baseball, football, and basketball. Thanks to his Seventh Cavalry days at Fort Bliss, he also received an Excellent rating in equitation. But he was behind on his academics and knew it. Every day, he went to the PX to buy two flashlight batteries so he could study physics and Morse code under his blanket after the mandatory 10:00 P.M. lights-out. Struggling with his code, Jack asked a friend, who also had once worked for Western Union, what the secret was. He was having trouble finishing a measly six words a minute and needed at least ten to pass. He was told to study the sixteen-per-minute tables instead of the six he had been studying and quickly became adept with code. He said the trick was to "have the sound dit-dah-dit replace the letter R in your mind and so on." The nine-week course wound down, and the cadets needed a minimum score of 70 or they'd wash out. After final results were in, the instructor read out the grades alphabetically to the 100 students in the class. When the instructor got to Rencher, "he stood up and said, 'I've been teaching this class forever, and Jack Rencher is the only student I ever had to get a perfect score, 100. Congratulations." Finally, in June of 1943, as a private in the Enlisted Reserve Corps, Jack would get near an airplane again.

9

TEX RANKIN

Jack was sent to Tulare, California, for a ten-week training program at the Rankin Aeronautical Academy, a civilian-run flight school that had contracted with the army air corps in 1940 to teach cadets. It was where Jack acquired critical flight skills that, he said, "saved my life ten times over, thanks to Tex Rankin."

John Gilbert "Tex" Rankin, the flight school's owner and operator, was the famous and colorful aviator who, over fifty-four months starting in 1940, would train more than 10,450 cadets to fly. Rankin's graduates included twelve WWII ace fighter pilots, among them the "ace of aces," Maj. Richard Ira Bong, the highest-ranked American fighter pilot in history.

Rankin instructed Bong beginning in June 1941, and Bong went on to break Maj. Eddie Rickenbacker's WWI record of twenty-six kills. For that achievement, Rickenbacker sent Bong a case of Scotch. Bong racked up a total of forty kills on 200 combat missions consisting of more than 500 combat hours in the Pacific theater, during two years of combat. He received the Congressional Medal of Honor from Gen. Douglas MacArthur in 1944. After being commanded home by the brass for his safety and a publicity tour, Bong returned briefly to his native Wisconsin and married his girlfriend, Marge, on February 10, 1945. After a quick California honeymoon, Bong went to work as a test pilot on the Lockheed P-80 Shooting Star jet fighter program at Wright Field in Dayton, Ohio. After being checked out in the P-80, Bong flew it eleven times during the war's final summer. On August 6, 1945, the same day that the atomic bomb was dropped on Hiroshima, Bong took to the sky for the last time. Just after takeoff the jet stalled and Bong was killed trying to eject at low altitude. He was twenty-four years old. The P-80 became the first fighter jet used operationally by the U.S. Air Force and saw extensive combat as the F-80 in the Korean War.

Tex Rankin, born in 1894, became a pilot in 1913. Three years later his unit in the Washington State National Guard was ordered by President Woodrow Wilson to the Mexican border under General John J. Pershing during the Punitive Expedition against Pancho Villa. Pershing's staff included a young George Smith Patton, who "had been known to Americans ever since he had strapped the three corpses to his vehicle" in 1916. The army chased Pancho Villa around northern Mexico following his raid on Columbus, New Mexico, the first attack on U.S. soil in a century. During WWI, Rankin was mustered into the army and served in the Aviation Section of the U.S. Signal Corps, as the military aviation service of the army was then called.

Although posted in England, Rankin never saw combat and returned to the United States in the summer of 1919. The next year, Rankin opened a flight school in Washington State with an old military surplus airplane and charged students the whopping sum of $1 per minute of flight time. Sixty dollars an hour will get flight instruction even today. He also began to barnstorm and competed in air derbies around the country. In late 1922, he moved his business to Portland, Oregon, and opened the Rankin Flying Service, where, by 1927, he had more than 250 students.

When not teaching or barnstorming for cash, Rankin published a series of booklets called *The Rankin System of Flying Instruction,* which became the standard text for at least sixty flight schools nationwide in the late 1920s, exactly when the world was transfixed with aviation following Charles Lindbergh's solo flight across the Atlantic in 1927. Although Rankin emphasized safety, he became famous for wildly dangerous stunts and "superstition-defying antics which included painting a large black number 13 on his fuselage."

In the 1928 Portland to Cleveland air race, he won $1,500. While he and his mechanic were returning to Portland, the engine on Rankin's Great Lakes Trainer cut out in a cloud bank. Flying on instruments, he crash-landed on a hilltop in the jagged Cascade Mountains; both men walked away.

Rankin was the first pilot credited with flying nonstop from Canada to Mexico in 1929. By 1931, he specialized in aerobatic stunts, and in Charlotte, North Carolina, he set the world record of 131 consecutive outside loops in 131 minutes, almost tripling the previous record. He often roared over the runway, inverted at low altitude, and snatched a flag with a wingtip. At the 1935 National Air Race in Cleveland, Rankin was judged U.S. aerobatic champion.

Hollywood beckoned and Rankin moved to Los Angeles to fly in numerous films, including Paramount Pictures' 1938 feature *Men with Wings,* which included Andy Devine, Fred MacMurray, and Donald O'Connor and was filmed in the San Fernando Valley. Rankin performed aerial stunts in the classic 1927 Paramount Pictures silent film about WWI fighter pilots called *Wings,* directed by William A. Wellman. It was not only the first film to win the Academy Award for Best Picture but also the only silent film ever to win it. The box-office hit starred Clara Bow and Charles "Buddy" Rogers, and featured Gary Cooper in a scene that launched his star in Hollywood and ignited an affair with Bow, the iconic 1920s flapper and "It" girl.

Rankin gave lessons to film royalty and was elected president of the powerful Hollywood Motion Picture Pilots Association. In 1938, he won the International Aerobatic Championship's $2,000 first prize in St. Louis, Missouri. In 1939, Rankin was featured with an aerobatic team called Tex Rankin's Hollywood Aces at the Golden Gate International Exposition and performed hair-raising routines, including flying under the new bridge, upside down, almost daily. In 1940, Rankin signed a lucrative contract with the War Department to train pilots.

As an air cadet, Jack met Rankin in June 1943, and during the ten-week primary flight training course, he learned the aerobatic skills that saved his life "a dozen times during the war." Awed by Rankin's records, skills, and fearlessness in the air, Jack blossomed as a natural pilot. He was an excellent student studying under an experienced flight instructor, and before long he became quite a good aerobatic pilot, flying underneath bridges and doing inverted loops. On one occasion, he almost burned out a plane's engine by flying upside down for twenty miles from Visalia to Tulare. The plane, not equipped for aerobatic flight, couldn't circulate oil while inverted. After Jack landed, the mechanics were dumbfounded by the smoking, red-hot engine. Jack kept his mouth shut and learned yet another important flight lesson.

Jack practiced all the time. If he was climbing he practiced power-on stalls; if he was descending he practiced power-off stalls. "That is just my nature."

The "world was stunned" when, after decades of instruction emphasizing flight safety, fifty-three-year-old Rankin (and two businessmen, charter passengers) died suddenly on February 23, 1947, in Klamath Falls, Oregon. Rankin died like his most illustrious student, Richard Bong—from engine failure just after takeoff.

10

FLIGHT TRAINING

After completing primary training at Rankin's school in Tulare, Jack was sent, in the fall of 1943, to Minter Field near Bakersfield, California, for basic flight school. Minter was a facility where nearly 12,000 WWII pilots received instruction in a variety of trainers, including PT-19s, BT-13s, and the AT-6.

He started out flying sixty-six hours in an open-cockpit PT-19 Cornell, manufactured by the Fairchild Aviation Corporation in Farmingdale, New York. The two-passenger trainer was powered by a 175-horsepower, 6-cylinder, air-cooled engine. During the war, 7,742 PT-19s were built. He then graduated to the Vultee BT-13, one of the most widely used American training aircraft of the war. Jack logged seventy-three hours in the BT-13, which had an enclosed canopy, seated two with the cadet in front and the instructor behind, and had dual controls. It was equipped with "blind-flying" capabilities to teach instrumentation flight principles.

John Pyram King Sr., a Jacksonville, Florida, native and a WW II B-24 copilot who also trained on the BT-13, recalled that the plane's nickname, the "Vultee Vibrator," fit its flight characteristics perfectly.

By war's end 11,537 B-13 Valiants had been sold to the army, although the company's owner didn't enjoy the planes' huge success. Jerry Vultee, along with his wife Sylvia, died when the plane he piloted crashed and burned in a blizzard near Wilson Mountain at Sedona, Arizona, in 1938. Today, a bronze plaque memorializes the Vultees at the crash site in Coconino National Forest. Despite the BT-13's instrument-training capabilities, Vultee, who had failed to avail himself of the plane's capabilities and had no instrument training, was trapped and doomed in the white-out.

The next plane Jack trained in was the North American AT-6 Texan trainer, considered one of the most important aircraft of the era, with a production run more than 17,000 units. First built in 1935, the Texan was in continual production for a decade and remained in active military use for the next twenty-five years. In the mid-1930s, North American Aviation sold a few of the planes to licensee Mitsubishi Industries of Japan. The AT-6 saw service through the Korean War; the air force and Marine Corps outfitted the low, slow Texans with white phosphorous rockets and used the aging planes for forward air control of jet fighters, bombers, and artillery before finally retiring the plane in the 1950s.

North American Aviation's technical representative for the AT-6 was Jack Canary. In 1966, Canary built two Fokker triplane replicas for 20th Century Fox's World War I German fighter-ace epic, *The Blue Max*. In 1968, Fox hired Canary to create a Pearl Harbor–bound Japanese fighter squadron for the film *Tora! Tora! Tora!* Canary, who assembled a small air force for the film, including several B-17s, chose to adapt BT-13 and AT-6 trainers to resemble the iconic Japanese fighters. Modifications and re-painting were under way at Long Beach Airport as Canary traveled the country buying up old planes. In August 1968, Canary died when a BT-13 he was ferrying to California caught fire in the air.

Jack flew eighty training hours in the AT-6, and when he graduated from cadet to second lieutenant, his younger sister, Gladys, who married a trainee pilot buddy of Jack's, Roger Ashton, proudly pinned his silver wings onto his chest. Jack promptly requested assignment to P-38 twin-engine fighter training in late 1943.

The army, in its infinite wisdom and desperate need for multi-engine pilots to man the thousands of four-engine bombers then coming off the massive B-17 and B-29 production lines at Boeing's Seattle, Washington, and Wichita, Kansas, plants and Ford Motor's enormous consolidated B-24 Willow Run plant in Ypsilanti, Michigan, denied Rencher's request and sent him to B-17 training at Williams Field in Yuma, Arizona, instead. Jack, incandescent with rage, protested "I am a fighter pilot," to no avail. "I was very pissed," he recalled, but off to Yuma he went. Rencher was upset because, in a classic military catch-22, and despite his sterling record, having selected fighters and been denied them, he was automatically placed in a copilot slot, whereas cadets like Werner, who had initially selected bombers, were trained as pilots and aircraft commanders.

Assigned to the 306th Flight Training Group, Jack again earned an Excellent rating, and, after completing copilot training, he was told he would not be shipping out to war since he had been selected as a B-17 instructor. For the next several months, Jack flew an average of eight hours a day, six days a week, racking up flight hours while training cadets in the Flying Fortress. "They were mostly high school kids," recalled Jack, who, then twenty-three, was deemed an "older guy."

After 200 flying hours in the Fortress, he checked out as a first pilot but remained stuck in the copilot-instructor slot. Eventually, after completing nearly a thousand hours, in February 1944, Jack received orders to join the Eighth Replacement Wing in Salt Lake City.

The Eighth Army had been losing aircrews at a staggering 10 percent rate in Europe in 1943; the odds of coming home unharmed after "the normal maximum tour of twenty-five (later thirty-five) missions in a heavy bomber (the most dangerous) left a crew member with less than a 50 percent chance of escaping death or physical harm. Only one-fourth of the crew members could expect to complete all twenty-five missions." The army was scrambling to field replacement bomber crews in the dark days before long-range escort fighters, especially the P-51 Mustang, were available.

After arriving in Salt Lake City, Jack found himself cooling his heels. He would get up in the morning, report for roll call, and then have the rest of the day to do nothing. Week after idle week went by, while around him men were being formed into crews and shipping out to combat assignments daily. "There was no duty, absolutely nothing to do," recalled Jack. What he didn't know was that the FBI had been investigating him for a special assignment—to shoot Werner Goering.

11

THE NAZI'S NEPHEW

"So this is the guy I'm supposed to kill—maybe," Jack thought as he shook hands with Werner for the first time at Fort Douglas air base in Utah in late February 1944. The big Nazi's nephew. Jack up sized Werner silently. Although Werner was captain of the plane and outranked him, he was three years younger than Jack and had only about one-tenth the flight hours that Jack had, and it pissed Jack off.

At six feet Werner was taller than Jack. He was Hollywood handsome, with blond hair, piercing blue eyes, a trim waist, and symmetrical facial features. He was fastidious about his perfectly pressed uniform and "didn't seem to sweat." He was remote, calm, quiet, and reserved. "He didn't say much," recalled Jack, "then, or ever." Werner looked like he had been sent from Central Casting for the role of heavy-bomber flight commander. He also could have been a poster boy for the Nazis, which is exactly what concerned Hoover. Only nineteen, Werner had a heavy responsibility, and because of his name, a steep uphill battle proving himself in the Eighth, whose men were dying by the dozens daily at the hands of Hermann Göring's Luftwaffe pilots and flak gunners.

The day before they first met, Jack was ordered to report to the commanding officer at 1300 hours in his Class A full-dress uniform. The bird colonel ordered him to wait and walked out of the room, soon returning with two beefy civilians in dark suits and white shirts. After introducing Jack to two men "from Washington," the CO left and shut the door behind him. It struck Jack as odd and ominous. He'd recently received a letter from an aunt in Eager, Arizona, who wrote, "I hope you didn't do anything wrong, but I wanted to let you know that two FBI agents were here last week asking questions all over town about you." A letter from his favorite high school teacher followed with a similar message: two FBI agents had been asking about him in Phoenix. An instructor for the last several months, he was now eager to fly combat missions. Yet he had been hanging around Fort Douglas with nothing to do for weeks. Jack thought his past had caught up with him.

Was it punching out the assistant principal before leaving high school at age fifteen? Consorting with a known bank robber who bribed his way out of a New Mexico prison with stolen loot that Jack's father retrieved from its hiding place in the mountains? Welding stills for boot-leggers? Doing armed bodyguarding for a professional gambler? Maybe it was the whole shooting match. It's all guilt by association in a court of law, but even the wartime military, scrambling for pilots, was starchy about conduct unbecoming an officer.

The FBI men pulled their badges, and the younger one said, "We have come to you with a top-secret voluntary assignment. If you choose not to accept it, there will be no blemish on your military record, providing you don't say a word regarding what we are about to ask of you." Jack, frustrated with his wait and copilot assignment, thought to himself that his military career "meant nothing anyway" and nodded in agreement.

The agent continued, "We have a pilot we don't trust. We have checked him out and can't find anything wrong with him, but his uncle is Hermann Göring, a top Nazi and head of the German air force. This pilot, Werner G. Goering, was born right here in Salt Lake, but he speaks fluent German, and headquarters in Washington said we can't take the risk that he might land one of our bombers in Europe."

Jack asked exactly what they wanted him to do. The two men glanced at each other and then the older man spoke for the first time. "We want you to join his crew as his copilot, go to England, and fly missions with him, but if he ever tries to land the plane in Europe or if the plane has to ditch, he can't fall into German hands. We want you to shoot him dead before he can ever be captured or land the plane for whatever reason. We just don't trust him because his uncle is Hermann Göring, the number two Nazi and the head of the Luftwaffe." The identification was unnecessary. Like most everyone, Jack had watched Göring strut around in fancy uniforms in newsreel shorts and had seen his picture in the newspapers. "Washington says we can't take the risk that he will desert or even be captured alive. We have been looking for someone who is an expert in small arms, a solid B-17 pilot, and who can do the job. We think you might fit the bill, and we want you to volunteer to sign on as his copilot."

Jack was stunned, partly with relief. He had figured he was going to be broken in rank and stripped of his pilot's wings. Instead, the FBI and military intelligence wanted him to be their hit man! If that's what it takes to remain a pilot and fly B-17 missions, he could handle it. He was not ruthless at all, but he was tough and knew from his days as a bodyguard that looking ruthless went a long way. "Why, hell," Jack said, "I'll shoot him and dump his body out of the plane."

"No, no, don't do that," the older FBI agent said. "Shoot him in the head, if you have to kill him, and then try to bring the body back. Dead or alive, we want to keep him out of the Germans' hands. But dead is okay if the plane goes down and you're in danger of being captured."

Jack understood their concern about Göring's nephew. Göring was the last commander of the legendary Richthofen Squadron and the first commander of the Gestapo and the Luftwaffe; speaker of the German parliament, prime minister of Prussia, and president of the Prussian State Council; Reichmaster of forestry and game; the führer's special commissioner for the Four-Year Plan; chairman of the Reich Defense Council; Field Marshal, then Reichsmarschall of the Greater German Reich; chairman of the Scientific Research Council; and head of the giant industrial conglomerate that bore his name.

He wondered why the army would let Werner fly at all, especially in Europe, and why fate had placed him in the assassin's seat next to Werner. But it was his job, it was war, and he would do it. The two largely uneducated lower-class outsiders who successfully became pilots against the odds were now strangers joined at the hip in what started off as an uneasy, and potentially deadly, shotgun marriage in which the FBI played matchmaker.

The memory of his near-washout pre-solo flight embarrassed and scared the hell out of Werner. Compared to Jack, who always excelled in flight tests and had hundreds of hours already under his belt, Werner was a rookie in the cockpit and he knew it, but he was the commander, despite being three years younger and having only a fraction of Jack's flight hours and mechanical expertise. Unaware of Jack's secret orders, Werner was nevertheless acutely conscious of Jack's initial dissatisfaction and reflexive criticisms as a former instructor. Like an old married couple, they got on each other's nerves—immediately and for the next seventy years.

Werner's view was that "basically the copilot is there to step in if something happens to the commander. It was really a thankless job. I knew Jack was several years older and had a lot more experience than me and I could imagine him thinking, 'What the hell am I doing next to this nineteen-year-old kid?' I would let Jack do some of the flying once we were airborne, but the takeoffs, the bomb runs, and the landings were the pilot's responsibility, and I did them." Werner figured Jack was just an unlucky fighter pilot candidate with an attitude who'd been put into the copilot slot, as was routine.

Werner and Jack were assigned a crew and started training as a ten-man team. For weeks, rivalry between them was quiet yet palpable. The tension was fueled on Jack's side by his resentment and secret assignment, and on Werner's by his pride in command. It was exacerbated because neither loner had ever been forced into such tight professional and physical quarters with another. They spent their waking hours together and slept in adjoining bunks. Then there was the constant danger that training crews faced. Death was all around them. Fully one-third of USAAF airplane losses from December 1941 to August 1945—21,583 of the 65,164—occurred within the continental United States.

Thanks to his aerobatic training with Tex Rankin, his mechanical expertise, and hundreds of flight hours as an instructor, Jack's contribution was invaluable and, he often felt underappreciated by his curt, chilly commander. For his part, Werner proved to be a superb formation pilot and a detail-oriented and confident commander. Jack was the master of poor-visibility instrumentation flight and instantaneous mechanical, hydraulic, and electrical diagnostics and jerry-rigging. From his experience as a heavy-equipment mechanic and continual study of the B-17 manuals, Jack knew the plane inside out. "There was nothing in that plane I could not take apart and put back together, except the radio."

The Werner-Hermann connection was never discussed openly by

the crew, but the information had been published in *Collier's Weekly* and became common knowledge wherever they were stationed, to Werner's annoyance.

Because of his name and nature, the remote, gruff Werner, a self-described martinet, was initially mistrusted, unpopular yet feared by his crew. He stayed to himself, and when he spoke, it was usually to chew someone out, but always in a quiet, reasoned tone. He was a stickler, but not an abusive, insecure hothead. He showed no emotion and did not care that he was considered by some a "Kraut." He only cared about performance and led by sterling example.

On March 4, 1944, the crew transferred to Dalhart, Texas, where they underwent four-hour training flights in the morning, four hours of classroom instruction, then another four hours in the air before dinner. They roared over the desert in the thirty-two-ton bomber at a hair-raising 150 feet at 150 miles an hour, learning air-to-ground tactics that they never used in Europe, as it turned out. They trained in air-to-air combat, with a plane towing a target. The gunners had different-colored bullets, so it could be determined who had actually hit it. The pilots' combined experience and discipline paid off: the Goering crew rarely scored less than an Excellent rating.

They trained in Texas until May 1, logging 50 flight hours before being shipped to Tampa's MacDill Field, where they flew another 100 hours perfecting gunnery, bombardment, and, above all, critical close-order flight formation skills. It was during this period that Jack realized how cool and competent Werner was while flying in the tightly packed combat boxes. Any tiny miscalculation by the pilot could be disastrous. While at MacDill, on June 6, they learned about the success of Operation Overlord, the D-day invasion of France.

Werner and Jack finally bonded as training drew to a close. They went out a few times in Tampa together, and, for the first time, the two loners realized that they somehow complemented each other's skills and personalities, and that together they had become greater than the sum of their parts, thus giving them a better chance of survival. Neither smoked or drank at a time when both vices were accepted parts of the tight fraternal social life centered on the officer's club. The pair stayed apart from their brother officers and built a mutually protective bond unlike any they had ever had before or after. The fact that both were lower-class reservist outsiders in the status-conscious West Point and college-educated "regular army" air corps contributed to their shared insularity.

Werner's name, peremptory leadership style, and obvious conviction that he was born to command initially fueled the crew's misgivings. Jack acted as a buffer between Werner and the men. Werner's relationship to the head of the Luftwaffe, then responsible for tens of thousands of aircrew deaths, gave the fearful green crew second thoughts. Shortly before departing for England, the enlisted men cornered Jack and asked him if he thought their chances of getting home alive might be better in another crew.

In the movie *Band of Brothers,* just prior to shipping out for England, the sergeants of Easy Company told the colonel in charge of their regiment that they did not want to go into action under their current company commander, whom they considered incompetent, and requested transfers to other companies. The colonel solved the problem by removing the officer in question and putting Lieutenant Richard Winters, whom the sergeants trusted and respected, in command of Easy Company. But this wasn't a movie: Jack couldn't remove Werner from command, and he didn't want to.

"We're the best crew in the squadron," he told them. "Good crews have a better chance of survival than bad crews. I don't think you have anything to worry about, but it's your call."

He'd wanted to say, "I'm glad to fly with Werner Goering, and you should be, too," but he kept his reply simple.

"Well, Jack," said Sgt. Orall Gustafson, the top-turret gunner, "I go where you go."

"I go with Goering," said Jack.

"That's good enough for me," concluded Gustafson as the other men nodded in agreement. To Jack's relief, the sergeants all decided to remain in Werner's crew. He never mentioned it to Werner because he couldn't see any good coming from it.

Yet Jack still had his own misgivings. Werner's stubbornness, arrogance, and aloofness—qualities that his acquaintances repeatedly commented on to the FBI and military intelligence while also vouching for his patriotism—would irritate anyone. Beyond that, he still bristled whenever Jack offered suggestions for improving his flying technique, especially with regard to instrument flight, Werner's biggest weakness.

While at MacDill, waist gunner Sgt. William LaPerch got it into his head to get married before shipping out. Most of the guys thought he was crazy or, more likely, had been "shotgunned," but all, including Werner, showed up for the hastily arranged afternoon wedding in the base chapel and, later, at the reception in a small Tampa bar and restaurant. Tables and chairs were pushed aside to make a dance floor. The crew was having a good time dancing with the bride's girlfriends. Jack recalled the prettiest ones clustered around the tall, handsome Werner in his perfectly creased uniform. Everyone was sweating on that humid Florida afternoon, but Werner, as always, looked like he'd stepped out of a movie magazine. Always the gentleman, Werner didn't take advantage of his looks with the ladies. Jack watched the bridesmaids flutter around Werner and felt both jealousy and admiration.

Too shy to strike up a conversation with one of the girls or ask for a dance, Jack sat alone with LaPerch's mother. Suddenly she grabbed his sleeve and leaned across the table. He could see tear tracks in her pancake makeup. The unpleasant scent of alcohol on her breath reminded him of his dad and of tense days spent as a bodyguard at poker tables in bars full of rowdy drunks.

"Please promise me you'll look after my Billy, Lieutenant Rencher," the sobbing Mrs. LaPerch said while honking into a paper napkin. "Take care of him and bring him home alive." Jack almost recoiled and wanted to say, "The hell with him. He's a grown man, same as me, and has got to look out for himself," then realized that as LaPerch's senior officer, he was in fact responsible for him. He cleared his throat. "We'll do our best, Mrs. LaPerch. We're one of the top crews in the squadron, and we have a better chance of getting through this." The woman dissolved in grateful sobs while Jack looked across the room at Werner's broad shoulders and for the first time felt grateful their positions were not reversed. He was happy not to bear the weight of command. It struck him as funny that, not long before that, he'd said the same thing to the sergeants when they asked him what he thought about flying with Göring's nephew. Their crew had just been certified as battle-ready with highest marks. The teamwork and friendship that had developed with Werner were the most rewarding things he'd ever experienced in his life, and together they'd molded the crew into a proud, confident, crackerjack outfit.

Over the months spent training the crew, Jack realized that he did not like commanding men or having ultimate responsibility for others. The irony of his ultimate responsibility for Werner increasingly weighed on him. It was a tough break that he couldn't become a fighter pilot, but despite the burdensome task Jack had sworn to complete for the government, he decided it was good to be paired with Werner, who had command presence in spades.

As a poker-trained expert in odds and percentage calculation, whenever Jack thought about what measure of courage it would take to endure the deadly game of musical chairs they faced, he realized that Werner's grim determination, pure guts, and rigid sense of duty gave Jack the inspiration he needed to do his own duty, no matter how terrible that might be. Werner, less introspective and privately more religious than Jack, didn't dwell on or seem to fret about the deadly odds, and he was unaware of the particular circumstances that lessened his personal odds of survival immeasurably. Werner had become Jack's anchor in the deadly tide sweeping them inexorably toward war, yet he was an anchor Jack knew that he might have to cut loose one terrible day. "What the hell have I gotten myself into?" he wondered, not for the last time.

Werner and Jack's crew earned the highest scores in the squadron and were approved to ship out. Following the rigorous four-month training regimen they'd undergone in Utah, Texas, and Florida during the spring of 1944, the distinction was an early tribute to both of their skills and their crew's ability. Jack's prior experience as a B-17 training officer in Yuma paid huge dividends, as did Werner's ability to focus during dangerous flight formation and aerial tactic training. Not all crews were fortunate enough to have commanders as skilled as Werner and Jack. Thousands of airmen died during stateside training, never once having seen combat.

Having forged the best aircrew in their squad, both men were proud and confident. On one of their last nights in Tampa, Jack prevailed on Werner to join him for a night on the town. They received permission for an overnight pass and took off to explore Tampa's sultry nightlife. In Class A dress uniforms, the two baby-faced aviators took a bus from the base to Tampa's waterfront district, which was packed with bars, seafood restaurants, MPs, drunk servicemen from all branches of the military, and throngs of lovely women pretending they didn't want to be noticed.

Jack and Werner hit the town with plenty of cash. There hadn't

been many spending opportunities during the months of intensive training, and with their Depression-era upbringings, neither parted with cash
easily. Jack and Werner met two cute army nurses, invited them to dinner,
and then allowed themselves to be taken on a tour of Tampa's hotspots.
The women, who Jack doubted would normally have given him the time
of day, seemed happy enough being accompanied by two gallant and
generous pilots—officers and gentlemen. Jack beamed while a detached
Werner took it all in with his usual sangfroid.

Although neither man drank, they bought the girls glass after glass
of champagne in bars frequented exclusively by fellow officers. Enlisted
men had their own racially segregated, cheaper, and rowdier watering
holes. Evening stretched into early morning as the four young people,
barely out of their teens, swanned from club to club, ending in nearby
Ybor City, on the racier side of the tracks. They jived to big bands, swayed
to Cuban music, and experienced a night so carefree and sultry that one
wouldn't have known it was wartime.

With Werner at his side, Jack realized his social status had greatly
improved since he had enlisted two years earlier. Then he was nothing
but a high school dropout; now he was an officer and a gentleman. His
best pal looked like a Hollywood leading man, and Jack was his faithful
wingman. The bar-hopping wound down; the two pilots invited their
giddy, tipsy dates to an after-hours café for a steak-and-eggs breakfast and,
more important, hot coffee to sober them up.

In the wee hours they waited patiently for a taxi to ferry the nurses
home safely. They paid the driver an extravagant tip and noted his cab
number. While this Old World chivalrous behavior seemed to come naturally to Werner, it was enlightening, self-conscious, and ennobling for
Jack, the kid from the wilds.

Hanging out with Werner, Jack felt a part of something larger than
himself—something extraordinary. He loved the camaraderie and the
status that came with his uniform and from having a handsome, cool officer as a close male friend, his first, and he found that he cared for and
respected Werner in the only way men of the era could—silently. Recall-
ing their bond seven decades later, he said, "Werner was the only friend I
took away from the war, the only friend I really ever had."

As the taxi pulled away, the frugal duo realized they were both flat
broke. Each thought the other had an emergency fiver. They cracked up at

their predicament until they were weak, laughing stone sober until their sides ached, leaning on a streetlight for support.

"Hell, Werner, it's four in the morning and we're ten miles from the base." Jack chuckled. "We're going miss roll call and get written up for it."

"The hell we are," Werner replied, grinning, "but we'll have to double-time it. Let's go."

They had no choice but to hoof it home.

In the predawn cool of the late spring tropics, the pair walked ridiculously fast and heard Tampa Bay's gently lapping waters along Beach Front Park as they headed south. The wind stirred the palms along South West Shore Boulevard and prompted the morning salutation of egrets, parrots, and pelicans.

The pals trudged ever southward, took a left onto West Gandy Boulevard, a right onto South Manhattan Avenue, and cut across Rembrandt Gardens to MacDill's front gate. It took nearly two hours to get back to base, and they made it just in time for the mandatory 7:00 A.M. roll call.

A bond had been forged, one they would rely on many times in less bucolic settings. Jack found in Werner the older brother he never had and the man he could never be. Werner was his leader, his friend, and his target. Werner had opened up to Jack more than he had previously, and the men were enriched by each other. They knew they faced war, and possibly death, but from that day forward, the two ambitious lone wolves shared a fragile, unspoken, shared sense of not being alone.

12

TO ARMS

On June 17, the crew was certified as combat-ready for the European theater of operations. The pilots had assumed they'd fly a B-17 to England, but were told they would make the transatlantic crossing on *Aquitania,* the longest-serving Cunard ocean liner of the twentieth century. They set sail for the United Kingdom on July 15, 1944.

Launched in 1913, just after the *Titanic* disaster, *Aquitania* was the first ship to boast lifeboats for all passengers and was then the largest and most luxurious ship afloat. Nearly 900 feet long and 100 feet wide, it could race across the seas at 23 knots and was the only liner in its class to serve in both world wars.

Aquitania's maiden voyage to New York, on May 30, 1914, began on an ominous note; only one day earlier, the *Empress of Ireland* sank in the Saint Lawrence River after a collision with a Norwegian collier. In that little-remembered maritime tragedy 1,021 perished: 8 more than did during the *Titanic*'s sinking just two years earlier.

When WWI erupted, the British government seized the *Aquitania* and pressed it and its crew into the Royal Navy as an armed merchant cruiser. During its second military outing, just two weeks after joining the Royal Navy, on August 22, 1914, the *Aquitania* collided with the ocean liner *Canadian* in a heavy fog bank. The following year it served as a troopship and transported thousands to the ill-fated Gallipoli campaign in which 44,000 Allied soldiers died. Then it was converted to a hospital ship it brought home many of the same men who had sailed to Gallipoli on its outbound voyage, as casualties of war.

When the United States entered WWI in 1917, the ship brought American expeditionary forces to France and later returned American and Canadian troops home. During the interwar years, the refitted *Aquitania* cruised the Atlantic and the Mediterranean, and when WWII broke out, it was requisitioned as a troop transport on November 21, 1939. It sailed the world during the war, transporting Canadian, Australian, New Zealand, and finally American troops.

The three liners, *Aquitania, Queen Mary*, and *Queen Elizabeth*, were at the core of the "Atlantic shuttle service," according to Satchell; lacking escort from the navy, they used speed and intelligence decoding to avoid U-boats.

Jack, disappointed at not being selected to fly a B-17 to England, recalled the smelly, cramped conditions aboard the *Aquitania* and welcomed an opportunity to stand watch for German U-boats on the ship's bridge. Gus Gustafson recalled troops being "let onto the deck for only a half hour a day and then sprawling on mountains of Idaho potatoes in the steamy third-level hold."

Three days out, a hypervigilant Jack spotted a U-boat on the ship's starboard side and raised the alarm. The "sub" then spouted a column of water thirty feet high and, with a wave of its great tail, sounded to the great relief and amusement of British naval officers on the bridge. Approaching the United Kingdom, Jack also spotted a convoy that turned out to be a chain of rocky islands off the Irish coast. While aboard ship, the troops were entertained by Spike Jones and the City Slickers, a popular band that performed humorous arrangements of songs of the era. "Ballads and classical works receiving the 'Jones treatment' would be punctuated with gunshots, whistles, cowbells, and ridiculous vocals." Werner was impatient to get into action and passed time studying training manuals, including a pamphlet given to all soldiers by the War Department. It included instructions on how to behave in wartime England: "Remember you are coming from a country where your home is still safe, food is plentiful and lights are still burning. But you are now in a war zone. British soldiers and civilians have been living under a tremendous strain. They have been bombed night after night, month after month." The soldiers were instructed not to brag that U.S. soldiers were better paid than British troops; not to make fun of British accents, warm beer, and lack of soap; and to "never criticize the king or queen."

The abysmal weather of the British Isles was also mentioned. The guidebook promised the Americans that they'd get used to the weather. "But many never did. Warm beer and unwashed women they could learn to live with. But not the cold, wet, cloudy, horribly unpredictable weather."

The bombing campaign that the Goering crew joined in the summer of 1944 had been ordered by Winston Churchill and Franklin Roosevelt during the Casablanca Conference of January 1943. There, the two leaders had formally decided that the combined Allied offensive war in western Europe would begin in the air with round-the-clock bombing of Germany's military, oil, industrial, and transportation infrastructure. Churchill and FDR had to placate a furious Josef Stalin, who had expected and demanded a land invasion of the continent in 1943. Says Ferguson: "The more Stalin pressed the Western powers to open a second front in Western Europe, the more Churchill extolled the virtues of strategic bombing, promising attacks that 'would shatter the morale of the German people.'"

The bombers were the only way to strike Germany until the Allies could mount D-day, still eighteen months away. To some extent, bombers were used as a card in the high-stakes game being played between the three often-fractious Allied leaders. Roosevelt and Churchill knew, yet were forced to accept, that without long-range escort fighters like the P-51 Mustang, which had not yet arrived in sufficient numbers to make a difference, the bombers would suffer heavy losses. It was the price they paid to ensure Stalin would not be tempted to find a separate peace with Hitler. So they committed to bomb Germany round the clock; the Royal Air Force would take the night shift and the United States' Eighth, Ninth, and Fifteenth Air Forces would bomb by day. The communiqué issued at Casablanca included the following unambiguous goal for the Allied air forces:

> The progressive destruction and dislocation of the morale of the German military, industrial and economic system and the undermining of the morale of the German people, to the point where their capacity for armed resistance is fatally weakened.

A moral Rubicon had been crossed by the democracies, despite Roosevelt's high-minded pronouncements against "bombardment from the air of civilian populations or of unfortified cities" following the Luftwaffe's attack on Warsaw in 1939 and Neville Chamberlain's 1938 declaration that "air attacks against civilians are a violation of international law." The advent of "total war" put paid to gentlemanly peacetime nostrums.

When Werner and Jack joined the fight, the air war had been on for a half decade but was just getting into high gear, and there was plenty of fighting and dying to come, despite a widely held hope that D-day would end the war by Christmas of 1944. Fully three-quarters of the bombs dropped on Germany would fall during the last twelve months of the war. Of the 1.7 million sorties flown against Germany during the war, 1.4 million were flown in 1944 and 1945.

Incredibly, despite all the bombing missions by the Allies, 1944 represented the pinnacle of German fighter production, thanks to the logistical and production miracles orchestrated by Nazi armament minister Albert Speer. Despite the two-year-long Allied bombing offensive, more German fighters were produced in December 1944 than in July of that year. By early 1944, Speer had doubled the 1943 monthly production level of fighters, and by fall of that year he had more than tripled it. Newly introduced V-1 and V-2 German rockets rained on London; Messerschmitt-262 jet fighters appeared in combat for the first time; the Allied march toward the Rhine had become a bloody slog; the invasion of Italy was an ongoing and agonizing near-disaster; the Allied Italian offensive was a running sore. And ahead lay the Battle of the Bulge, the biggest and bloodiest battle American soldiers ever fought—one in which nearly 80,000 Americans were killed, wounded, or captured. The Allies just kept on bombing night and day.

Unlike Germany, the United States didn't have jets or new aircraft to throw into the mix, except for the P-51. For bombing, it was totally dependent on the aging B-17s and B-24s in Europe. Although the $3 billion B-29 Superfortress program had been in development since 1942, early test flights of the initial prototype experienced a serious chronic problem: the plane's engines often caught fire or simply cut out.

Worse, on February 18, 1943, the second B-29 prototype had two engines ignite simultaneously on the same wing, killing Boeing test pilot Edmund T. Allen and an entire crew of ten men; in addition, the plane crashed into a meatpacking plant three miles from the end of the Boeing runway. One fireman and nineteen meatpackers died on the ground. The third prototype almost crashed in a very close call, and many more accidents were to occur.

Harry S. Truman, chairman of the Senate's Special Committee to Investigate the National Defense Program, looked into what many now saw as a $3 billion boondoggle. Even after the B-29 was first deployed in Asia in April 1944, five crashed during a single week as a result of engine fire or overheating. The B-29 would never contribute to the air war over Germany.

Arriving in Britain in early August, Werner's crew was first sent to Bovingdon, England. This training base was the closest Eighth Air Force facility to London, and it was where General Dwight D. Eisenhower's personal air transport, a North American B-25 Mitchell, was based. At Bovingdon, Jack and Flight Officer Rex H. Markt, the navigator, learned to use a radar-based English navigational aid called the GEE box, short for ground electronic equipment. The British had built three transmitters about one hundred miles apart. Each sent a signal several hundred miles into the European mainland. Airborne receivers triangulated the signal and, if it was not jammed by the Germans, the navigators calculated their location. Pyne explains:

> As bombers flew in a particular direction, the navigator took a fix, which was accurate within a thousand yards. He took a successive number of fixes, connected the lines, and that was their heading in degrees. The box had a timer and navigators could measure the distance between the two points and, by knowing the time it took to get from one to another, they could compute ground speed.

Jack thought the GEE box was tremendous. He felt that the Goering crew's weakest link was its navigator, Markt, and was happy to see Markt quickly became adept with the GEE box. "Rex was a lousy navigator and the GEE box was literally a lifesaver for us." After two weeks at Bovingdon, the Goering crew went to Molesworth, home of the 303rd Bombardment Group, the Hell's Angels, their home for the rest of the war.

13

FRUIT OF A POISONED TREE

Hermann Göring's ancestors and relatives included German aviation pioneer Count Ferdinand von Zeppelin, a German army officer who developed his famous airships in 1897. The common threads of pioneering military aviation, love of adventure, willingness to take huge risks, and service to empire flowed through the family's history, along with darker and deeper currents. Two of Göring's nephews died in aerial combat, on the German side.

A Göring somewhere or another was involved in military aviation from the time when the first German dirigibles took to the sky a decade before Kitty Hawk, and two decades later when Count Manfred von Richthofen, the Red Baron of WWI, commanded his eventual successor, the twenty-four-year-old captain Hermann Wilhelm Göring.

The first zeppelin flew in July 1900 and a few were purchased by the Imperial German Army. By the start of WWI, the army had seven zeppelins, which reached a maximum speed of eighty-five miles per hour and could reach an altitude of 14,000 feet. The zeppelin had five machine guns and carried a bomb load of 4,400 pounds. The monumental airships had the dubious distinction of being the first aircraft to bomb civilian populations when, in January 1915, two 623-foot-long zeppelins bombed Yarmouth and King's Lynn in the south of England. The first zeppelin raid on London took place on May 31, 1915, and by the war's end about 550 British civilians had been killed by Germany's 115-strong zeppelin fleet.

The irony of the zeppelin's pioneering of terror bombing would be highlighted by both Hermann Göring's bombings of England and Werner Goering's personal role in the bombing of Germany. Göring's more distant relations included the nineteenth-century German romantic author and nationalist Hermann Grimm, a proponent of the concept of the German hero as a mover of history whom the Nazis claimed as one of their ideological forerunners; the pharmaceutical industrial family Merck; and even the highly respected Swiss diplomat and postwar president of the International Red Cross, Carl J. Burckhardt, who served as the last League of Nations high commissioner for the free city of Danzig from 1937 to 1939, until the Nazi invasion of Poland.

Göring's father, Heinrich Ernst, was a widower who married his housekeeper, fathering nine children in total. Hermann was related to the Chicago-based American engineer and steel industrialist Herman A. Brassert, whose family controlled H. G. Brassert & Company and contracted with Nazi Germany during the 1930s to build blast furnaces for the Hermann Göring Works.

On October 24, 1942, the United Features Syndicate published influential political columnist Drew Pearson's "Washington Merry-Go-Round," which contained a section about Göring's relations in the United States. Pearson reported that in 1939, an American engineer, H. A. Brassert of Chicago, an American citizen and steel industrialist and distant relation of Hermann Göring, had constructed blast furnaces for the Hermann Göring Works, the huge military industrial complex Göring headed. The U.S. Treasury, reported Pearson, put Brassert "on the blacklist and froze his funds." The column kicked open a hornet's nest and resulted in a congressional inquiry that revealed that Brassert had also given the State Department a report regarding a conversation he had had with Roberto María Ortiz, the former president of Argentina. Brassert had made a study for the Argentine government, which wanted to establish a steel mill, but the pro-American Ortiz told him it would be impossible to have the mill constructed by an American, since "the German and Italian elements in my country are very strong . . . and . . . they have been strengthened by the arrival of thousands of 'tourists' who are actually agents and spies. . . . These agents declare that Germany is about to win the war and will come over here to run Argentina."

14

THE BLUE MAX

When WWI erupted in August 1914, Göring was already a junior officer in the Prinz Wilhelm 112th Infantry. Göring, a spoiled youth yet a successful military academy graduate, was by all accounts eager for battle and was one of the first German officers in the war to experience it, literally within hours of the war's outbreak.

His unit was based in Mülhausen, on the west side of the Rhine River in the Alsace-Lorraine, and was exposed to a sudden French army advance. This was territory that France had lost in the Franco-Prussian War in 1870 and was determined to regain. Göring's unit fell back across the Rhine, and forward elements of the French army promptly filled the vacuum. A general hoisted the French flag in Mülhausen and welcomed its stunned inhabitants back as French citizens.

During the celebration, Göring led a platoon that crossed back over the Rhine in an armored train and conducted a series of small spoiling raids, almost capturing the French general in the process and causing the French army to withdraw. Göring returned with four French prisoners and early glory. Although the action had little effect on the war, his name was mentioned in dispatches—one of the first officers to have that distinction. Following his initial burst of adventure, however, Göring discovered that the life of an infantryman was not to his liking when his regiment was ordered into the trenches and rain turned them into freezing, deadly mud pits as stalemate enveloped the Western Front.

Fortunately for Göring, he developed rheumatic fever following a streptococcal infection caused by the filthy trench conditions. His knees became grossly inflamed and he was effectively crippled. The illness probably saved his life, since he was invalided to a military hospital and thus missed the first Battle of the Marne in September 1914, in which both sides experienced about 250,000 casualties and saw disproportionally high death rates among young line infantry officers, which Göring had been.

While convalescing in a Freiburg hospital, he was visited by a friend who had transferred to the German Flying Service and become a pilot. Determined not to return to the trenches, and envious of his friend's more glamorous posting, Göring immediately wrote to his commanding officer requesting a transfer to flight school; after receiving no reply, he forged a signature on the necessary documents and joined his friend in the air service. Initially a photographer, he rode in the backseat of a German biplane, leaning out with the cumbersome cameras of the period to take photographs of enemy trench emplacements. Occasionally he took potshots at enemy planes with his service revolver. He was already flying when his commander's response arrived. To Göring's horror, his commander denied his request for a transfer and ordered him back to his unit immediately. "Technically, he had laid himself open to a charge of forging transfer papers and deserting his unit," says Leonard Mosley, "the latter being the second most serious crime an officer could commit in wartime (the first being desertion under fire)."

Not only Hermann's career but his liberty, and possibly his life, were at stake. When his outraged commanding officer demanded a court-martial, Göring contacted his godfather—also his namesake and his mother's lover—Dr. Hermann von Epenstein. (Göring's family lived for almost two decades in von Epenstein's castle, along with Hermann's often drunk, openly cuckolded, much less wealthy and older father, Heinrich Ernst, who was not even allowed onto the second floor, where his wife and von Epenstein had adjoining bedrooms.) Dr. von Epenstein, a wealthy Jew turned Catholic physician who had purchased his honorific "von," conveniently produced a medical certificate declaring Hermann unfit for trench service, possibly saving his skin in the process.

Narrowly evading the court-martial, Göring was accepted by the aristocrat-dominated air service only after the personal intercession of Crown Prince Friedrich Wilhelm, whom Hermann had impressed during a debriefing session after a particularly successful air reconnaissance.

By the end of 1914, Göring had proved to be a brave airman albeit a photographer, earning an Iron Cross 2nd Class in March 1915. In May 1916 he daringly photographed the breastworks at Verdun in such detail he was presented to Commanding General Erich von Falkenhayn and received the Iron Cross 1st Class personally from the prince in the field. By October, he had earned his wings and had engaged enemy aircraft for the first time as a pilot. He served in several units with increasing success until November 1916, when he was shot down and wounded by a British Sopwith Camel. He managed to fly back to the German lines and luckily landed next to a hospital unit, which again probably saved his life. He fully recovered from a gunshot to the thigh and returned to duty in 1917. Between May and October 1917 he shot down about a dozen planes and was awarded two other high decorations. By June 1918, he had racked up twenty-two kills and was awarded the highest of all awards for a German imperial officer, the Pour le Mérite, or Blue Max. Capping off his WWI laurels, he was selected as commander of the world-famous Richthofen squadron, following the death of both the Red Baron and his immediate successor within a matter of days. After that, Göring did very little flying. At war's end, he defied orders to turn his squad's aircraft over to the Allies and ordered them destroyed.

In the early 1920s, Göring met Hitler in Munich and promptly joined the Nazi Party as its best connected and most decorated member, marching next to Hitler during the ill-fated Bavarian Beer Hall Putsch of 1923. Göring was shot in the thigh, but unlike Hitler, he escaped arrest and imprisonment and fled to Innsbruck, Austria.

His extended recovery, in a penurious Austrian exile, led to a lifelong morphine addiction and several years in the wilderness, during which he was in and out of drug rehabilitation clinics. Once he was straightjacketed and nearly declared insane after attacking a nurse during a violent demand for morphine. It came close to ruining his reputation, but he hushed it up and by the late 1920s, with Hitler out of prison and the Nazi Party on the rise, he was able to regain his status, second only to Hitler and nominally head of Germany's Flying Clubs, a clandestine effort to build up military aviation under the guise of civilian glider training.

In 1928, Göring was one of twelve Nazis, including Joseph Goebbels, first elected to the Reichstag, and he began to wield influence with, and extract bribes from, industrialists who were vying for aircraft contracts from Lufthansa, Germany's national airline. Göring's increasing influence over aviation-related matters translated into ever more expensive gifts. By the time the Nazis came to power in early 1933, Göring's rise was unmistakable. On August 30, 1932, prior to Hitler's assuming the chancellorship, Göring was elected president of the Reichstag, and, in April 1933, premier of Prussia. This was, according to Roger Manvell and Heinrich Fraenkel, "a personal triumph for the man who only five years previously had been in exile with neither place nor prospects in Germany, and who only seven years before had been confined in a straitjacket."

"From this period, Göring's financial status was inextricably entangled with the perquisites and prizes of office," and through blatant graft, he became one of the most conspicuous, fattest, and wealthiest politicians in Europe. Göring starred in international newsreels in 1935 when he married his second wife, the divorced actress Emmy Sonnemann, following the 1931 death of his first wife, Baroness Carin von Kantzow, a Swedish aristocrat who left her first husband and their son to marry the then-penniless but dashing Göring in the 1920s. By all accounts, he was a loving and faithful husband to both wives and fathered a daughter in his second marriage. In 1935, when Göring married Sonnemann, the führer personally honored him by standing as his best man in the Berlin social extravaganza of the year.

During the Spanish civil war, Göring commanded the Condor Legions in civilian bombings. With the September 1939 invasion of Poland, which Göring had his doubts about, and the resulting start of WWII, Hermann Göring turned the family name into a source of increasing shame for the Utah Goerings.

He oversaw the brutally efficient air war over Poland and authorized civilian bombings of Warsaw and, later, England during the Blitz, following the loss of the Battle of Britain in late summer and fall of 1940. His career was at its peak and was praised by Hitler during the opening stages of the Russian campaign, in 1941, when the Luftwaffe decimated the sleeping Soviet air force on the ground during the initial phase of Operation Barbarossa. The Reich Marshal's reputation and standing with Hitler went into decline after promising and failing to relieve the trapped and doomed Sixth Army at Stalingrad in late 1942, and as the Allies began to retaliate with ever more intense bombing of Germany.

15

MOLESWORTH

After the navigation course, Werner's crew was assigned to the 303rd Bomb Group (H) Hell's Angels in Molesworth, not far from Cambridge. The Molesworth name was among the oldest in the history of the British Isles. The first members of the clan arrived from France during the Norman Conquest of 1066, which proved to be the last successful invasion of England. The three major-power invasion threats over the next millennium—by Philip II of Spain, Napoleon Bonaparte of France, and Hitler—all failed or were abandoned.

King Edward the Confessor, who commissioned Westminster Abbey, named William of Normandy his successor in 1051. After Edward's death in early 1066, Harold, Duke of Wessex, a pretender to the throne with some valid historical claim, was quickly crowned. William assembled an invasion force of 5,000 knights and successfully crossed the English Channel, defeated Harold's army, and killed Harold, who was shot through the eye by a Norman archer at the Battle of Hastings on October 14. William, "the Conqueror," was crowned in Westminster Abbey on Christmas Day 1066. Halley's comet was visible for an extended period in March 1066, and was thought to be an omen. The comet is prominent in the 700-year-old Bayeux tapestry, a British-made 210-foot-long woven history of the Norman Conquest that can be viewed today in Bayeux, France, not far from the D-day invasion beaches. The tapestry was seized twice in seven centuries: once by Napoleon and once by Hitler.

The Molesworth family settled in Cambridgeshire on land that includes the airfield site. The family name suggests their early occupation; in

Old English, *mulesword* was an enclosure for mules. During WWII, Lt. Gen. George Noble Molesworth served in the British India Office. He died in 1968.

The Royal Flying Corps selected Molesworth for an air base during WWI. The base and runways underwent renovation following the 1940 Battle of Britain and again in 1942 before the arrival of the American heavy bombers.

In February 1942, Gen. Ira Eaker, then head of the Eighth Air Force, flew to England with a staff of six and inspected and selected Molesworth as one of the first of dozens of American air bases in England. The facility was improved to Class A standard for heavy bombers; the runways were extended and support facilities were constructed, including the ubiquitous Quonset huts to house the men. A Quonset hut is a lightweight prefabricated structure of corrugated galvanized steel with a semicircular cross section. In 1941, the military needed an all-purpose lightweight structure that could be shipped anywhere and assembled without skilled labor. The George A. Fuller Construction Company, the inventor of the modern skyscraper, including New York's iconic Flatiron Building, got the contract, and the first Quonset huts were in production in Rhode Island within weeks. The huts' ends were covered with plywood, with cutout doors and windows. The interior was insulated and had pressed wood lining and wood floors. The 720-square-foot building could be placed on concrete, on pilings, or directly on the ground. It typically housed twenty men in two rows of ten bunks in an open and flexible interior space that allowed them to be used for as barracks, latrines, offices, medical and dental offices, isolation wards, kitchens, and mess halls.

Between 150,000 and 170,000 Quonset huts were manufactured during the war. After the war, the U.S. military sold off surplus Quonset huts, and some still stand today. The huts were heated with two coal burners, one at each end. In England, they were notoriously chilly and damp and the men were only given four days' worth of coal each week. Inevitably, pilfering of coal became an art, except of course in Werner's hut, at least as far as he knew. Jack was a natural scavenger, a jack-of-all-trades and a pack rat. Somehow, he always came up with whatever was needed. The men were allowed a short, "almost warm shower a couple of times a week at best." The damp weather, the funk of twenty sweaty men—most of them smokers—and their soiled flight suits gave off a tang that one could both taste and smell.

After the Eighth Air Force took over Molesworth, it was designated Station 107 and became one of the most active and historic American airfields of the war. Home to four B-17 squadrons—the 358th, the 359th, the 360th, and the 427th—Molesworth had three intersecting runways, including one almost a mile and a half long. The base, about seventy miles north of London, housed thousands of American aircrews during the war.

In addition to the bomber and ground crews, the base housed a military police unit, an ordnance unit, a weather unit, a chemicals unit, a firefighting unit, a quartermasters company, a finance section, a hospital, a dental department, and a gas defense company. A total of 841 Molesworth-based airmen died during the war, and 747 were taken prisoner; 210 B-17s from Molesworth were lost in combat and training. The 303rd compiled 364 combat missions, the most of any Eighth Air Force B-17 group in the war, and flew 10,721 individual sorties. Molesworth had the distinction of more postwar shotgun weddings and war brides than any other air station in England because eligible, young British men were at war, and an earlier generation of British men had been lost in WWI.

16

INTO THE FRAY

In early 1942, as Jack and Werner trained, the Allies were under pressure worldwide. "The beginning of 1942 was a relentless cataract of defeats . . . German U-boats were sinking hundreds of U.S. ships . . . Japan's army and navy far outmatched the U.S.," and Midway had yet to happen. The impregnable fortress of Singapore fell to Japan, and Germany won significant back-to-back victories, first in the Soviet Crimea at Sevastopol, which threatened vital Russian oil fields, and second, Gen. Erwin Rommel, the "Desert Fox," threatened British-held Egypt and the Suez Canal from Libya. Churchill was despondent, and Stalin's pressure to produce results caused the Americans to rush poorly trained and underprotected air crews into the war.

On July 4, 1942, just four months after Gen. Ira Eaker's initial visit, the first Eighth Air Force mission over Nazi-occupied Europe was launched from Molesworth. Six American crews from the Fifteenth Bomb Squadron joined six RAF crews for an attack on Luftwaffe airfields in the Netherlands, becoming the first American unit to bomb Europe during the war. The attack, specifically ordered for Independence Day by Gen. Henry H. "Hap" Arnold, USAAF's chief of staff, with Roosevelt's enthusiastic approval, was a disaster. Three of the twelve crew flying that day did not return. It was an inauspicious beginning that portended the heavy losses that could be expected flying daylight missions without escort fighter cover over German-held territory. The British knew the horrendous costs of aerial bombing. "Among every hundred RAF Bomber Command aircrew in the course of the war, fifty-one died on operations, nine were lost in crashes in England, three seriously injured, twelve taken prisoner, one was shot down and escaped capture, and just twenty-four completed a tour of operations." The heavy losses in 1942 set back the Eighth Army's European bombing plans. In July, Roosevelt committed to Operation Torch, the invasion of North Africa. Army Chief of Staff George C. Marshall ordered two Eighth Air Force bomber units, the 97th and the 301st, transferred from England to North Africa and diverted other, formerly British-bound B-17 bomber crews directly from stateside to support Operation Torch.

General Dwight D. Eisenhower, slated to become supreme allied commander later that year was flying from his Algiers headquarters to attend the crucial January 1943 Casablanca Conference with Roosevelt, Churchill, and the combined chiefs of staff when his B-17 "lost two of its engines flying over the Atlas Mountains, and Eisenhower was obliged to spend part of the flight standing in the bomber's open doorway with his parachute on waiting to bail out." Roosevelt remarked on seeing him, "Ike seems jittery."

Another B-17 sent to Africa became the center of a controversy that greatly contributed to the deterioration of the already prickly relationship Ike had with Gen. Bernard L. Montgomery, commander of the British Eighth Army. While recognizing Montgomery's talents and recent success in saving Egypt from Rommel, both Marshall and Eisenhower considered him a difficult subordinate as well as a prima donna. Monty thought he should have been offered Eisenhower's job, and denigrated Ike's lack of battlefield experience, writing to another British officer that Ike "obviously knows nothing whatever about fighting." Ike thought Monty conceited. The relationship grew worse over a wager Monty made with Eisenhower's normally cautious chief of staff General Smith:

> Monty boasted that he would break through the Gabès Gap onto the plains of southern Tunisia and capture the port of Sfax early in April. Smith, who thought Monty could never bring it off, uncharacteristically told Monty he could ask for anything he liked if he did that, and Monty said he wanted his own B-17 Flying Fortress "complete with an American crew on their payroll," the whole thing to be "his personal property until the war ended."

Monty captured the port on April 10 and immediately demanded the plane and crew, asking that the captain report to him personally. An angry Ike was forced to honor the bet, which caused eyebrows to shoot up in the Pentagon and the USAAF, much to Eisenhower's embarrassment. Monty, of course, went to dinner on the story, hilariously repeating it often as part of his personally embroidered legend. Eisenhower was furious, and the incident did much to worsen their relationship, with adverse consequences for the Allies. Ironically, Monty's B-17 crashed less than three months after he took possession of it and was never replaced.

17

WHAT FRESH HELL IS THIS?

When Maj. Curtis E. "Old Iron Ass" LeMay flew into England for the first time in October 1942, he was shocked by the fog. When the control tower asked the pilot of his aircraft if he could see the runway lights, the pilot replied that he couldn't even see the man sitting next to him.

LeMay, the new head of the 305th Bomb Group, refined heavy-bomber tactics in a manner that changed the air war from then on. The Ohio native and former foundry worker failed in his attempt to gain admission to West Point and entered the army after ROTC training in the late 1920s. He was blunt and intellectually and physically intimidating. Stricken with Bell's palsy, which paralyzed facial muscles near his mouth, LeMay never smiled because he couldn't.

> [LeMay] masked this facial paralysis by constantly chewing on a cigar. His speech was so slurred as to be almost incomprehensible.

His soft-spoken but curt and often brutally frank assessments terrified subordinates, but LeMay based his opinions solely on facts and performance and was considered a tough though judicious commander.

LeMay made two innovations designed to better protect the unescorted bombers: prohibiting evasive action during the bomb run; and instituted a lead crew, whereby following aircraft were ordered to bomb on the leader's drop to improve the Eighth's heretofore dismal accuracy. He organized his bomber armadas into the tightly packed "combat boxes," which in theory would maximize their protective firepower. The wing box, a 54-plane formation made up of three 18-plane boxes, evolved from the need to provide defensive fire in all directions. Like the combat box, the firing box followed a triangular design, with a leading bomber in the center and two bombers immediately behind in a V shape, one at an altitude above and one below the center in close proximity for mutual defense.

The new combat boxes continued to be used, but groups were placed in a horizontal column and stacked at one-thousand-foot intervals to decrease their vulnerability to attack. This resulted in the rear formations lagging behind, which impacted both defensive tactics and bombing performance.

The most serious disadvantage of the wing box was that the lowermost and uppermost bombers at the ends of the formation had the least protection. An additional risk was that an aircraft might be struck by falling "friendly" bombs if it strayed from its position. Following an attack on Berlin, 303rd Bomber Group pilot Richard Riley Johnson recalled:

> Directly below us in the path of our falling bombs was a B-17 out of position. Later pictures show a B-17 having his left stabilizer shorn off by a five-hundred-pound bomb dropped from above. That plane went into a steep dive, out of control, and was lost.

The combat box required pilot strength, practice, and discipline. Turbulence from leading bombers added to the difficulty of maintaining formation. The box served as a defense against fighters, however, and as flak became the much greater threat in May 1944, the 36-plane box was resurrected in a looser formation and became the standard through the remainder of the war.

LeMay saw poorly trained bombardiers and navigators. Pilots, in the early days, took evasive maneuvers trying to avoid flak, which inevitably surrounded the most important targets. The result was dismal bombing accuracy. LeMay picked the best pilots, navigators, and bombardiers and placed them in the lead plane with orders to fly straight and level when approaching targets. When the leader dropped its payload, it was the signal for the following planes to do the same. LeMay improved accuracy, but flying the tight formation was always a nail-biter and often deadly. Long-range air cover did not exist in the European theater until the P-51 Mustang arrived more than a year later.

B-17 copilot and writer Bert Stiles recalled how difficult formation flight really was. While still in college Stiles had been published in the *Saturday Evening Post* and *Collier's Weekly*. "From the ground a formation is always static and always beautiful. It looks deadly simple and easy." But once in the air, Stiles realized it was an illusion: "Pilots were screaming at squadron leaders, 'Get us out of here, we're in prop wash.'" Stiles wrote that the B-17 was a "big heavy monster that has to be heaved around the sky."

After Stiles completed a tour in B-17s, he qualified as a fighter pilot and died in a crash over Germany, aged twenty-four, on November 26, 1944. Stiles's mother commemorated him by having his book published in 1947, in England. The first U.S. publication was in 1952, by W. W. Norton. Entitled *Serenade to the Big Bird,* the book achieved cult status among aviation enthusiasts for its intense depictions of bomber combat, and it won favorable literary reviews.

The Germans caught on to the new tactics and adjusted their own accordingly. Assisted by radar, central ground fire control, and swarms of fighters, the Luftwaffe continued to take a devastating toll on the unescorted daylight bombers attempting to enter German airspace.

The American fighter escorts in 1942 and most of 1943 were the P-38 Lightning and the P-47 Thunderbolt. Robust fighters both, they simply did not have the range to penetrate deep into the German heartland. It was not until North American Aviation's P-51 Mustang appeared in the late fall of 1943 and long-range drop tanks were added to the P-47s that the bombers could fly complete missions past the Rhine with full fighter escort. Until then, the bombers suffered appalling losses.

On January 3, 1943, sixty-eight bombers attacked U-boat pens in Saint-Nazaire, France. Seven of the bombers were lost, fourteen damaged so badly as to never fly again, and forty-seven others damaged. The toll on the crew was equally shocking: thirty-six casualties and fifty men missing in action. Three weeks later, on January 23, again on a mission to bomb U-boat pens in France, fifty-four B-17s made it to the target at Lorient, five were lost, and thirty damaged. Among the crew there were twenty-eight casualties and fifty men missing in action. While bombing accuracy had improved, the losses of planes and crew, hovering at 10 percent, were disastrous and unsustainable.

18

HELL OF A MESS

The Eighth Air Force was one of the U.S. military's most dangerous WWII postings. From 1942 to 1945, for about a thousand days, Mighty Eighth airmen, all based in England, perished at an average rate of two dozen a day. The horrors of combat were brought home after nearly each mission. Lt. Walter E. Truemper from Aurora, Illinois, graduated as a navigator after washing out of the pilot's course in 1943. In the B-17 *Ten Horsepower,* the ball turret gunner was Sgt. Archibald Mathies. On a mission to Leipzig, their plane was attacked by two German fighters, the copilot was killed outright, and the pilot, Lt. Clarence Nelson, was badly wounded and unconscious. Truemper took the controls. Although not a qualified pilot, he knew enough from his pre-washout training to make it back to England, allowing the six other crewmen to parachute to safety. Truemper and Mathies could have parachuted out themselves but decided to remain with the gravely wounded Nelson. After two failed landing attempts, *Ten Horsepower* crashed on final approach, killing all three men. Truemper and Mathies posthumously received the Medal of Honor.

The aftermath of a crash landing would never leave the minds of those who witnessed the results. Copilot Jim O'Connor saw a P-51 Mustang overshoot the runway and crash into a nearby forest. He ran to help.

> Two doctors . . . were collecting the remains. . . . I found a GI shoe with a foot still in it. At the base of a huge smoking tree, one of the doctors lifted up a pile of intestines like a string of

steaming sausages. He said that we each had 29 feet of them inside us. Up in a tree we saw the victim's skull, rib cage and spinal column wrapped around the trunk. Just about all the flesh had been blown off the bones.

Almost half of noncombat accidents happened during landing. Maj. James J. Carroll, a USAF officer, later wrote:

In 1944, 2,835 aircraft of the Eighth Air Force were involved in 2,562 non-combat related accidents, of which 47 percent were completely destroyed and 17.4 percent resulted in the death of one or more persons. Twenty-nine percent of aircraft losses occurred during in-flight accidents, including hundreds of mid-air collisions. An additional 16.1 percent of losses happened while planes taxied on the ground and 11.5 percent occurred during take-off, and 3.4 percent involved parked aircraft. The total number of accidents per month averaged more than 200, ranging from 148 in February to 271 in July, with well over half the accidents occurring during non-combat flights.

Wesley Frank Craven and James L. Cate reported that by mid-1944:

Low morale among the aircrews, particularly in the Eighth Air Force was a nagging problem. The intensive scale of operations, high operational losses and wastage, the absence on occasions of sufficient fighters for escort and the almost unbearable pace of missions on consecutive days all contributed to fatigue and a pessimistic outlook on the part of the flyers.

Before the Goering crew could fly as a team, Werner and Jack each had to fly an introductory combat mission in the copilot seat with an experienced bomber pilot in command. It was as much of a gut check as it was a skills test.

On August 18, Werner flew his first mission, with the rest of the crew minus Jack, under the watchful eye of 2nd Lt. Ernest A. Whittall in a B-17G nicknamed *The Floose,* one of 39 B-17G Flying Fortresses that the 303rd contributed to a mission force of 772 bombers and 858 fighters. Sent to attack rail bridges in two Belgian cities in order to support Allied ground forces' approach to the Rhine River, the 303rd bombers had a fairly short five-hour mission with no fatalities, two wounded airmen, and battle damage to four planes. Although one damaged plane wasn't able to make it to Molesworth and had a forced landing at another English base, all the 303rd's planes and crews made it safely back to England.

For the 303rd, August 18 was not a "milk run," the term reserved for missions with no enemy opposition either in the air or from antiaircraft guns, but no bomber crew could completely relax until their plane touched down safely at the end of the mission. But the Hell's Angels got off easy compared to other units aloft that day. The Eighth suffered battle damage to 101 bombers and 7 fighter planes, but more important, seven men were killed in a crash landing following a midair collision, eight were wounded by enemy fire, and thirty-nine went missing.

Of the thousands of airmen reported missing by the U.S. Army Air Force during the 1,042-day air war, a rare few, including P-51 Mustang fighter pilot Chuck Yeager evaded capture; a much larger number, also to be counted among the lucky, parachuted into captivity and became prisoners of war. Others perished at the hands of enraged civilians or drowned in the English Channel, the North Sea, or the Bay of Biscayne. Some who bailed out died of injuries received in the air or on hitting the ground. In all, 3,603 Mighty Eighth airmen went missing in action and were declared dead. Many simply vanished forever, vaporized in cataclysmic explosions or burned beyond recognition in crashes. After the war, except for the released POWs, the fates of many of the missing were never determined.

Werner's crew was approved as combat-ready, and on August 24 Werner commanded his first combat mission in the pilot's seat, again minus Jack; 2nd Lt. George Conley occupied the copilot's seat. Jack flew his own maiden combat sortie on the same mission as copilot, with 1st Lt. Donald P. Stark in B-17G 42-97949. Not every B-17 had a nickname, and many bore only a numerical designation. Crews did not always fly the same plane, and men were sometimes shuffled between crews because of sickness or injury.

Once in the war zone, Werner and Jack quickly absorbed what air combat really meant. Reporter Bob Considine described an episode in a 1943 *Cosmopolitan* magazine article in which a Focke-Wulf 109 shell

> struck poor pilot Lt. Bob Campbell, from Liberty, Mississippi, in the side of the head. The shell exploded with such terrible force that it not only blew off the pilot's head, but blasted the arm off the top turret gunner behind him, Sgt. Tyre C. Weaver of Riverview Alabama.

Campbell's blood coated the windshields and controls, and his body slumped over the wheel. Considine's description of Campbell's death differs greatly from the version in *The Mighty Eighth*, by Roger Freeman, considered the definitive group history. Freeman reported that Campbell was fatally shot in the head yet struggled in the cockpit for over an hour. During the hellish return flight, Copilot John C. Morgan realized that Weaver wouldn't survive the several freezing hours back to England. He tried to tie the arm's stump off with a tourniquet, "but there was too little of the arm left, and it continued to pour blood." Weaver's only chance of survival was to be parachuted into captivity, and the crew threw him out of the plane. Woozy from shock and blood loss, Weaver had just enough strength in his remaining arm to pull the rip cord. Details vary, but not the horror of the circumstances.

In mid-August 1944 Werner and Jack bicycled onto the runway at Molesworth as a stricken Fortress was coming in to land. As both recalled, incorrectly, as the record would show, the pilot had been killed. A dead pilot in a shot-up B-17 is a serious matter, since so many copilots had only minimal flying hours. A heavy bomber, on only two or three engines, with damaged flight surfaces, little or no hydraulic pressure, and damaged landing gear is an extreme challenge even for an experienced pilot, much less a terrified, horror-stricken nineteen-year-old rookie copilot.

Considine continued:

> Landing a Fortress is a two-man brake job at best . . . what Morgan did that awful day was miracle flying, an unparalleled saga of fortitude, determination and muscular strength . . . He had manhandled that huge bomber into subjection.

Entire crews died in similar circumstances, a half mile away from their bunks in the final moments of a nine-hour, 1,500-mile mission. This time, as Werner and Jack watched transfixed, the copilot shot off two red flares to get priority landing permission and alert medical personnel, and amazingly got the plane roughly, but safely, onto the landing strip. It shuddered to a halt at the end of the runway. Emergency crews extracted the wounded; the dead waited be taken to a discrete morgue at Cambridge Cemetery for postmortem analysis.

Werner and Jack, eager to learn combat lessons, scrambled up onto the plane and looked into the bomber. They saw a dead crewman's headless corpse strapped upright in his seat. He was killed instantly by a flak shell. "The interior of the cockpit looked like spaghetti and meatballs had been smeared all over the inside," said Werner. All Jack could think about was the "hell of a mess a human head can make," and of the very real possibility that any day he might have to make a similar landing with Werner's corpse at his side in a similar state.

The army's June–August 1944 air corps medical study made the following determination:

> Approximately 86 percent of the casualties were hit by flak fragments. Less than 4 percent were hit by shells or shell fragments fired from enemy fighter planes. Practically all of the 7.8 percent of casualties hit by secondary missiles were the result of flak hits on the aircraft. Secondary missiles include fragments of Plexiglas . . . objects in the plane; bulletproof glass; brass fittings; and parts of electrical heating and radio equipment and .50 caliber machinegun ammunition. . . . The high casualty rate for waist gunners was partially due to the fact that heavy bombers frequently carried two waist gunners.

The highest casualty rates were among the bombardiers, which, considering the fact that waist gunner casualties were divided between two positions, "was to be expected from their positions in the nose of the aircraft. They lacked the protection provided by other personnel and portions of the ship's structure and by being in the most forward compartments of the aircraft; they were exposed to the greatest density of flak."

Surprisingly, among the lowest incidence of casualties occurred in the ball turret gunner's position, but this was partially due to the fact that only one of the two types of B-17s involved in the study carried a man in that position.

The origin of the word "flak" is *Flugabwehrkanone,* the German word for antiaircraft cannon. Flak, so the saying went, was a word long enough to walk on. When flak filled the air with exploding shells that sent shrapnel tearing through metal, flesh, and bone, calling B-17s by their nickname, Flying Fortress, seemed like a bad joke.

Every man responded to this experience differently, from Werner's icy calm to Jack's grim determination, Gus Gustafson's constant prayer, and Tex Mahan's salty jokes. Rex Markt, the navigator, was the most problematic member of the crew in this regard, because his nerves interfered with his already poor navigating (faulty navigation was a common problem throughout the war for all sides). Yet Markt earned the sympathetic respect of his fellow crew members for never cracking under the strain, as many men did. Werner, for one, decided Markt was a brave man simply for holding himself together and not "bugging out." Sgt. Chester "Chad" Brodzinski, full of nervous energy and chewing Wrigley's gum nonstop, when he wasn't smoking or doing both at the same time, was always ready with a big-city wisecrack or a snappy line he'd picked up from some Bogart or Cagney movie.

To compensate for Markt's chronic difficulties in fixing a position, Jack became expert at locating ground landmarks, weather permitting, which in northern Europe's winter was iffy at best. Markt developed a critical skill with the GEE box, but it was often useless because the Germans were so adept at jamming it. Yet it was invaluable on the approach to landing back at Molesworth in poor weather during instrument-only conditions. The pilots could not land their plane safely, time after time, without Markt's assistance in lining them up over the center of the runway despite fog, rain, crosswinds, mechanical failure, and frequent battle damage.

The 303rd's mission on August 25 was to bomb the Leuna Works at Merseburg, Germany, the heavily defended synthetic oil production site. Antiaircraft fire was intense and accurate, and one airman was killed by flak during the eight-and-a-quarter-hour mission. For the 1,319 bomber crews and 739 fighter pilots of the Eighth Army Air Force involved in the mission, the butcher's bill totaled 4 men dead, 45 wounded, and an astounding 247 missing. A total of 550 planes sustained major battle damage. Merseburg always was and would be a very tough target.

Werner and Jack flew together with their crew for the first time on August 26, attacking an airfield at Anklam, Germany. For the Hell's Angels, it was a long but relatively safe mission, with meager flak and no enemy fighters. The Eighth Air Force lost only one man killed. Twenty-eight were wounded, and 165 missing. The fact that 194 casualties in one day was considered light spoke volumes about the army's willingness to sacrifice airmen.

On August 27, bad weather prevented the 303rd's bombers from reaching their primary and secondary targets, an aircraft assembly plant and an airfield in Germany, so instead they bombed a Luftwaffe airfield in Denmark. The battle reports described the flak over the Danish airfield as "moderate," yet it was the bloodiest day to date. One bomber broke in half after taking a hit in the fuselage. No one bailed out, and although eight men plunged to their deaths, it was later learned that one of the crew survived and was taken prisoner. Another bomber had portions of its tail blown off by flak, instantly killing the tail gunner. Despite badly damaged elevators and stabilizer, and no rudder, pilot Bert Hallum Jr. managed to fly the plane to England, where he ordered the crew to bail out. After trying several approaches to see if he could control the plane at landing speed, Hallum pointed it out to sea and parachuted to safety over land.

The number of men lost doesn't convey the sheer terror bomber crews experienced as they risked daily capture, injury, or death. The balance of airpower was in the Allies' favor at this stage of the war, but the Eighth Air Force remained the military's most dangerous regular assignment by far.

19

ASSASSIN'S DILEMMA

Since the FBI had ordered Jack to shoot Werner, he'd wrestled with his conscience. He spent nearly every day and night for almost a year in close quarters with Werner and slowly found he liked and admired his gruff, taciturn commander. Jack, who had been on his own most of his life, found comfort in the bond that had formed between them. Of course, he and Werner never spoke about it, but Jack increasingly felt that he was important to Werner, beyond the airborne and mechanical skills and flight experience he brought to their partnership. During the months of stateside training and combat sorties, the pair had forged what Jack considered the "best damn B-17 crew in the entire army."

Although Jack was three years older than Werner, he looked up to Goering as the older brother he had never had and the childhood friend his youth in the Arizona wilderness had denied him. Jack was impressed with Werner's preternatural calm under fire and ability to focus completely on flying no matter what was going on around him. The man "appeared fearless, which both inspired and terrified" the crew. Jack, the former instructor, considered Werner "among the bravest men" he had ever met and "the best damn formation pilot" in the army.

By late summer of 1944, Werner's relationship to Göring, despite the secrecy the military tried to impose, was an open secret at Molesworth. Werner's glacial remoteness and unwillingness to drink booze, fraternize, or even enter the officer's club made him an outsider and an oddball and only heightened the aura of mystery surrounding him. Werner neither noticed nor cared what others thought or said. His military bearing was always impeccable. He said he greatly appreciated Jack "keeping the crew squared away" since he didn't mix well with other people, especially enlisted men, whom he sensed mistrusted him because of his heritage. Jack was more sociable and accessible. Although he spent many long hours in the Quonset hut he shared with Werner pouring over maps, manuals, and mission reports, Jack also made time to help mechanics fix bombers at night and to engage in his one very profitable vice—poker.

Jack, like Werner, avoided the officer's club, but he loved to bet on poker in the barracks or in the repair hangars. He didn't drink or smoke and was painfully shy around girls, but he was the squad's acknowledged poker champ. Usually, when they knew they were not flying the next day, the other crew members and officers headed to their separate clubs or bars or to carouse in London. During the war, Werner went to London only once and visited the Molesworth officer's club only once as well.

The crew got upset because Werner would volunteer for any and all missions. Some, including Gus Gustafson, Werner's top-turret gunner, feared he was "rank-happy and wanted to make major before the war ended." Werner just wanted to fly and be the best pilot he could be. Jack found that his unique relationship with Werner made him a minor celebrity, and he was often approached by men who were curious about the German Reich Marshal's nephew. There was always scuttlebutt about Werner and "Uncle Hermann" during their training and combat tour. At the very least, Werner knew some people questioned his loyalty, and Jack thought he "must have suspected" that the authorities were keeping a close eye on him. Gustafson said that if the crew had found out about Jack's secret orders, "no one in the entire 303rd would have been shocked."

"The army strongly discouraged officers from fraternization with enlisted men," said fellow pilot Maj. William C. "Iron Ass" Heller. Even new junior officers were largely ignored since they so often died or disappeared into German POW camps before anyone got to know them. The first missions were the most dangerous; there was not a lot of time or incentive to get buddy-buddy, and Werner made few attempts to develop friendships. Heller, an experienced pilot, the handsome son of German immigrants, and a distant relative of Oskar Schindler, of *Schindler's List* fame, became one of Werner's few friends. He remembers Werner as a respected but remote commander. Heller, who was also fluent in German, connected with Werner through their common German roots: after a drink or two or three, Heller would routinely seek out Werner to practice military commands in the mother tongue, to the consternation of fellow pilots and intelligence officers alike.

Yet many officers and enlisted men, including members of his own crew, were wary of Werner. His sober, hard-as-nails work ethic made other officers seem slack by comparison, and forced his air and ground crew to work that much harder. The disdain he sensed only caused Werner to work twice as hard to compensate. He did not care that his crew, including Jack, would just as soon not have flown "every damn mission" if they did not absolutely have to. "I tried to play everything as safe as I can. If it was dangerous and I did not have to do it, I wouldn't," said Jack, but when the commander ordered a mission, the crew had no choice but to obey. As Heller noted, in the era before continual communications with ground-based commanders was possible, an aircrew commander, like a navy captain, "had awesome powers during the war and his word was final and absolute."

Heller's moniker, "Iron Ass," referred to his attitude toward combat. He had no hesitation ordering a man to his death to save others.

My crew was stellar. The radio operator gunner was a Felix Spoerri, German-Swiss born, who lived in a Parish near New Orleans as a beekeeper. . . .

On one mission, after bombs away, it was Spoerri's job . . . to clear the bomb bay. He would get up from his seat and check into the bomb bay to assure all the load had been dropped. He would then shout "Bomb bay clear!" and the bombardier would close the bomb bay doors.

After bombs away on this particular mission, I noted our two wingmen had both pulled away from us, and I heard Spoerri on the Intercom shouting . . . "We have a hang-up . . . and it's burning!" I knew what this meant, and why the wingmen had moved; they did not want to be next to a B-17 clearly about to blow up.

I shouted into the interphone. . . . "Spoerri! Get that bomb OUT of there, even if you have to go with it!" Our crew monitored the interphone and knew what was going on.

George Payne, the right waist gunner, heard and saw all of this as he looked toward the bomb bay. He immediately grabbed a walk-around oxygen bottle, ran over, pulled Spoerri, who'd passed out from lack of oxygen, by his legs and resuscitated him. Spoerri with no gloves, no oxygen mask and no parachute had saved the plane by instantly following orders, and then passed out with the upper half of his body dangling from the open bomb bay.

What a brave man . . . Upon return to base, we wrote up the incident and I recommended Spoerri for the Silver Star. It is the third highest award and is given for Gallantry in Action. The higher-ups awarded him the DFC. What his actions had to do with Distinguished Flying I will never know. I learned a lesson. Had I perhaps recommended him for the DSC (second highest) they may have then awarded him the Silver Star.

NBC did a fifteen-minute radio skit based on his actions and the mission.

Later in his tour, when I became Squadron Commander of the 360th Squadron, Felix, fluent in German, did some special intelligence work for the air force. He would go on missions monitoring the Luftwaffe frequencies, and if they gave locations of our wings and divisions, he would countermand German orders or otherwise mix them up so as to attempt to fool the German fighter planes.

The evening after the mission, Spoerri came to my barracks . . . He told me he understood how difficult it was for me to give him an order that may have meant his death, but he carried out the order to the letter.

Werner had no ability for or interest in small talk or horsing around. He was determined to survive, thrive, and, above all, redeem his family name. Except for one quick look around, he refused to go to the officer's club and avoided social situations, including ones where lonely British women, who were clearly attracted to him, would be present. He was not a skirt chaser. "Werner was a very good dresser, always sharp and neat," recalled Jack. Period photos universally show a trim, handsome, strapping young blond man with a grim, unsmiling face. A smile to a stranger was as foreign to Werner as was a glass of whiskey or a whorehouse. Words did not come frequently or easily from his mouth.

Heller said Jack was "well liked by both officers and men alike and always tried to please, but had a palpable inferiority complex." Werner "kept to himself and was an object of much speculation and rumor," but "eventually became a highly respected pilot and squad commander."

20

MURDERSBURG

The jackrabbit's head flickered in and out of the .22 caliber rifle's iron sights in the shimmering Arizona desert before exploding into chunks of bone and flesh. A clean first kill, yet that memory, sickeningly real, remained with Jack Rencher eighteen years later. At 20,000 feet, next to his best friend and commander, his prey was so much closer to him, too close he thought.

One early afternoon, Tuesday, November 21, 1944, Lt. Jack Rencher prepared to blow his best friend and flight commander's brains all over the cockpit with one of the three Colt .45 pistols he always carried within easy reach during combat missions. Jack discreetly carried one pistol in each thigh pocket of his flight suit and the third in an M3 brown leather shoulder holster under his left armpit. The pistols each held seven bullets, were eight and a half inches long, and weighed two and a half pounds: the army's weapon of choice for in-your-face combat.

That cloudy morning, in the midst of 2,245 American planes rumbling across Germany in a 100-mile-long armada, Werner ordered, "Oxygen check." Jack calmly recited the crewmen's surnames over the interphone of their Flying Fortress *Teddy's Rough Riders* and silently counted off eight replies.

Every few minutes, Jack repeated the routine to keep the men focused and ensure they were still breathing in the thin deadly air four miles over Merseburg, Germany. Werner flexed his jaw and rotated his head to work the kinks out. They'd been in the air for four hours and knew it was about to get as hairy as the south end of a northbound grizzly.

Beneath and forward of the cockpit, in the Plexiglas nose cone, sat bombardier Lt. Donald L. Birkenseer at the Norden bombsight and the bomb bay controls. Birkenseer was new to the crew that day: a replacement, an unknown quantity. Werner and Jack didn't like flying with strangers and kept an eye on him. Bill Sachau, their stolid regular bombardier and choirmaster had the trots so bad he was grounded by the flight surgeon. You didn't want a man with bad trots on a ten-hour mission in a plane without a crapper. Sachau loved to lead the crew in singing off-key and off-color ditties like "Roll Me Over." He would bellow the first line into the interphone: "We've tried it once or twice, and found it rather nice," and the rest of the enlisted kids hollered the chorus: "Roll me over in the clover, roll me over lay me down and do it again."

Sachau had about a dozen different stanzas to the popular tune, each one racier than the last. When the airborne choirboys would start in on a song, Werner's face wouldn't change expression, but Jack, who always cracked a smile, could spot a twinkle in Werner's eye. The boys were always better off singing than worrying about what awaited them. Although he'd never admit it, Werner missed the sound of happy singing. All he heard was the heavy throbbing of four engines, the howl of wind in the open cabin, and an occasional machine-gun burst as the boys checked to ensure their Brownings didn't freeze solid.

Behind him to the left sat navigator Lt. Rex H. Markt at a shelf covered with charts beneath a small Plexiglas bubble that allowed him to see the stars. Behind and above the cockpit was flight engineer Sgt. Orall "Gus" Gustafson, in the rotating top turret equipped with twin machine guns. In the open, freezing midsection, aft of the bomb bay and racks that held ten 500-pound bombs, waist gunner Sgt. Clarence W. Houseman stood at the firing port with a .50 caliber machine gun on a swivel mount. At the other waist gunner position, back-to-back with Houseman, was Sgt. Donald E. Skinner, who doubled as the plane's photographer when action permitted. He stood just behind the radio operator, Sgt. Chester "Chad" Brodzinski. Brodzinski was the only crewman, other than Werner, who spoke fluent German, and Jack suspected it was no coincidence he was flying with Werner, probably under secret orders to monitor any German-language transmissions that Werner might make. The FBI was indeed very thorough, Jack thought. Almost directly under the radioman was the hatch for the tiny belly turret gunner's position, manned by Sgt. Joseph

Blinebury. Behind the waist gunner was an ammo storage box and main entry hatch, and in the farthest aft and most dangerous compartment sat Sgt. Weldon Mahan, their dead-eyed Texan tail gunner.

Over their recently developed and often unreliable electrically heated leather and fleece flight suits, the crew, mostly teenagers, also wore DuPont "ballistic nylon" twenty-pound flak jackets with manganese armor plates sewn into sweat- and cordite-stained waistcoats. Piss-stained, too: when the crew relieved themselves during five- to ten-hour missions, usually out the midsection machine-gun port, the slipstream spattered them with freezing back spray. There were those, usually in the navigator and radioman cubicles, who preferred to sit on their flak jackets to protect their balls. Pilfering of extra flak jackets from other crews, for added protection by panicky crewmen, was not uncommon but considered cowardly and disgraceful. When Werner learned that his own often-terrified navigator, Rex Markt, had stolen a flak jacket from another plane, he lost his glacial reserve in a way no crewman ever forgot. A commandment had been broken. Werner didn't shout, but his personal shame and contained fury at seeing one of his men commit such a craven act was so intense that the entire crew, many older than their twenty-year-old commander, learned the lesson instantly and permanently: the Goering crew shall not steal, especially not another man's life-saving gear.

The precious flak jackets, developed by the Eighth Air Force's chief surgeon with assistance from medieval armor specialists at New York's Metropolitan Museum of Art and Britain's Wilkinson Sword Company, gave men wearing them more than twice the survival rate of those without body armor.

The new, often problematic electric flight suits were one of the ways flight surgeons fought the intense cold, a deadly enemy that threatened crewmen on every mission. High-altitude combat occurred in temperatures as low as −60 degrees Fahrenheit, and at fatally low oxygen levels. Both presented bomber crews with previously unknown physical and psychological dangers and stresses. Any exposed skin immediately adhered to subzero metal. An unprotected hand that grabbed exposed metal in an emergency or a moment of distraction could result in the whole skin of the palm being left hanging on the metal "like half a bloody glove." Frostbite was a killer and wounded thousands so severely that "drastic amputations" of fingers, toes, noses, even eyes, were part of the over-whelmed flight surgeon's regular caseload. Early in the war, the cold wounded more men than did German fighters and antiaircraft flak com-bined. The wounded, losing blood and in shock, were particularly vul-nerable to the cold. Stories abound of wounded or dead men frozen fast in their own blood to the metal decks of the bombers. In addition to the immediate physical threat to the men, the cold caused the windows to ice over and the guns to freeze up. Ice formed around face masks and, more dangerously, heavy white contrails steamed out behind each bomber, providing both an unmistakable indicator to ground observers and an effective smoke screen into which enemy fighters could slip unseen, to shield their approach from the tail gunners. During freezing sleet and foggy conditions ice formed on the bomber's wings at altitude, forcing pilots to descend to lower, warmer, and more dangerous altitudes. "In a single cloud front a bomber could pick up a ton of ice." "It wasn't unusual for flights of B-17s to fly at 25-foot altitudes [over water] so pilots could follow the sea wake of the airblast from the leading planes propellers." "The weather goes up and down [as fast as] a whore's drawers," said one pilot. After a February 3, 1944, raid on submarine pens in Wilhelms-haven, Germany, Brooklyn-born tail gunner John Gabay recorded the following entry in his diary:

> Flak was heavy, but over on our left. We were to come out by way of the North Sea. A sleet storm reached our altitude and we couldn't see to stay in formation so we got orders that ev-eryone was on his own. Ice was forming on our wings as we let down through the storm. The last thing I saw before the weather enveloped us was a Fort running into the tail of another and chewing it up so bad the gunner fell out over the North Sea. We dove at great speed trying to get to warmer air.

On another foggy mission, Gabay described how an American crewman in a parachute "floated into a low Fort—he was churned up by the propellers and took the Fort with him. It just rolled over into a dive." Gabay also describes having frostbite on his face, chin, and knees.

In the fall and early winter of 1944, "the weather in central Europe was worse than it had been since the beginning of the century," as the army would discover in the December Battle of the Bulge. On rare clear days, bomber weather, elite interconnected German flak divisions, and radar sites quickly spotted the contrails, making the armada's swath across the continent that much easier to plot. Like modern air traffic controllers, they tracked the bomber formations and then handed them off after relaying the information to their colleagues, alerting fighter squadrons and hundreds of antiaircraft batteries about the bombers' location, altitude, heading, and airspeed. On the ground, everybody was ready to greet them.

Germany's famed .88 millimeter guns, the best artillery pieces of the war, weighed five tons and were wired to a command center consisting of a generator trailer and a radar targeting device. The operators of the system tracked formations of planes as they lumbered toward flak batteries and transmitted angle and elevation readings to each gun's crew.

The massive .88s fired more than a dozen twenty-pound shells a minute that reached as high as 37,000 feet, well past the Flying Fortress's flight ceiling of 36,000 feet. The shells had two types of fuses: barometric fuses detonated shells set to specific-altitude air pressure and time-delay fuses set to go off at specific heights, given the trajectory of the antiaircraft batteries firing them. No matter what triggered them, their red-hot, jagged steel fragments could easily carry away a man's head, a leg, or an entire crew. Fatal flak injuries were often caused by pieces of steel no heavier than two nickels—10 grams—while others were the size of razor-edged grapefruits. During the last year of the war, more than 80 percent of our casualties were flak-related.

On that day, November 21, 1944, Werner and Jack spotted puffy black smudges of flak barrages blossoming around the bombers ahead of them. The vast petrochemical complex was blanketed by heavy haze from the armada's contrails, black smoke, thousands of antiaircraft flak bursts, ground-based smoke pots, and natural cloud cover. Luftwaffe fighters covered the vital refinery at a distance; German pilots knew to keep well out of the "flak box" protecting the target. Although much diminished after five years of ceaseless combat, the Luftwaffe was still producing about 3,000 new fighters a month, double the rate from the previous year; it was a lack of experienced pilots and fuel that hamstrung them. By 1944, many German pilots were dangerously green from lack of training due to limited fuel. The ones who survived, like Luftwaffe Fighter Commander Gen. Adolf Galland, who had flown combat sorties since the Spanish civil war nearly a decade earlier, were the most experienced airmen in the sky.

The German pilots let the flak from their comrades on the ground do its work, and then swarmed and preyed on wandering or wounded bombers, the ones that, because of poor flying or damage, were separated from the protective formation's hundreds of interlocking fields of machine-gun fire. They reminded Jack of wolves attacking a lamb separated from the herd. The Luftwaffe flak gunners let loose an intense barrage and hit thirty-one of the thirty-nine Hell's Angels bombers, twenty-six of them badly, including *Teddy's Rough Riders*. Despite the bucking and battering, all forged ahead in tight formation. The army air force prided itself in never having been turned back by the Germans, despite the cost.

As planes formed up for the bombing run, they were at their most vulnerable, and the crew, the ground gunners, and the German fighters all knew it. In order to have any chance of hitting the targets from high altitude and in poor visibility, the Fortresses had to fly the "LeMay way," in a straight, level, constant-speed formation, wingtip to wingtip behind the squadron leader, and bomb on the leader's release. There was no such thing as evading flak bursts on a bomb run. The pilots had to stay exactly in line with the tight formation; any sudden evasive maneuver not only spoiled the bomb run's effectiveness but also exposed the plane to a mid-air collision with the other planes flying mere feet away.

Werner's crew was at a pre-bomb-run altitude of 19,800 feet when a shell hammered *Teddy's Rough Riders* with a loud crash and passed clean through the plane, blowing basketball-sized holes through both sides of the thin aluminum fuselage. Almost immediately, the plane was shredded by repeated hits.

The battering increased in volume and intensity as hundreds of shell fragments smashed into and through the plane, which rattled, crashed, and bounced through the black, flak-filled sky. The men heard the pitch of one another's voices spike with adrenaline and fear as they spoke over the interphone. Everyone knew the cataclysmic consequences if either the bomb load or one of the wing fuel tanks was hit. The contagiousness of fear concerned Werner. In the plane, there was no running away, no place to hide; if a man lost his nerve or his mind, it distracted all aboard, with potentially deadly consequences for the entire crew.

"Within the vast daily effort of the Eighth Air Force there were sometimes human tragedies unrelated to the course of operations," observed one historian. On October 25, 1944, shortly after takeoff, the pilot of *Deepseat-Baker*

> was informed that a ground man, a Corporal, had stowed away on board. The pilot radioed the Air Leader for advice and was told to continue the mission, as there was flight clothing aboard and an oxygen mask in the bomber. The Corporal was originally in a distressed state but appeared to settle down in the rear fuselage.
>
> When the bomber reached 19,000 feet . . . the stowaway suddenly released the side door and jumped out. He was not wearing a parachute.

Werner, a deeply devout man, prayed all the time, but as commander, he couldn't be seen doing so or discussing it. It would just have scared the crew even more and undermined their confidence in his command, and that was the one thing he would never abide—any hint of doubt regarding his ability and authority.

Werner looked over at Jack. "Settle 'em down, now."

Jack got on the interphone and in his calm southwestern drawl, learned from watching his dad arrest unpredictable and often violent men, he said casually, "Let's just do our jobs like we were trained to, boys, and we'll drop our load and get the hell out of Dodge in a minute."

In the upper turret, Gustafson, a tall, blond, devout Minnesotan Swede, began to pray silently. "Oh Lord, this is really it, we're not coming back from this, please God." But he never stopped scanning the sky for incoming fighters, especially the new Messerschmitt jets that were giving everyone the willies.

A red-hot chunk of flak striped the sole clean off of Houseman's left flight boot. As a waist gunner in the midsection of the plane, he found it increasingly hard to keep his balance, trying to swivel his .50 caliber Browning machine gun while slipping atop a growing pile of discarded brass casings. "Like a donkey on ice," was historian Donald L. Miller's perfect description. Houseman instantly felt the intense cold gripping his foot and quickly working up his leg, but he was happy he still had the foot.

A shell crashed through the ball turret gunner's Plexiglas canopy, barely missed Gus, and hit the armored partition directly behind Jack like Thor's hammer striking an enormous gong. It ricocheted off the partition into Jack's combat helmet and his side, scorched his flak suit, deafened and knocked the wind out of him. Everything changed in a heartbeat. The twenty-pound cannon shell's impact hurled Jack into the silence of a tomb. If it exploded in the bomber's cockpit, they'd be vaporized or would simply plunge to their deaths onto German soil from four miles up. The screaming and the roar of the engines went silent as Werner and Jack awaited the explosion. In his bones, Jack felt the vibration from the .50 caliber machine guns firing all around, but he no longer heard the "familiar, reassuring violence contained in the sound of each bullet." An aural void replaced the industrial thunder of air combat. A ghostly shroud descended over the concussed and deafened copilot, leaving Jack alone in his head: not a good place to be. He felt the fear in the pit of his stomach clawing up his throat; if it got into his head, it would seize him. He wouldn't let that happen, so he shoved it back down into his gut, slowed his breathing and, with it, his pulse. He needed his hand steady. He wouldn't let Werner down, even when he shot him. His best friend, commander, and target deserved a clean death. "Is there a purpose to this?" he wondered, reaching for his pistol, convinced they were about to crash. Werner looked at Jack and said something, but Jack, deaf, concussed, and in shock, couldn't hear a word. The aluminum fuselage was being shredded by flak. Jack was sure they were done for and tried to read Werner's lips for the inevitable bailout command. He rotated his shoulders away from Werner as if he were looking back at the plane's right-side fuselage and quickly slipped off his right glove, slid his hand into his pocket, and fingered the familiar contours of the Colt. He clicked off the thumb safety. He'd do it fast and clean so Werner would never see it coming. Jack waited for Werner to turn his head away to check the left wing and engines, as he did every few minutes. Werner manhandled the thirty-ton shuddering beast through cloud banks full of their fellow bombers mere feet away. He knew his life was in danger but never suspected the most immediate threat was from his best friend sitting in the copilot seat.

From his 360-degree perch atop the plane, Gus saw a nearby B-17 explode in a fireball and then watched open-mouthed as another B-17 flipped onto its back, "Oh, Christ, they're Tango Uniform," he yelled, watching it spiral down into the haze and crash before the crew could parachute out. "Tango Uniform" was the military phonetic alphabet for the letters *t* and *u,* shorthand for "tits up." The instrument panel contained a miniature representation of an airplane that showed the flight attitude—climb, dive, bank, etc. One symbol on the indicator was shaped with V forms between the dot—representing the fuselage (body)—and the dashes—representing the wings: –V*V–. The *v*'s were frequently referred to as tits; "tits up" meant the plane was upside down. Werner swiveled his head to the left just in time to see the B-17 explode, and just as quickly refocused on keeping his own plane in formation.

He couldn't dwell on the deaths—his crew needed him focused now, more than ever. "Air war is impersonal," he said in 2009. "You're five miles up and you don't hear a thing from the ground. When I saw other planes explode in a ball of fire killing ten men, I'd take a quick look—like you would at some horrible roadside accident—but no more than that. No, I was just glad it was not us, and didn't dwell on it." The shock wave from the nearby explosion stunned Jack and without ever knowing why, he clicked the safety back on his pocketed pistol. "Werner is fighting like hell to keep me alive," he thought. "What am I doing?"

Werner ordered another oxygen check, but Jack, head swimming and ears pounding, couldn't hear a thing. The noise from the flak hitting his helmet had his ears ringing like fire alarms. But from the corner of his eye, he saw Werner's lips move. Jack tapped his ears and turned up the volume on his headset as loud as it would go. Werner looked him in the eye and repeated, louder but as flat as ever and with no hint of tension, "Jack, oxygen check, now."

"If he can stand it, I'll stand with him," Jack decided, and wheezed the crew members' names. Breathing was painful, and he wondered if he had internal injuries. The men all answered "Check," as they'd been trained to do. The routine procedure took its calming effect on the crew and, luckily for Werner, on a badly stunned Jack, who had decided to ride it out since Werner clearly had no intention of bailing out. The flak was heavier than Werner and his crew had ever experienced.

The replies of the eight terrified men behind, above, and below the cockpit confirmed they were still alive and getting oxygen. If a man's hose was punctured or disconnected from the plane's internal system, his breathing didn't feel any different; he had to see the problem, before he suddenly passed out, to realize something was wrong. Without oxygen in an unpressurized plane flying above 10,000 feet, a man blacked out within sixty seconds and suffocated in as little twenty minutes. Anoxia was the silent, ever-present killer. A hundred "bomber boys" died that way during the war, usually in the isolated rear turret gunner's position in the heat of battle, or in a panicked attempt to assist desperately wounded airmen, when skippers forgot or were unable to order the mandatory oxygen checks.

In September 1944, a Hell's Angels formation was hit by intense flak and fighters north of Berlin. Navigator Lt. William A. Malone described it in the daily journal he kept throughout the war:

> They came in from nose and went around to tail. Our tail gunner was hit on first attack—whether by German shells or one of our own which strayed is only a matter of conjecture. His oxygen hose was severed and although none of his wounds were fatal he died of anoxia before the attack ceased and we could go to help him. There was nothing we could possibly do to save him before it was too late. We all felt his death was a terrible blow. He was a wonderful fellow with never a cross word and an everlasting grin.

Sgt. Miles R. Bruce suffocated alone in the tail gunner's seat. That would never happen in Werner's plane.

Despite its imposing nickname, a Flying Fortress was far from indestructible. In the months since their first mission, the crew saw plenty of B-17s vaporized in cataclysmic explosions or chopped into fragments by enemy machine gun and cannon fire. Dangers also lurked above. Aside from enemy fighter fire, "friendly" bombs released from planes flying at higher formation took out one or more bombers on several missions. In the air, death approached from all angles and often arrived at a leisurely pace.

When a wing was blown off, the plane often spiraled slowly toward earth. From a distance, it looked like a gently descending leaf or a broken toy. Werner, Jack, and the rest of the crew knew that inside such a plane, men were screaming. They'd heard them over the radio. The g-force of a spinning one-winged bomber pinned most of the crew to the bulkhead or whichever Plexiglas bubble they occupied. If a man was stationed near a firing port or happened to be near the main hatch and was able to shed his flak suit and grab and don a parachute within seconds, he had some chance of survival by jumping. If not, in a spinning plane a man needed the strength of nearly four men to compensate for the g-force that caused a 150-pound man to weigh 525 pounds. Men were pinned like butterflies at a science fair exhibit. During those slow, seemingly gentle spins, all aboard usually died on explosive impact, which from four or five miles up, if visible at all, appeared as little more than a silent match igniting in a distant mist. From five miles up, a 65,000-pound, 100-foot-long bomber appeared the size of a dime.

In the howling, hole-filled plane the five machine gunners had no time to dwell on the fate of other crews; Sergeants Skinner, Blinebury, Mahan, Houseman, and Gustafson were all filling the air with lead from their Brownings as German fighters made deadly screaming passes, probing for the formation's weaknesses.

Werner again ordered an oxygen check and Jack recited the names. Gustafson, Birkenseer, Houseman, Markt, Mahan, Skinner, and Blinebury all answered in turn, but not Chad Brodzinski, the radioman. "Brodzinski," Jack called out again. "Chad!"

All anyone heard was roaring silence.

Jack, still shaking off his concussion, ordered Gus to check on Chad.

Gus wriggled down out of the ball turret, inhaled deeply, took off his regular oxygen mask, and strapped on one of the portable oxygen units clipped to the bulkhead behind the cockpit. He lumbered back along the frozen, eighteen-inch-wide catwalk to the radioman's cubicle. Chad, a small, wiry, fast-talking, gum-chewing "New Yawker" was on the floor, unconscious and pale. Flak had severed his oxygen hose and blown apart the plane's radio. After pulling the ever-present wad of gum from Chad's mouth, Gus grabbed an oxygen canister and strapped it to the radioman's face. The "walk-around" canisters supplied enough oxygen for only short periods of time, so Gus quickly found a spare piece of hose to reconnect Chad to the plane's central oxygen system. He waited a few moments until Chad's color came back and his eyes fluttered open, then quickly made his way back to the cockpit, tapped Jack on the shoulder, and gave him the thumbs-up. Back in the upper gun turret, Gus reported what had happened.

Werner and Jack shared a knowing glance. If another crewman was incapacitated or killed, it would not necessarily mean the whole crew's instant doom, the way it could if either of them screwed up or died. The thought entered Jack's mind that everybody's chance of getting home alive was enhanced by Werner's skill and cool command. The pilots never talked much, in the air or on the ground, and no superfluous chatter passed between them. But when Werner quietly spoke to Jack, and then Jack to the crew, they instantly followed orders.

During their two dozen previous combat missions together, Werner and Jack had brought every man home alive. The crew did not understand either man, or the bond between them, but given the casualty rate on other planes, they were grateful to be flying with them, despite the workload and missions counts their commander demanded from them.

21

IRON ASS

Earlier that morning, the crew had been awakened at about 3:30 A.M., the officers politely by a sergeant, the enlisted men "with less propriety. 'Drop your cocks and grab your socks, boys, you're flying today,' an orderly would bellow, banging the heel of his hand on the hut's low, corrugated steel roof." Werner's ears were still hot from what Jack had told him the previous evening.

Some soused, Ivy League WASP had teased Jack about "babysitting the fat Nazi's nephew" over a round of seven-card stud. Jack studied the man's flushed face for a long moment and spotted the white skin around his tightly pursed lips. "I'll match your twenty and raise you fifty," he said, and slowly peeled fourteen fives off his fat wad, making sure the Yale guy got a good long look at his stack of cash. As Jack knew he would, the drunken preppy folded like a lawn chair. Jack cleaned him out on a bluff with a pair of fours, but made the mistake of mentioning it to Werner, thinking it was a funny story. He wanted to make the point that the preppy had paid for his loud mouth with cold hard cash, but Werner just grunted as he stared into the glowing coals in the heater at the rear of the Quonset hut, iron poker in hand. It pissed Werner off. He couldn't help his last name; he was born with it. Hell, Molesworth, their home base, like the entire military, was full of German Americans: Vogel, Heller, Schlottman, Reider, Osterman, Auerhamer, Richter, Braun. Even Vosler, the 303rd's only surviving Medal of Honor recipient, had been a Kraut. Werner could have gone on for an hour, but what was the point, he thought. None were related to the man heading the Luftwaffe, which was killing his buddies daily. Werner understood, but after two dozen hairy missions, he felt that it was high time for that "Nazi shit" to have ceased, certainly among his fellow group officers, but he knew it never would. Too many guys had died, and nerves were frayed and raw. He jabbed at the embers, sending a shower of sparks into the hut. Jack realized he'd stepped in it, stomped out the embers, and crawled onto his cot. Werner lay down across from Jack, his long arms behind his head, and stared at the ceiling. Jack turned his back, punched his thin GI-issue pillow into shape, and dropped into an uneasy asleep.

After a greasy breakfast, the Goering crew trudged through the dark, wet mist of early winter, predawn East Anglia to the briefing hut. The hut was jammed with men and, as usual, full of smoke, which both Jack and Werner found disgusting.

Following takeoff, when oxygen started flowing at about 10,000 feet, the men couldn't light up, so they nervously chain-smoked their Luckys in the new trademarked white package with a red circle, which reminded Werner of both RAF fighter markings and a bull's-eye.

Lucky Strike's traditional prewar dark green pack was changed to white in 1942. In a famous American Tobacco ad campaign, "Lucky Strike Green Has Gone to War," the company claimed the change was made because copper and chromium used in the ink were needed war materials, which was accurate. However, Madison Avenue consumer surveys showed the new white package modernized the label and increased its appeal to growing numbers of female smokers who, then out of the home and working in war production plants by the millions, had regular smoke breaks for the first time and were the fastest growing segment of smokers. The war provided "a convenient way to make the product more marketable while appearing patriotic" and even better, without the copper- and chromium-based dyes, the package used less ink overall and was cheaper to produce: a win-win for American Tobacco.

The men shuffled into the briefing hut and found places to sit on the long wood boards set on cinderblocks. The 303rd's executive officer, Maj. George Mackin, entered from the rear and yelled, "Ten Hut!" The men jumped to their feet as the CO, Col. William Raper, followed Mackin down the center aisle and mounted the platform. "At ease," said Raper as the bleary-eyed men removed their "covers" (hats and caps) and sat down.

115

Mackin and Raper were living testaments to the speed with which officers advanced in the air force. Just two years earlier, both had been mere lieutenants—Raper a pilot and Mackin a "second louey" copilot. Their quick rise was due to brutal attrition and ability. Mackin was a tall, handsome guy who looked like Mickey Rooney and smiled a lot, but he took no shit and allowed no slack. Raper had black hair and a round face; new to the job, he usually wore a quizzical expression. But it was his eyes the men recalled: the sad, penetrating eyes of an officer who sent his boys to the grave on a wholesale basis almost daily and then had to write letters to their families.

Some pilots, including Major Heller, didn't like Raper and called him "a namby-pamby, Goody Two-shoes." Raper had only been CO for three weeks and some senior guys, like Heller, who was the 41st Combat Wing commander and flew lead for the Hell's Angels, thought Raper lacked the "type of leadership"—meaning balls—of his predecessor, the much-loved Col. Kermit D. Stevens.

November 1944 was the "prime month of the war for the offensive against German oil production. . . . The Eighth, sometimes operating in weather that would have been regarded as unflyable a year earlier," carried out thirteen missions against oil facilities that month alone.

Raper nodded to Mackin, who pulled open a curtain exposing the day's flight route and destination. The aircrews faced a movie-screen-size map of Europe. The thick red yarn pinned to the map indicated that the target was the Leuna synthetic oil refinery at Merseburg, Germany, 700 miles away. "No fucking way," mumbled an anonymous voice from the back, "not again."

A not-so-low groan swept the room. Mackin instantly snapped, "Men!" and the muttering fell silent as Raper, brows furrowed, hands on hips, scanned the men's faces. Heller looked over to Werner a few seats away and silently mouthed "Kraut," and both shared a smile.

Heller, a handsome, dark, square-jawed Clark Gable type with a thin moustache, had a distinguished forty-two-mission career as a top bomber commander. He volunteered for a second tour and had been flying combat since August 1943, but because he, like Werner, spoke German and both had first cousins in the Luftwaffe, Iron Ass got special scrutiny. Heller and his kid brother, Emerson, also a copilot in the 303rd, regularly had to report to the rear-echelon intelligence desk jockeys who interrogated them after the flight surgeon injected them with sodium pentothal, a rapid-onset short-acting barbiturate and general anesthetic known as "truth serum." Iron Ass considered it an outrage. Werner was never called in for an injection. They already had his number covered in the roulette wheel of air war.

"I know what you're feeling, but this damn oil plant has got to be wiped out, no matter how many times we have to go back. General Doolittle wants it gone and we're going to do it for him, isn't that right?" Raper challenged.

"Yes sir," was the muted, mumbled reply from the benches.

"What was that?" demanded Mackin.

"YES SIR!" was the full-throated reply Mackin expected.

"It's all right, Major," said Raper quietly, knowing that he would likely never see 10 to 15 percent, or about forty, of the young faces in front of him ever again. That was the math. He hated his job, but, like his men, Raper had no say in the matter.

Everybody in the room knew what had happened on a mission to Leuna less than three weeks earlier, on November 2, when a sister bomb group, the 91st, sent thirty-six B-17s to Merseburg. Thirteen failed to return, 130 men, for a 42 percent loss rate, among the highest suffered by the Eighth Air Force during the war. SNAFU (Situation Normal All Fucked Up), in the biggest way. It was musical flying chairs of death with too many seats removed; the guys understood the odds of coming home unhurt were about the same as playing russian roulette every mission day.

The Allies had been bombing Leuna since the previous May, and it cost them dearly. The site became "so dark from flak, German smoke pots, and exploding oil tanks, that 'we had no idea how close our bombs came to the target,'" said Tom Landry, a B-17 copilot and later the Dallas Cowboys football coach and two-time Super Bowl champ.

Even in the best conditions, "precision bombing" was not very precise. An early British analysis indicated "one aircraft in three had got within five miles of its target." As Miller documents, reconnaissance photos showed that on clear days, only 29 percent of the bombs aimed at Leuna actually landed inside the plant gates. On radar or cloud-covered raids, the number dropped to 5.1 percent. A postwar analysis revealed that only 334 Leuna workers were killed during a total of twenty-two

Allied raids on Leuna between May 12, 1944, and April 5, 1945, twenty by the U.S. Eighth Air Force and two by the RAF. "Over [that] period of ten months a total of 6,630 American bombers tried to put Leuna out of business. It was, said one writer, the 'grimmest fight to the death ever attempted by an air force.'" The Allies dropped a total of 18,328 tons of bombs on Leuna yet achieved only sporadic production interruptions at the site. The Eighth Air Force's twenty raids cost the lives of 1,412 airmen. The Eighth lost 119 planes in three of those attacks, during which not a single bomb hit the Leuna works.

"We'll form up in three groups, A here, B here, and C here," said Raper, smacking three red circles over Cambridgeshire with his pointer.

The red circles again reminded Werner of the new Lucky Strike pack, but this mission looked anything but. He scratched a tingle on his scalp and wished he could take a hot shower, but that was still four days away. The fug smelled of cigars and unwashed men.

"Heller will lead Group A, Newton will take B, and Johnson's got C. Today is a big show and just about whole air force, over 1,200 'heavies,' are going, so keep your eyes open and don't stray an inch out of formation," warned Raper.

Heller, hearing his name, theatrically yawned, and his buddies cracked up. "Just another day in paradise," he said under his breath. Raper didn't know how to handle Iron Ass because there *was* no way to handle him. Raper knew that Heller had a personal relationship with the "big boss," Brig. Gen. Robert Falligant Travis, commander of the First Division, and that Heller had been the Hell's Angels squad leader during the famous attack on Schweinfurt's ball-bearing factory during Big Week, last February, when 226 heavies (heavy bombers, such as B-17, B-24, or B-29) were lost in just five days of furious combat. It was one of the deadliest weeks of the war, and Heller had lived up to his nickname.

Heller flew the December 16, 1943, mission to Bremen for which the Hell's Angels was awarded a unit commendation by Travis, who noted the "fine esprit de corps and a very high degree of training and determination in the Group." Travis also commended the unit for "the utmost in efficiency, cooperation, diligence and untiring effort."

Everybody, including Raper, knew Travis thought Iron Ass "walked on clouds as well as water." All the senior guys in the First Division knew that "Travis's hand rested on Iron Ass's shoulder," and that Heller was being groomed for high command. Iron Ass was the very last officer that Raper, a new and still untested CO, wanted to tangle with.

General Travis, a handsome West Point graduate of the class of 1929, was a Georgia-born eldest son of WWI hero Maj. Gen. Robert Jesse Travis and the only brother of USAAF Col. William Livingston Travis. Travis was said to have "brass balls that clanged when he walked," and his rise had been meteoric: in little more than a decade, he rose from lieutenant to general, commanding one of the most important and active divisions in the USAAF. By comparison, it took Dwight Eisenhower, a 1915 West Point graduate, twenty-six years to get his first star, in 1941.

Travis, who flew a full thirty-five-flight tour during the war, personally commanded the First Division during the January 11, 1944, Oschersleben raid in which eleven of forty Hell's Angel's bombers were lost attacking a German fighter factory. In one day alone, the Eighth lost sixty heavies, of which forty-two belonged to Travis.

The First, Second, and Third Divisions were airborne when the weather socked in and the entire Eighth was recalled by headquarters. Travis claimed "he never received the recall order" and pressed on. Most of the Second and Third Division aircraft, including fighter escorts, elected to return to England, leaving the First alone and exposed. While there was some fighter support on the penetration, and other fighters were able to provide withdrawal support, most obeyed the recall and left Travis's bombers to fend for themselves. One who didn't was Lt. Col. (later General) James Howell Howard, the only fighter pilot in the European theater of operations in WWII to receive the Medal of Honor.

German fighters, sensing advantage, attacked in groups of 15 to 30. Up to 300 enemy fighters were observed on single occasions, and an estimated 500 attacked the reduced armada overall. Howard was leading a group of P-51 Mustangs. As his group met the bombers in the target area, Travis's force was attacked by swarms of fighters. Howard and his group at once engaged the enemy and he personally destroyed a German fighter. During the melee, Howard lost contact with his squad, yet instantly banked around in a "high-G roll" so as not to lose contact with the enemy.

Seeing the bombers were being slaughtered and no other friendly fighters were at hand, Howard, who could have waited to reassemble his group before engaging the enemy, instead single-handedly attacked a formation of more than thirty German fighters. With "utter disregard for his own safety," he pressed home accurate attacks for some thirty minutes, during which he destroyed at least three more fighters while scattering the Germans. Despite damage to three guns and being low on fuel, Howard continued the attack to protect the bombers from the rampaging Germans. His actions undoubtedly saved scores of bomber crews.

Travis said, "For sheer determination and guts, it was the greatest exhibition I've ever seen. It was a case of one lone American against what seemed to be the entire Luftwaffe. He was all over the wing, across and around it. They can't give that boy a big enough award."

> The following week, the Air Force held a press conference in London at which Major Howard described the attack to reporters. . . . The story was a media sensation, prompting articles such as "Mustang Whip." "Fighting at 425 Miles Per Hour" and "One Man Air Force." "An attack by a single fighter on four or five times his own number wasn't uncommon," wrote a fellow WWII fighter pilot in his postwar memoirs of Howard's performance, "but a deliberate attack by a single fighter against thirty plus enemy fighters without tactical advantage of height or surprise is rare almost to the point of extinction."

Captain Jack P. Fawcett recalled the most "terrifying" part of the infamous January 11, 1944, mission to Oschersleben, Germany, for him was the return to Molesworth. As his Fort approached the fog-covered air base, another squad of undetected B-17s suddenly "drifted by" in the pea soup mere feet away, only to disappear again as pilots, low on fuel and carrying wounded and dying men, struggled to find a runway. He estimated thirty bombers were lurking unseen in the immediate airspace, flying 300 feet off the ground, close to stall speed. The landing conditions at Molesworth were deadly. Fawcett said pilots had no way of knowing if planes were in front of him on the runway or if another would suddenly pop out of the murk and land on top of his plane on the overcrowded and chaotic runway.

For the successful and costly mission, Travis's First Division and all its bomb groups, including the Hell's Angels, received the Presidential

Distinguished Unit Citation. Some thought Travis should have been ca-shiered, but he'd shown he was a fighting general, and Doolittle backed him up.

The "I didn't hear the recall" episode was exactly mimicked in the 1949 film *Twelve o'Clock High,* in which "General Savage," played by Gregory Peck, continued on a mission after a general recall order was issued. Mirror-ing the Travis incident, Peck's fictional unit, after a serious mauling by the Luftwaffe, received a Unit Citation. The incident has also been ascribed to the first strike on Berlin on March 4, 1944, by the 95th Bomb Group, as well to other units. It is likely a composite of several Eighth Air Force episodes.

In the film there was a fictional German American aviator named Lieutenant Zimmerman, who made a navigational error that caused his unit to arrive at the target three minutes late and out of formation. Sav-age rips the kid a new one and blames his error for the loss of fifty men. Zimmerman's commanding officer, Colonel Keith Davenport, is relieved of duty for not having grounded Zimmerman and, haunted by his par-ents' prewar association with the pro-Nazi German American Bund, Zim-merman commits suicide on base the same day.

Although there was never any connection between Werner's family and the Bund, there were as many as 200,000 enthusiastic supporters of the Bund, 25,000 card-carrying, dues-paying members, and on George Washington's birthday in February 1939, 20,000 American Nazis attended a goose-stepping Heil Hitler rally in Madison Square Garden.

The Travis-led Oschersleben raid proved to be one of the most di-sastrous 303rd missions, even though 210 enemy aircraft, the largest number ever claimed by any division of the Eighth Air Force for any one mission, were confirmed as destroyed, 43 probably destroyed, and 84 damaged. The division lost 42 heavy bombers, and many more were badly damaged. Four hundred and thirty men failed to return.

One Hell's Angels pilot who survived was Vern L. Moncur, com-mander of the *Wallaroo.* Vern Moncur, whose son Gary is currently the group's historian, later said the Oschersleben "mission was the toughest mission thus far, and as later events proved, it was the toughest mission we had in the whole combat tour. It was rated as one of the three tough-est missions that the 8th Air Force ever flew."

Raper knew that Heller was his best pilot, but he remembered what had happened the previous month, on October 20, just nine days after Raper took command of the Hell's Angels. Iron Ass was coming in to land at Honington Field in Suffolk, on a soggy grass runway in a rainstorm blowing sideways, and immediately after touching down in near-zero visibility, skidded across the grass, took out two Quonset huts, and killed Sgt. Paul A. Thompson, a sad-sack ground crewman, in his bunk. The army interrogated everybody on board and on the tarmac and determined that the accident was "unavoidable," but some poor bastard had the uncomfortable duty of explaining the mess to Travis and, worse, to Thompson's mother—how her kid, in a safe ground crew job, had been cut nearly in half by a ten-foot-long propeller, in his own bed.

The review determined that two improperly parked Mustangs blocked the main runway, forcing Heller to make the fateful grass landing. Not a good way to impress General Travis, especially since the general was tight with Heller. Raper was glad it hadn't happened at Molesworth, where Iron Ass had taken off from, but from then on, he made double-damn sure his runways were squared away at all times.

Iron Ass and Raper never saw eye to eye, especially since Iron Ass was taller than his CO, but Raper needed him, and both knew it. Not only was Heller a great pilot with political juice, but, at twenty-five, he was one of the older pilots and was so popular with the men that one of the 303rd's own Forts, *Heller's Angels,* was named for him by the ground-crew chief. In a sad coincidence of war, Heller, Werner, and Jack all helplessly watched as the plane named after Heller was shot out of the sky that late November Tuesday morning over Merseburg.

Raper announced that the thirty-nine crews were to be divided evenly into three squads, and Werner's crew was in C, two planes behind Lieutenant Johnson to the left. He then ordered the weather briefing.

The meteorologist, a thin mousy-looking guy with a weak chin, glasses, and a pencil-thin moustache, mounted the platform. The pilots didn't like him. He didn't fly and they thought he was affecting British mannerisms, or was a homosexual—almost the same thing in their eyes. Raper and Mackin at least had flown full tours and still flew on occasion and thus had the men's respect, but not the weather "Mouse," as they nicknamed him. Mouse reported that there was "a thick belt of haze from 18,000 to 28,000 feet over the target."

"Exactly our bomb-run altitude, just perfect," thought Werner. Iron Ass grinned and discreetly flashed two thumbs down to Werner and Jack. They knew that meant that Iron Ass would taking them below the cloud belt instead of a 22,000-foot bomb run, Iron Ass would take them in at 16,000 feet, a hell of a lot closer to the 88s and to eternity. What looked like a bad day had just turned into a "lead shit storm." Iron Ass was untouchable. He had "I will live through this war" written all over him, thought Jack, who then got to his feet and quickly headed to the latrine to empty his suddenly watery, bloody bowels as Werner stared after him.

"The visibility over England is eight out of ten, about as bad as it gets," squeaked the Mouse, before scurrying off the platform. The pilots were matadors, and as far as they were concerned, if you were not in the ring facing the beast, you were in the audience. Mouse occupied a nose-bleed seat.

Merseburg was surrounded by up to a thousand flak batteries and well known as one of the deadliest targets in Germany. The Mighty Eighth had bombed Merseburg numerous times in the previous six months—crews nicknamed it "Murdersburg."

Lt. Bob Welty, a copilot who flew six Merseburg missions, including on November 21, the deadliest day in his unit's history, recalled:

> "You couldn't get into Germany without being shot at because they had a ring of flak all around—all away around the border . . . Merseburg was the worst target in Europe . . . there were twelve hundred 88s in the Merseburg area. And when they threw a flak barrage it was unbelievable. We lost sixty B-17s one day to flak ground fire alone at Merseburg." Welty continued. "The one thing I discovered about fear was . . . you read about fear rising in your throat, that sort of thing. And sure you feel that, but I always had a feeling that if it could go no higher . . . than my throat, I'd be alright. I always felt that if it got up into my head, I'd go berserk."

"We all know that more of our guys are being shot down by flak than by fighters, so don't let your guard down anywhere over the continent," said Raper.

What Raper couldn't tell the men was that top-secret "Ultra" intercepts from the supposedly "uncrackable" Enigma decoding machine showed German fighter production had more than tripled in the past year, thanks to the meticulous organizational skills of Nazi armaments minister Albert Speer. Speer had "effectively dispersed aircraft production from 27 main plants to 729 smaller ones, some of which were located in quarries, caves, mines, forests or just in villages." Production of German fighters rose from 1,016 in February 1944 to 4,103 in September 1944. While the Eighth's bomber strength and sortie rates soared during the same period, "there had been no corresponding rise in the number of fighter escorts."

"Aerial recon shows that as these bastards retreat from our Red brothers-in-arms in the East, and from our guys in the West, they're pulling their 88's back with them. Leuna is probably the most heavily defended target in Europe, more than Berlin," continued Raper. "Hell, what the Brits don't seem to realize is that Berlin's buildings can all collapse and this damn war will continue, but without synthetic fuel, gentlemen, every damn Nazi fighter, U-boat, tank, and truck will grind to a halt."

While true, the unspoken reality was that 350,000 laborers were exclusively devoted to oil facility repair.

> The Nazis were able to reconstruct . . . the refineries at a much faster rate that the Allied Air commanders had considered possible . . . and [the Luftwaffe] was concentrating heavy flak guns around chief oil installations in numbers that probably would have made Berlin's inhabitants resentful had they known of it.

Hitler protected his oil more than his precious architecture. In the führer's calculus, civilians were the most expendable commodities of all.

Heller had heard it all before and knew the day's mission would be bad.

"Leuna's gas is critical to the German war effort and may supply half or more of Germany's fuel," droned Raper in conclusion. "Hitler needs this refinery like you need your next breath and we're going to deny it to him. Romanian and Hungarian oil fields are almost inaccessible to the

Nazis thanks to the valiant two-year-long efforts of our noble brothers in the Ninth and Fifteenth Air Forces," he said.

"Those guys only have wings because they're fairies," said someone sotto voce. After a beat, the room exploded in laughter, which brought a grin even to Mackin's stern mug.

"And now, it's our turn to finish it, let's choke the bastards dry," concluded Raper. "Go get them. Godspeed. Dismissed. Heller, a word please."

As the men shuffled out, Iron Ass rolled up to Raper, a toothpick jutting out of his mouth and his cap tilted back on his head, both at a forty-five-degree angle.

"Sir?"

"What's the dope on the new guy? Mackin tells me there are some rumors." Mackin nodded. The pilot had flown only a handful of missions—new-pilot jitters, he thought.

"Way I see it, he isn't green, he's yellow," said Iron Ass flatly. They were talking about the new pilot of *The Duchess' Granddaughter*, named for a hot-blooded local blue blood one of the guys was sleeping with in some ancestral manor nearby. The lieutenant had flown four consecutive missions in the past couple of weeks, and the scuttlebutt about him from both the enlisted men and the ground crew was not good. He had been overheard bitching about everything in general, but nothing in particular. His own guys didn't trust or, more important, fear him. That was enough for Iron Ass. He knew the type and had seen the symptoms before.

"What would you suggest, Major?" asked Raper.

"Personally, sir, I'd transfer him to permanent KP duty, if it doesn't involve using a knife, because even in a mess hall, he'll get someone hurt or worse."

Raper, ordered by Division to get all his birds airborne, paused. Sacking a flight commander moments before a mission based on rumors was unheard of; it meant paperwork and, worst of all, an explanation to Travis, none of which would reflect well on Raper.

"We need the whole wing airborne today. I'll speak with him after the mission," he said.

"It's your decision, Colonel," said Heller. "And your ass," he thought.

"We both know that if we hit Leuna hard and not a bomber returned, Division would declare it a great success. It's not the commander

I worry about, it's the poor bastards who have to depend on his sorry ass." Iron Ass saluted, gave Raper his back, and sauntered out of the briefing hut like he was going for a country stroll.

That cocky son of a bitch was absolutely right, admitted Raper to himself as he and Mackin left the hut to salute the departing crews. The chaplin joined them at the edge of the runway and made the sign of the cross as each Fort rolled past. Non-Christians were largely left to their own devices.

As wing commander, Iron Ass was the first to roll down the runway. Grinning, with a cigar stub clenched in his teeth, he blessed the padre in return and ignored Raper's salute. He slammed his window shut, shoved the four throttles forward, and released the brakes. His thirty-eight chicks followed the leader. On to Murdersburg. Cloud cover and the Luftwaffe be damned.

Raper looked hard at *The Duchess' Granddaughter* as it rolled by and caught its pilot's limp salute and sullen features.

"You had no choice, sir" said Mackin as they watched the bombers claw slowly into the leaden sky that nearly matched Raper's pallor.

Across southeastern England people craned their necks skyward as the bombers and fighters roared overhead. One of them was sixteen-year-old Roger A. Freeman, a farmboy born and raised on land the U.S. 56th Fighter Group used as part of its base. He was mesmerized by the aerial wonders and horrors he saw as a child. As a boyhood hobby, he memorized unit decals and collected information, photographs, and patches from various Yank units he encountered. After the Yanks left in 1945, Freeman returned to the plough for two decades. In the mid-1960s he dusted off his memorabilia and organized his scrapbook. The farmer-turned-author wrote a series of books with the help of many veterans who shared their experiences and rare color photographs never previously seen by the general public. It was Freeman who'd coined the moniker "The Mighty Eighth" in his 1970 book of the same name, which is widely hailed as "the bible" of the Eighth Air Force. Freeman became a foremost authority on Eighth Air Force U.S. warplanes, the airmen who flew them, and the operations in which they were involved. In all, Freeman wrote seven books about the strategic air campaign and worked on radio, television, and feature films as a technical expert. Following his death, the Roger A. Freeman Eighth Air Force Research Center Library and Archive was dedicated at the Mighty Eighth Air Force Museum in Pooler, Georgia, in 2007. The Yanks fondly recalled and honored the local farm kid in shorts who tagged around with boys only a few years older than himself during those unique years in world history.

In *The Mighty Eighth,* Freeman wrote that "the price the heavies paid in denying the Germans oil was higher than any of the other priority targets on the Eighth's list."

I. G. Farben, the German chemical conglomerate and manufacturer of Zyklon B, used in concentration camp gas chambers, owned the Leuna refinery, which was Germany's second largest producer of synthetic oil and chemicals. Leuna didn't make gas; it used the Bergius process, named for a Nobel Prize–winning German chemist, to synthesize petroleum from lignite, a locally mined brown coal tar. Unknown to all in the briefing room, Leuna was also doing heavy water experiments for the Nazi atomic bomb program.

22

THE FORT

After the briefing, Werner, Jack, Markt, Birkenseer, and the noncommissioned officers piled into a jeep and were driven out to their plane. The ride out was one of the most stressful times, and arriving at the hardstand, men smoked and urinated one final time before climbing into the belly of the beast for the next ten hours—or for eternity.

The B-17G, designed by the Boeing Corporation in Seattle, Washington, was a remarkable plane for its era. It was massive and impressive from the outside, bristling with up to thirteen .50 caliber machine guns. It carried more than 5,000 pounds of bombs, both high-explosive and incendiary, depending on the target. That day they carried both. On the tarmac, the cockpit sat almost twenty feet off the ground. The bomber was 75 feet long, with a 103-foot wingspan. Four 1200-horsepower Wright radial engines took the plane 2,000 miles on a tank of gas, with a fully loaded top speed of 250 miles per hour.

A B-17 had four commissioned officers, usually first and second lieutenants, and six noncommissioned officers, all sergeants. Everyone was at least a sergeant to ensure that they were more decently treated as POWs by the Germans in stalag luft camps. The four officers were the pilot, copilot, bombardier, and navigator. Sergeants operated the radio and manned .50 caliber machine guns, each at the top-turret gunner, the belly turret gunner, and the tail gunner. When the plane was over the target or under attack, the navigator also operated machine guns. Some later models of the B-17 had a single .50 caliber machine gun pointing upward through a skylight position aft of the radio bay, the "dorsal gun," that the radio operator could fire at German fighter planes attacking from above. Finally, the bomb bay held more than two and a half tons of ordnance, which could be a variety of high explosives in various weights or smaller incendiary bombs. "They were intended to be flown in tight formations of a hundred aircraft and more, whose combined fire power could spew out up to forty tons of 50-caliber machine gun slugs per minute."

Despite the firepower, Göring assured Hitler that the B-17 presented no great threat. There was little truth in that despite the fact that on its first missions, the early B-17s lacked sufficient forward-firing capability, and Luftwaffe fighter planes downed scores of bombs simply by attacking head-on. The top-turret and belly turret gunners on the B-17 had some forward-firing capability but not enough. By the time Werner's crew entered combat, almost all Forts in the Eighth had the chin turret, directly under the nose, with twin .50 caliber machine guns operated by the bombardier.

The chin turret guns were directly forward of the top-secret Norden bombsight, named for its Dutch American inventor, Karl Norden. Norden bombsights cost a whopping $1.1 billion in WWII dollars to develop and manufacture, equivalent to 65 percent of the cost of the Manhattan Project to build the atom bomb and more than 28 percent of the production cost of the B-17 itself.

The men who flew B-17s knew it to be a claustrophobic, smelly, long, narrow aluminum tube, reeking of "grease, stale sweat, cordite, dried blood, and urine"—and vomit. It was packed with guns, first-aid kits, ammo boxes, bombs, oxygen hoses, bulky parachutes, radios, emergency oxygen canisters, and ten men in bulky flight suits and heavy flak jackets. In the cockpit, Werner and Jack sat shoulder to shoulder surrounded by a sea of instruments, dials, gauges, and switches spread out above, in front of, between, and to the sides of both pilots:

> the pilot and co-pilot sat at the top of the bomber, riding "as on the bridge of a ship," able to see "the sky and the curve of the far horizon but not the swell of the sea or the rich details of the earth." They were "embedded in instruments": over 150 switches, dials, cranks, handles, and gauges, any one of which might save or doom the entire plane."

Werner and Jack took regular turns at the controls during the four-hour flight to Leuna. As always, Werner had the controls when they formed up with the other bombers from their group about fifteen minutes from their target.

The crews were wary of a squadron of German fighter pilots known as the Abbeville Kids, supposedly Göring's handpicked "all-ace" squadron.

On the day of the Leuna raid, German radio announced that a Luftwaffe squadron of aces with five or more kills each had decimated nearly an entire squadron of B-17s from the 398th Bomb Group, the last thing Werner wanted to hear.

"We got them all," was the English-speaking German announcer's boast. The Abbeville Kids had an understandable hard-on for B-17s: recently, when a group of their fighters had surrounded a B-17 and were about to blast it from the sky, the American pilot lowered his landing gear, the universally accepted sign of surrender and submission to forced landing and captivity. The Germans accepted the surrender and were escorting the captured Fort to a German airfield when the Americans opened fire, killed two German pilots, and escaped to neutral Switzerland. It was a violation of the accepted rules of air war. The last vestige of chivalry among international airmen was history.

The Luftwaffe usually treated captured aircrew much better than any other prisoners. Most American and British fliers who were captured and imprisoned survived the war. And several instances were recorded when German military police saved Allied fliers from the vengeance of the bomb-weary German populace.

23

BLOODRED SKY

The planes took up to an hour and a half getting to altitude and into formation over England. While forming up, two bombers from the 389th collided, killing seventeen men before they ever left British airspace. As the horror of the collision, explosion, and crash unfolded, the 12,683 men in the air simply roared past the catastrophe. Some, like Werner, said silent prayers, and all thanked God it wasn't them and then quickly refocused on their responsibilities and fates.

After the collision there was silence on the airways. Iron Ass eventually called Werner. "Hey, Kraut, looks like the shit is getting flaky fast today." Werner didn't reply as the 1,291 heavy bombers, both Forts and Liberators from the Mighty Eighth, lumbered across the sky over southeast England and the Channel. To help neutralize Luftwaffe fighters, 954 long-range fighters, mostly P-51 Mustangs, escorted the bombers.

The collision, although tragic, was not uncommon. During the 1,042-day European air battle, pilot error and weather caused planes to collide, on average, about once every ten days, with disastrous results for the crews. For every American airman who died in combat in the Mighty Eighth, another died in noncombat-related accidents.

In another assembly crash, Sgt. Fred Walsh, a top-turret gunner, watched in horror as a Fortress slammed into his B-17 from above. Walsh was knocked senseless, and when he regained consciousness at the base of the turret, he saw the cockpit completely engulfed in flames as the plane entered its final dive:

I could see the skipper and co-pilot slumped in their seats, their bodies burned almost black. I thought of getting out, but discovered my chute was gone. It was a terrible realization—almost as if I was doomed to die. I glanced at the escape door leading into the bomb bay and found myself looking into the sky. The plane had been blown in half by the explosion and wind was whistling through the opening. . . . I saw my parachute dangling in space, held only by part of the harness which had caught on a jagged edge of metal a few feet from me. . . . Finally I grabbed it and slipped it on.

Before jumping, Walsh looked back toward the cockpit and saw the wind-driven inferno. The plane lost so much altitude that Walsh's chute popped opened just a few feet above the ground and he landed with a tremendous jolt.

Sgt. Louis Conser, the tail gunner in the other B-17, also attempted to reach his chute:

Every time I stood up, the tail section would lurch and throw me to the floor again. Then the force of gravity would nail me there. I must have died five times before I finally crawled to where my parachute hung.

Conser was just about to jump from the spinning death trap when he thought to check the ball turret gunner's tiny cocoon dangling under the plane's belly. The belly gunner was barely conscious as the plane fell from the sky. Conser knew they had no time. He did the only possible thing, which proved impossible. He tried to secure the belly gunner to his own body, and the two men jumped out, clinging to each other. "I only remember the hard jerk as the chute opened . . . the gunner was gone. He didn't have a chance."

Heller led his air wing in *Mercy's Madhouse*. Flying lead was a tribute to Heller's crew since the rest of the formation followed the leader and dropped on his signal. It meant that the best pilot, navigator, and bombardier were all on his plane. It also meant that Iron Ass's plane was the one the Germans wanted to hit at any cost.

After a couple of hours, two Hell's Angels planes developed mechanical problems and were forced to return to base, a real bitch for the men on board since it meant the mission didn't count toward their completed totals despite all the angst they'd gone through preparing themselves. Later, most considered themselves blessed.

When Heller encountered heavy clouds at 18,000 feet, approaching the target, he called *Blue Boy High* at thirty-three Angels (33,000 feet), who reported he couldn't see a thing, so Heller knew they couldn't go up there. Then he called *Blue Boy Low* at sixteen Angels, who reported he was totally in the clear and could see the entire target.

Just before reaching "initial point," where the bombers got into tight attack formation, Heller's electronics suddenly cut out, and he couldn't lead the bomb run, so, with no radio, he ordered two yellow flares shot off, the signal for deputy wing leader J. D. Mickle to take over the lead. As Mickle slid his Fort past, Heller handed the yoke over to his copilot and showed Mickle the open palm of his left hand, his right thumb pointed first up and then down toward the ground, like a Roman emperor in the coliseum. It was their sign meaning "down to Sixteen Angels," or 16,000 feet. Mickle pointed to the earth and raised his eyebrows, and Heller nodded in the affirmative: they dropped to 16,000 feet to better see and bomb the refinery. That was 2,000 feet below regulations and everyone knew it. Iron Ass wanted Leuna dead.

Heller's decision, which he quietly worried about under the bravado, meant that he could possibly lose his job if it turned to shit. But if they were to attack the target, they had to go lower, and he knew his formations must drop very far down. It was a tough call and would be a rough ride, he knew, but "that's why they pay me so well," thought Heller, who really had only two options: either go down and attack the target or turn tail for home. The way he saw it, it was a Hobson's choice, no choice at all, and he had to attack. Consequences be damned.

The Mighty Eighth had never once been turned back by the enemy, only by weather or recall, a decision that could be made only by Doolittle at Bushey Park, Eighth's headquarters. But since Heller's radio was out, along with everything else, Iron Ass would have a plausible excuse for descending into the belly of the beast without reporting in to HQ.

Until his men found the blown fuse, Heller was blind, incommunicado, and furious at being socked in the clouds. Mickle led the bomb run, with Heller on his wing and the thirty-five other bombers trailing them, swooping down like a flock of baby birds following their gun-metal gray mother.

Lt. Sidney L. Underdown's plane was one of the two bombers that had mechanical problems, so B-17 serial number 44-6600, a new plane as yet unnamed, piloted by 1st Lt. Andy Virag on the final sortie of his thirty-five-mission tour, took over Underdown's position in the lead high slot.

Planes were usually named either by the pilot or the crew chief responsible for the plane on the ground. As thousands upon thousands of heavies entered the European theater of operations, many went on their first several missions without having been christened or decorated. There simply wasn't enough time to paint every new plane with racy nose art; the ground crews were too busy patching up the squadrons after each mission.

Over the refinery, the bombs began to pour out of Virag's plane, the "bombs away" signal for his combat box. Aboard *Teddy's Rough Riders,* bombardier Birkenseer took over control of the plane and pressed the Norden bomb release button. Nothing. He pressed it again and again. Nothing.

"A bomb is hung up in the rack," Birkenseer yelled, anxiety taking his voice up a notch in pitch. When flak hit anywhere near the bomb rack, it often bent the track from which bombs slid out of the bay. The application of crowbars, elbow grease, and kicks, along with urgent curses, usually solved the problem. Werner looked over at Jack. "Get that thing the hell out of my plane," he said and told Birkenseer to stay put. Normally, Werner would send his regular bombardier, Sachau, but he didn't yet trust Birkenseer and knew Jack would get it done right and fast. There was no time to lose.

As the steel storm perforated *Teddy's Rough Riders,* Jack strapped on an oxygen canister and waddled back to the bomb bay. The bomb that was hung up, holding all the others, was a high-explosive 500-pounder. "A direct hit on this baby will vaporize us all," he thought. He removed his flak suit for mobility and glanced down through the open bomb bay doors to kingdom come, four miles below. Best not do that again. He gripped a stanchion with both hands, planted his left foot and, with half his body hanging over the gaping bomb bay in 250-mile-an-hour freezing winds, started kicking the live bomb with his right foot. It didn't budge. He squirted some grease onto the rack. Ignoring the pain in his side, the ringing in his ears, and a stabbing pain in his gut, he grabbed the stanchion tighter and kicked harder. Once, twice, three times, and the bomb squeaked against the steel. He gave one more kick with all he had, and the bomb slid off the bent rack. He held on to the stanchion as the rest of the bombs tumbled out, and then he took a peek. Still over the target. Kicking the shit out of a live 500-pounder was an experience Jack would never forget.

Live bombs got hung up all too often. On another Leuna-bound Fortress, bombardier Lt. Chuck Wilbur discovered that his bomb bay doors were frozen shut, which meant he had to hand-crank the huge doors open while fighting a 250-mile-per-hour slipstream, not an easy feat at any temperature, much less at −45 degrees. Wilbur ran back to the nose and toggled the bomb release switch. No luck. Three 500-pounders were hung up on the right side. Wilbur again ran for the bomb bay. Straddling the catwalk over Leuna without a parachute, Wilbur released the stuck bomb by hand and worked others loose with tools. One bomb slammed into his leg as it fell, nearly breaking it and taking Wilbur along for the ride. Since Wilbur was his box's lead navigator and the planes in his squad were waiting for his signal to start bombing, he could only imagine where the squad's entire bomb load fell as he limped forward to his position.

Jack just got back to his seat when a flak burst hit Virag's plane. The pilot in *The Duchess' Granddaughter,* who was flying next to Virag, seemingly panicked; he couldn't believe Heller had brought them so low as to be sitting ducks. In an inexplicable act, the pilot jinked his yoke to the left and slammed into Virag's Fort, which instantly dropped under the already low formation by another 5,000 feet.

It was exactly what the German fighters were waiting for. Fighting the yoke of the damaged plane, Virag managed to release all his bombs except one, which got hung up. As Virag struggled with the yoke and lost speed and altitude, the German fighters pounced. Virag conceded the inevitable; he ordered his crew to bail out, and, amazingly, the entire ten-man crew parachuted into captivity as the B-17 crashed near Sangerhausen, Germany. "As he floated toward the ground, Virag bitterly recalled that his regular bombardier, Lt. John C. Rhyne, had died on an earlier Merseburg mission on August 24. On the final mission of their 35 flight operational tour, Virag's crew found Merseburg to be its nemesis," recorded the group's historian. The Hells Angels, climbing into the clouds after the bomb run, didn't see the Virag crew's chutes and believed they were all dead. *The Dutchess' Granddaughter* had wing damage but remained aloft, a testament to the Flying Fort's toughness. Werner and Jack were stunned speechless. They understood how Virag's plane might have jinked to the right after getting slammed by flak, but it was the *Dutchess'* pilot who had cut to the left, dooming Virag's crew and threatening his own. Werner had heard about the pilot's bitching, and what he saw confirmed his worst fears. Jack's mouth hung open in what Werner called "his hang-dog look."

"Iron Ass is going to put his boot so far up his butt he'll need a dentist to get it out," said Jack. "I wouldn't want to be in his seat."

"He won't be in it for long," opined Werner.

Two weeks before the Murdersburg raid, a fellow 303rd bombardier, Lt. Karl Ulrich, told his close friend, Lt. James O'Leary, pilot of another crew, of a recurring dream in which Ulrich saw his bomber take a direct hit in the right wing, in the starboard fuel tank, and explode in flames. In Ulrich's nightmare, the plane rolled over onto its back with the bombs being flung out and upward from centrifugal force. Ulrich's dream "closely paralleled the actual downing of his Fortress," recalled O'Leary as he watched in horror when it crashed near Leipzig, Germany, that afternoon. Seven men, including Ulrich, died. O'Leary learned later that some crewmen who parachuted out were pitchforked to death by civilians before the German military police were able to take them into custody.

So it went all that bloody morning. O'Leary also saw *Heller's Angel,* named for Iron Ass himself and piloted by Lt. Arthur F. Chance, shot out of the sky by a Messerschmitt 110 fighter. Yet intermingled in the chaos of burning and exploding heavies were the American fighter escorts. One of them, leading a P-51 Mustang squadron, was Capt. William Whisner. Whisner was credited with six kills and two probable kills at Merseburg, making him an instant ace. By war's end, Whisner had fifteen and a half kills and was one of only fourteen air corps officers to win two DSCs in WWII. He received a third DSC in Korea and became an ace in that war as well.

24

HEAVING THE MONSTER

The big question was what kind of luck *Teddy's Rough Riders* would have getting home. On their previous twenty-four missions together, Werner and Jack had never had a plane suffer so much damage, yet they still had a lot of Nazi-controlled territory to fly over. After the bomb run, Werner banked the increasingly sluggish plane sharply toward its homeward heading, and Jack surveyed the damage. They didn't need to talk about it. In a B-17, they were as in sync as any two human beings could be.

Moving aft, Jack gave Gustafson a thumbs-up and got one back. At his navigator's station, a perspiring Markt was furiously scribbling on a pad, trying to fix their location. Jack wondered how the man could sweat in this frigid hell and moved on. He considered the navigator "a near-psych case." Werner was aware of Markt's constant terror but silently admired him for not "bugging out." At the waist gun port, Houseman shouted over the 200-mile-an-hour wind roaring through the gaping holes in the plane, "Are we gonna make it? Should we put our chutes on?"

Jack barely heard him. It felt like his head was in a sealed box. Although he wasn't sure it was true, Jack shouted, "It's not time to think about chutes yet." He moved on back through the plane to the tail gunner and tapped Tex Mahan on the shoulder.

Tex turned around and cracked his trademark grin. "That was a hell of a doozy, huh, Jack?"

"It sure was. But we're still flying."

"Amen to that."

Jack returned to the cockpit. He was buckling his harness when Houseman's voice, nearly hysterical, came on the interphone: "Are we gonna make it? Shouldn't we put our chutes on?"

The plane was vibrating like a cement mixer full of marbles in overdrive. The crew had kept it together over the target, but now Jack smelled their fear—and his own. Jack said into the interphone, "We're full of holes and the hydraulics are bad, but we're still over enemy territory, so stay put, keep your flak jackets on and your eyes peeled." Werner cocked an eyebrow at Jack and continued flying. With the hydraulic fluid leaking like it was, Jack knew that Werner was wrestling this monster to keep it steady. He saw the tension in Werner's grip as he strained against the yoke, but his thick forearms remained steady, and his face impassive.

Jack hoped to hell he hadn't been talking through his hat about the condition of the plane. He was trying to convince himself more than anyone. He could barely hear the engines and had a splitting headache and his guts ached something awful. He hoped he didn't have to take a crap—lately he'd seen blood in his stool but pushed the whole thought out of his mind. The nearest thing to a toilet was a "relief tube," which froze up at altitude with predictable and disgusting results, or something that looked like an oversized wax-lined airline "barf bag." "Crews often returned with uniforms befouled from long missions that precluded any chance to urinate or defecate."

One Mighty Eighth crewman, Hank Hall, recalled that men usually used a steel helmet to defecate in and would set it on the fins of a bomb to keep it steady as they did.

> "Of course it stayed there till bombs away, along with the odor. When it got into the oxygen system it seemed worse." Hall joked, "If some German was to find the helmet with its contents intact, he'd think they had blown some American's brains out."

Despite the cold, the Colt .45 in Jack's shoulder holster felt warm, and the two other .45s in his thigh pockets seemed to be pulling on Jack as the dilemma he hated to think about crowded his already fuzzy mind. If the shot-up plane faltered—a real possibility—and Werner gave the bail-out command, Jack would kill him instantly and take command. Jack knew the eight men behind, above, and below the cockpit were all wearing their oxygen masks and one more hole in the plane would not matter at all. Nor, from a flight safety perspective, would a dead Werner, since Jack, unlike almost any other copilot in the Eighth Army, had 1,000 flying hours to his credit, roughly ten times the flight hours Werner had when they met. He would have no problem flying the plane home, if it was at all physically possible, with his best friend's corpse at his side. If the plane couldn't make it, he'd give the bail-out command and leave Werner's disfigured body behind, after removing his dog tags and all personal papers, as instructed.

The crew was not only terrified and dying to bail out; they were also pissed off at their commander. It had been building for a while because Werner continually volunteered his plane for every possible mission, or so it seemed to the crew. Several guys wondered if Werner was "rank-happy, bucking for medals and promotions," said Gustafson. Since Werner didn't fraternize with his crew—which was frowned on by the brass anyway—they respected and feared him, but never warmed to him the way they did to Jack. Werner knew he wouldn't win any popularity contests, but he could not have cared less. He was driven by private demons and commanded his crew accordingly. A couple of weeks earlier, flight commanders had been offered an opportunity to take a week's R & R at an old Scottish manor where the USO had organized entertainment, free beer, dances with local lassies, baseball games, and hamburger cookouts. Werner decided that his crew would stay on flight rotation and continued to fly missions instead. The guys were furious and let Jack know. Jack, as always, backed Werner to the hilt, even though he personally would have loved the time off.

The men trusted Jack, and if he had shot Werner, the crew would have backed him up, he was sure of it. Gus Gustafson confirmed it. They had all heard about Göring. The possibility tore at Jack's guts like a dull razor; he knew he was not well, but he ignored it. Was he going to have to shoot Werner—blow his best and only friend's brains out the cockpit's portside window? Jack was sick to his stomach and bent forward slightly to ease the cramps. A wave of nausea left him covered in a slick, sweaty sheen that froze instantly against his oxygen mask's rubber lining. He understood then how Markt was covered in sweat. Psychological and physical trauma were immune to thermometers. His ribs ached like hell, but pain was a welcome distraction.

Jack saw Werner glance at him. "Let me spell you," Jack said, reaching out for the yoke in front of him. Werner gave him another quick glance, let the pilot-side yoke go, and settled back in his seat slightly.

Jack marveled at how quietly Werner had been flying. With low hydraulic pressure and damaged control cables, the yoke was like a dead weight. He had to keep his biceps and forearms continuously flexed, like an intense arm-wrestling match. Fortunately his physical strength and flying ability matched Werner's, but Jack knew his body's response to battle stress did not. Werner's cool under fire, one mission after another, was a source of continual amazement to him.

"He's not normal," thought Jack, "or is it me?" His own nerves were getting worse as the mission count mounted. Some nights he didn't sleep because of the images in his mind's eye. He was glad he was an expert mechanic and could help fix planes on those nights. So long as their crew wasn't slated to fly the next day, he'd tinker for hours inside damaged planes with the ground crew, trying in vain to forget his worries and the stabbing stomach pain he was regularly ignoring. Jack was the unit's handyman and master of all trades. He gave the men haircuts, fixed their sidearms and machine guns—"Hell, he could even resole shoes and cut hair," recalled Iron Ass. Although he was always busy, put up a good front, and maintained a high level of mission performance, the stress was beginning to tell on Jack. He had a hard time shaking off traumatic images and dreams, and his secret orders only added to the strain. He worried about yelling out something awful or secret while sleeping mere feet from his best buddy.

Did he have the courage to follow his orders and shoot Werner if the plane went down? Yes, he knew he would; it was his terrible duty. All it would have taken was for Werner to have thrown in the towel and given the bail-out command. Jack had accepted the assignment voluntarily, but that was before he knew and respected Werner, and before they had become best pals. Jack didn't have written orders, which he understood, but it still bothered him. If he failed to follow the orders and they wound up in German hands, and if they survived until the end of the war, the FBI would probably put him in jail and throw away the key, he feared.

Hell, to save face and shut his mouth forever, they might execute him for aiding and abetting Werner on some trumped-up charge of espionage. But if he followed orders, they might "take care of" him quietly and dispose of his body somewhere. Or they'd "stage something and say [I] cracked under the strain" of bomber duty. God knows, he felt close enough to cracking sometimes, and the FBI's promise to prosecute him if he ever opened his mouth still rang in his perforated eardrums.

"I've got the stick, Jack," he barely heard. It was as if he were at the other end of a tunnel with cotton stuffed in his head. He glanced at Werner's big hands on the pilot-side yoke and let him take over. Jack rested his hands on his thighs and again felt the two .45s in his flight-suit pockets. His hands itched to check the safeties, but he knew they were on. He felt responsible for the crew but knew in his aching guts that he couldn't handle the top job the way Werner did. For his money, there wasn't another pilot in the army who had Werner's grit and competence combined with such a calm and reassuring command presence. "The son of a gun really was born to command a heavy," he thought.

Ten minutes later, both port engines began smoking. Werner shut them down to avoid a fire that could melt the wing off, transferred fuel to the starboard tank, and increased power to the number three and four engines. This caused the bomber to slow down and the roar of the two remaining redlined engines increased even as the crew's anxiety ratcheted up another notch. Again, it was Houseman who couldn't contain himself. "What are we going to do? Are we gonna bail out?"

Jack heard Houseman as if he were in a dream. He glanced back down the aisle. Markt looked as if he'd swallowed his tongue. Sounds were so distant, he wondered if he'd hear the .45 go off. He was so close to pulling the trigger, the knot in his stomach seemed made of barbed wire. If Jack were in command, he'd order the men to bail out; capture was preferable to crashing or drowning. But Werner was still the boss, and their collective fate rested in his large, steady hands.

The odds of the plane going down were getting worse by the minute. They were dangerously low on fuel. Jack felt the crew's terror. "Why don't we just bail out now before we drown?" was the unspoken, urgent question on the crewmen's minds.

Werner gave the instrument panel a long hard look, exhaled sharply, puffing out his cheeks, and held his breath for a moment before inhaling deeply through his nostrils. He made his decision and calmly addressed the crew. "Sit tight, we're going home." The English Channel loomed low on the horizon, a deadly hurdle. Jack glanced over at Werner—cool, quiet, and as focused as ever—and trusted him to keep the shuddering, whistling, hole-filled plane out of the deadly drink.

After the German fighters faded away over the English Channel, Werner finally ordered the men to put on their chutes and life preservers. They huddled near the main escape hatch. Most of them smoked once they got below 10,000 feet, and repeatedly checked their chute and preserver straps while they nervously eyeballed the icy waters churning beneath them.

During the 1042 days of the Eighth Air Force's WWII service, about 450 heavy bombers, about one every two days, ditched into the icy English Channel's powerful currents, usually sinking within a minute and a half. Early in the war, a vast majority of the airmen who ditched in the water died, and despite the RAF's strenuous efforts to improve sea rescue, almost half still drowned. The crew would have much preferred to become POWs than to crash into the drink.

The Tweacheous Wabbit, also inbound from Leuna, had portions of its tail blown off. Despite badly damaged elevators and stabilizer, and no rudder, pilot Loye J. Lauraine, a twenty-six-year-old married Texan, had just crossed the English Channel and made a recorded radio contact with the control tower.

He knew he couldn't land.

Control:	"See if you can head the Fort out to sea."
Lauraine:	"It's all I can do to keep it going. We tried to tie the control cables together to save the plane, but it's no go."
Control:	"Use your own discretion."
Lauraine:	"Will try to turn around and head out to sea."
Control:	"Keep in touch with us."
Lauraine:	"We are ready to bail out, if we don't make it, good luck to you."
Control:	"I won't need the luck—good luck to you."

Lauraine held the Fortress steady just long enough for his entire crew to bail out safely over land. Trying to get near the coastline and

Maj. Werner G. Goering, circa 1955.

(Courtesy of the Goering family)

Werner Goering's mother, Adele K. Goering, circa 1915.

(Courtesy of the Goering family)

"The Devil's Count." Karl F. Goering's passport photograph, 1923. Age 48.

(Courtesy of the Goering family)

Jack Rencher, air cadet, 1942. "There was nothing in a B-17 I couldn't take apart and put back together again except for the radio."

(Courtesy of the Rencher family)

Major William C. "Iron Ass" Heller U.S. Army Eighth Air Force, First Bomb Division, 41st Combat Wing, 303rd bombardment group, January 1, 1945, Molesworth Station, England.

Courtesy William C. Heller

Werner G. Goering Crew—358th Bomb Squadron, standing in front of *Fearless Fosdick*. (Back, left to right): Lt. William D. Sachau, Lt. Jack P. Rencher, Lt. Rex H. Markt, and Capt. Werner G. Goering. (Front, left to right): Sgt. Paul A. Bishop, Sgt. Chester "Chad" Brodzinski, Sgt. William J. LaPerch, Sgt. Orall R. "Gus" Gustafson, Sgt. Clarence W. Houseman, and Sgt. Weldon T. "Tex" Mahan. August 10th, 1944.   *(Courtesy of Gary Moncur, 303rd BG historian)*

Brig. Gen. Robert A. Travis, January. 11, 1944.

(Courtesy of Mark Forlow)

Future SAC and USAF commander, Col. Curtis E. LeMay, circa 1943, England.

(Courtesy of Michael P. Faley, 100th Bomb Group Foundation)

Col. William S. Raper, less than a month after Raper took command of the Hell's Angels, November 6, 1944, Molesworth.

(Courtesy of Gary Moncur, 303rd Bomb Group historian)

Gen. Jimmy Doolittle, commander of the Mighty Eighth, circa 1944.

(Courtesy of the Congressional Medal of Honor Society)

"The flak was so thick you could walk on it" was how reporter Walter Cronkite described scenes such as this in which a squadron of nine B-17s is surrounded by hundreds of flak bursts, date unknown.

(Courtesy of Gary Moncur, 303rd Bomb Group historian)

A testament to the sturdiness of the Flying Fortress. Note damage to landing gear and left wing, date unknown.

(Courtesy of Michael P. Faley, 100th Bomb Group Foundation)

100th Bomb Group Foundation. B-17 Formation, lower right plane about to crash, date unknown. *(Courtesy of Michael P. Faley)*

Facing the brass. (Left to right): Gen. Carl Spaatz, U.S. Strategic Air Forces commander, and Gen. Jimmy Doolittle, head of the Eighth Air Force, interviewing Hell's Angels crews following the March 31, 1945, mission.

(Courtesy of Gary Moncur, 303rd Bomb Group historian)

June 6, 1944. "For Captain Bob Sheets—with a lifetime of gratitude for getting us back! Walter Cronkite."

(Courtesy of Sally Wiggins, daughter of Capt. Robert W. Sheets)

A B-17 with its tail shot off that is about to crash. The tail gunner's compartment is already gone. Date unknown.

(Courtesy of Mark Forlow)

The Molesworth Officers Club circa 1943: the center of USAAF social life. (Left to right): Capt. George T. Mackin, Capt. Walter G. Donnelly, and Maj. Eugene A. Romig.

(Courtesy of Mark Forlow)

Wounded crewmen being unloaded following the December 13, 1943, mission, Molesworth, England.

(Courtesy of Gary Moncur, 303rd Bomb Group historian)

The B-17 in the foreground has been hit in the bomb bay with catastrophic results. Note the string of bombs falling from the plane above and to the right of the stricken Fortress. Merseberg, Leuna oil refinery. Date unknown.

(Courtesy of Mark Forlow and Gary Moncur)

Bob Hope visits Molesworth, June 7, 1943. (Left to right): Col. C.A. Marion, Bob Hope, and Capt. B. Southworth.

(Courtesy of Gary Moncur, 303rd Bomb Group historian)

Sgt. Forrest Vosler, one of only two Hell's Angels who was awarded a Medal of Honor, 1944.

(Courtesy of Congressional Medal of Honor Society)

President Roosevelt shakes hands with T/Sgt Vosler as Under Secretary of War Patterson prepares to place Congressional Medal of Honor around his neck at award ceremony. The White House 31 August 1944.

The White House, August 31, 1944. Roosevelt shakes hands with Vosler as Under secretary of War Patterson prepares the Medal of Honor.

(Courtesy of the Congressional Medal of Honor Society)

The cockpit of a B-17.   *(Courtesy of the USAF)*

"All my love, Vern." Gary's father, Lt. Vern L. Moncur, surviving pilot in the infamous January 11, 1944, Oscher-leben mission.

(Courtesy of Gary Moncur, 303rd Bomb Group historian)

Wedding portrait, August 15, 1946, Salt Lake City, Utah, June and Werner Goering.

(Courtesy of the Goering family)

June and Werner Goering, Tucson, Arizona, July 2009.

(Courtesy of Stephen Frater)

Werner Goering, age 21, wearing the Distinguished Flying Cross, 1945.

(Courtesy of the Goering family)

JFK looks over Werner's shoulder in the U.S. embassy at Addis Ababa, Ethiopia, 1962.

(Courtesy of the Goering family)

Werner Goering's uncanny resemblance to Hermann Göring, Tucson, Arizona, July 2009.

(Courtesy of Stephen Frater)

Jack Rencher, age 88, Boise, Idaho, July 2009.

(Courtesy of Stephen Frater)

"Ace of Aces," Maj. Richard Ira Bong, the highest-ranking American Ace of all time with forty kills, dead at twenty-four. 1944.

(Courtesy of the Congressional Medal of Honor Society)

James Howell Howard, the only fighter pilot in the European theater of operations in World War II to be awarded the Medal of Honor during the deadly raid on Oschersleben. 1944.

(Courtesy of the Congressional Medal of Honor Society)

Walter Truemper. A navigator who washed out of pilot training, took the controls of a B-17 after the copilot was killed and the pilot left badly wounded and unconscious. Truemper flew the plane back to England, allowing seven other crewmen to parachute to safety. He and turret gunner Sgt. Archibald Mathis decided to stay with the pilot. All three men died. Truemper and Mathis both were awarded the Medal of Honor. Circa 1942.

(Courtesy of the Congressional Medal of Honor Society)

Goering, SAC commander. Werner would fly B-47 jet bombers carrying hydrogen thermo-nuclear bombs from Tucson to the Arctic Circle and back in twenty hour-long missions, refueling three times Circa 1955.

(Courtesy of the Goering family)

During the Cold War, an armed guard positioned next to a bomber signaled the presence of a live nuclear bomb inside the bomb bay. A bomber like this B-47 carried a 7,800-pound atomic bomb that was released near Savannah. Werner flew B-47s throughout the 1950s for the SAC.

(Credit: National Archives)

The Awash basin, Ethiopia, 1962. Werner sits atop a wild pig he shot with his cherished walnut Husqvarna 38 Swedish Mauser. Shortly after this photo was taken, Werner lost the gun while attempting to save Sgt. Landis, who drowned in the Awash River.

(Courtesy of the Goering family)

Werner, in full dress tuxedo uniform, pets a royal cheetah at the palace of Haile Selassie I, the last emperor of a dynasty that traced its origins to the thirteenth century, and by tradition back to King Solomon in biblical times. Ethiopia, circa 1962. *(Courtesy of the Goering family)*

Werner Goering retraces flight paths in his living room, Tucson, Arizona, July 2009.

(Courtesy of Stephen Frater)

A massive 18-carat solid gold ring that belonged to Hermann Göring, now owned by Werner Goering, July 2009.

(Copyright: Veneklasen Photography)

Declassified spy photo of Russian fighters taken by Werner Goering in East Germany. The jeep in the foreground races toward Werner as he snaps his photograph of a line of brand-new Soviet jets in East Germany. Werner was shot at but escaped. Circa 1950.   *(Courtesy of USAF)*

Site of the 1950 B-29 crash in which Gen. Travis died and an atomic weapon was destroyed in an explosion heard thirty miles away. Eighteen people, including Gen. Travis, died. *(Courtesy of USAF)*

(Left to right): Gary Moncur 303rd Bomb Group Historian (son of Hell's Angels pilot Vern Moncur) and Jack P. Rencher, Memorial Day 2010, Boise, Idaho. Sixty-five years after the fact, Jack is still wearing his wings.

(Courtesy of Gary Moncur, 303rd Bomb Group historian)

away from inhabited areas, Lauraine was in a desperate situation, but when he saw the coastline, he let go of the shuddering yoke and tried to make the thirty-foot dash from the cockpit to the hatch. But the *Tweacheous Wabbit* lived up to its name, instantly yawed out of control, and crashed from 9,000 feet, killing Lauraine instantly.

25

HOMEWARD

Teddy's Rough Riders was steadily losing altitude, and the risk of a water landing was quite real. Because the radio compartment was so badly damaged, Chad Brodzinski couldn't send a distress signal to the RAF's Air and Sea Rescue shore stations along the British coast. The plane had two self-inflating life rafts, but it was obvious that one of them was too shot up to be of any use.

Jack moved about the plane, inspecting the damage. Hydraulic fuel leaked everywhere and the plane's fuselage looked like Swiss cheese. Werner battled the crippled bomber and struggled to maintain altitude to reach Molesworth, 150 miles north of the white cliffs of Dover.

In an incident related by Jack, which Werner adamantly denied, as they finally approached Molesworth, Jack said, "You're coming in too high." Werner abandoned the approach and circled around for another try. They were flying on fumes and the plane was mushing badly, grossly underpowered, with only two engines. Heavy bomber pilots trying to land on two or three engines had a bad habit of coming in high because they didn't have enough thrust to compensate for a short approach. Jack knew from his instructor days that many men had died in similar approaches a half mile from their bunks after otherwise successful 1,500-mile missions.

On the second approach, according to Jack. Werner was again coming in too high. Without asking permission Jack instantly shut off the two remaining engines, the generator, the avionics, the navigational lights, the radio circuitry, and anything that would make a spark if they were to crash. Werner had to land a completely "dead stick"—the plane lost all propulsive power and was coming down one way or another. To this day, Werner indignantly denies Jack's account of the landing.

What's not in question, however, is that eight hours and fifteen minutes after takeoff, *Teddy's Rough Riders* hit the ground hard and collapsed a front tire that had been shot through. The landing gear collapsed with it, and the plane skidded in wild circles across the grass strip adjacent to the main runway. The smoking B-17, perforated with more than 245 holes, finally lurched to a stop as ground crews raced toward them. Another mission completed. For the Eighth Air Force as a whole, the numbers told the tale. That day, 567 of the 1,291 bombers were damaged, 25 bombers never returned, and 15 of the 954 escort fighters also vanished. As for the men, 22 crew were killed; 30 were seriously wounded, never to see action again; and 283 simply went missing, some to emerge from POW camps after liberation, some never to be seen again.

For the 390 Hell's Angels airmen sent aloft that day, the butcher's bill included 11 fatalities, accounting for half of that day's Eighth Air Force deaths and 25 men missing; 185,000 pounds of bombs were dropped on Leuna and 14,700 .50 caliber machine-gun rounds were shot off. But to Jack's great relief, and Werner's good fortune, not a single .45 caliber round was expended. Little did either man suspect they'd be returning to Murdersburg within days.

At another Eighth airfield that afternoon, Col. Frank P. Hunter, the 398's commanding officer, asked, "Where are the rest?" as he approached Lt. Warren Johnson, the squadron leader, more than eight hours after takeoff. "There are no 'rest,' sir," answered Johnson. Colonel Hunter himself, along with Chaplain James Duvall, had stood at the end of the runway early that morning and waved to each crew as the group's thirty-seven Fortresses took to the air starting at 7:51 A.M.

After they gave silent thanks to the Almighty and the Boeing Corporation, Werner's crew wearily dragged their gear out of the plane. Eight of the crewmen gratefully grabbed the double shots of whiskey from a platter offered up by a Red Cross nurse; Werner and Jack, as ever, waved away the booze.

Werner saw Heller, about fifty feet away, gesticulating furiously, and walked over to see what was up. But he already knew it was about *The Duchess' Granddaughter,* and its pilot, Mickle, was standing next to Heller.

"Kraut," said Heller, "what the fuck was that up there? You were behind them and I didn't see it, but I want to hear exactly what happened to Virag before he lands."

Werner told Heller exactly what he and Jack, who had wandered over to the group, saw. Jack nodded in agreement.

"You're both sure Virag wasn't blown into the other plane?"

Werner and Jack nodded glumly. This was going to be ugly. Mickle, binoculars to his face, spotted *The Duchess' Granddaughter* on approach. "Here he comes."

Heller ordered the MPs to detain the pilot as soon as he landed and to bring him to his quarters.

Before the propellers even stopped, Mackin was at the plane, closely examining the damage to its left wing, where it had hit Virag.

"Lieutenant, get your sorry ass out here right now," he yelled into the open hatch as the crew emerged looking at some invisible spot on the tarmac or anywhere away from Mackin's furious gaze.

The pilot climbed out looking like that jackrabbit in his .22's sights, thought Jack. No, more like a jackass, he decided.

The MPs escorted him to Heller's hut.

"What in God's name happened up there?" demanded Heller.

"It was my fault," said the lieutenant.

"I'm asking you again, what exactly happened?" Louder this time. Mickle slid over to Iron Ass's right side to face the hapless pilot.

"Spit it out."

"I just didn't want to fly anymore," mumbled the pilot.

"What?" exploded Heller, unable to accept what he had just heard.

"I want to be taken off combat status."

"Goddamn right you're not going to fly anymore," shouted Iron Ass. "I'm personally guaranteeing you that, but you didn't answer my question. What the hell happened?"

"I figured if I just bumped into him, you'd take me off combat missions."

"Are you saying you hit Virag on purpose?" Iron Ass couldn't believe his ears.

"Yes, uh, yes, sir."

Heller reached for his Colt, but Mickle grabbed his arm. "Sir, don't," he warned Heller.

"You yellow bastard, I should shoot you right here in front of the entire squad for failing to advance against the enemy as ordered in combat," shouted Iron Ass.

"You have cost us ten good men on their final fucking thirty-fifth mission," yelled Heller as other officers gathered around to watch the spectacle of a man's career going up in smoke.

"If it were up to me, I'd shoot you right here. Not only will you never pilot a plane ever again, anywhere in this man's army, but I'm bringing you up on charges and will make it my personal business to see your court-martial."

Heller turned to Mickle. "Now take this shit-bird out of here before I change my mind. I want him out of my sight and out of the squad."

He was escorted away by MPs. Iron Ass was as good as his word and filed charges against him. Heller wanted him in the stockade.

Eventually an officer from the Judge Advocate General Corps visited Heller and told him that since pilots were all volunteers, technically the lieutenant could stand down at any time, as any pilot could. Even though his actions occurred during combat, the army's lawyers and brass just preferred to make the whole mess go away quietly. Recognition of posttraumatic stress as a valid war wound or disorder was still decades away. Nobody wanted to deal with cases like this, since they were bad for both morale and careers. The men who cracked simply vanished to some other group and function. An Eighth Army unit historian wrote, "This happened more than records indicate. It was usually kept secret, and even the crew it happened on, to this day, rarely speaks about it so as to not offend the man's memory or family." When such unfortunate and shameful events occurred, the man was tagged RFS—removed from flying status—and instantly transfered off base.

The pilot of *The Dutchess' Granddaughter,* who never flew again in the military, left Molesworth immediately that night and eventually "wound up in some REMF"—rear-echelon motherfucking engineering job—Iron Ass told the guys later, shaking his head in disgust.

"I had the MPs charge him. I was so disgusted. Knowing so many brave and staunch men who had died serving their country, I could not resist myself from wanting to shoot him right there in my quarters. Had I been a commander in the field, I could have done so. Happily and legally," recalled Iron Ass sixty-five years later.

26

THE FINAL FLIGHT OF
JERSEY BOUNCE JR.

A Fort that ditched in the water the previous December became one of the Hell's Angels' most famous episodes, one that Werner, Jack, and the whole crew knew very well. On a freezing winter's day, *Jersey Bounce Jr.* crash-landed in the North Sea off Great Yarmouth.

Earlier, as the plane banked sharply in a tight 300-mile-per-hour evasive maneuver after having dropped bombs over Bremen, flak slammed it broadside "like hitting a brick wall."

Ball-turret gunner Ed Ruppel saw fire streaming from the number one engine and shouted to pilot Lt. John Henderson, who happened to be flying with a very experienced instructor pilot that day, Capt. Merle Hungerford. Henderson and Hungerford opened the cowling flaps on the burning engine and extinguished the flames. But *Jersey Bounce* was now outside the protection of the formation. Minutes later, another flak barrage killed the number four engine, leaving it windmilling out of control. Henderson and Hungerford knew they were in a major snafu far from home.

On only two engines, *Jersey Bounce Jr.* dropped farther and became the target of an assortment of enemy fighters, that lined up ten deep to get a shot at the crippled ship. Limping toward the North Sea coastline over Holland, the bomber that had survived twenty-eight previous combat missions shuddered violently in its death throes. As it got over the water in a slow, inexorable final dive, it lost power on the number three engine. It was only a matter of when and where in the water the plane was going to crash.

Ruppel glanced to his right and saw five B-17s under attack from fighters. One was almost alongside them.

> They cut one of his wings off and he went into a tight roll. Then they went after the others. They just kept pecking away until they got them all. They chopped up one ship and then another, and then they hit the third one . . . they went to work on that plane over to our left, and cut him up . . . I knew when the fighters were finished with them we were next.

Jersey Bounce Jr. was down to 15,000 feet and falling fast when the Luftwaffe turned its tender mercies toward it. To the crew, it seemed like the entire Luftwaffe was on them. Several fighters dove on the plane's rear, and, during a hailstorm of bullets, a German 20 mm cannon shell blasted the tail gunner's position. The shell went straight down the barrel of Sgt. George Buske's .50 caliber machine gun and exploded, peeling back the Browning like a steel banana.

> Just five months earlier, a 20 mm exploding shell fired by an attacking German fighter plane had caused deep wounds to his left hip. For that mission he had been awarded his first *Purple Heart,* another *Oak Leaf Cluster* for his *Air Medal,* and the *Silver Star* for conspicuous bravery. After 45 days in the hospital, he had finally returned to full duty.

All on board heard, and never forgot, the single gurgled scream from Buske.

"Help me . . . help, I'm hit."

"Tail gunner report," ordered Henderson. "Buske, Buske, report in." Buske failed to respond, and Henderson ordered top-turret gunner Bill Simpkins to go back and check on Buske and then had the waist gunner, Ralph Burkart, take over Simpkins's guns.

Radioman Forrest Vosler was also hit and several of the plane's control cables were severed. The waist and turret gunners poured .50 caliber bullets back at the attackers, shot down four fighters, and damaged others, but the ship, now low in the sky, was a fat, slow clay pigeon for every coastal Luftwaffe flak emplacement and fighter in sight. Shrapnel and lead tore into the plane from every direction. Vosler worried as much about losing his mind as his life. He was hit in both legs and hands. He stood for a moment in horror and felt hot blood pumping down into his cold flight boots. Vosler slumped into his armor-plated seat to avoid being hit again when it dawned on him that instead of hiding from the battle, his crew needed him to be in it.

As it turned out, Vosler's actions would make the difference in all their fates twice in the next few harrowing hours: once with a gun and the other with Morse code.

"If this is the way it's going to be, at least I'm going to die standing up," Vosler thought and staggered over to a machine gun near his position and returned fire at the swarming fighters. Ruppel shot at a fighter from the ball turret but missed, and the German pilot peeled off for another try. From above, eight or nine fighters swooped in, sun to their backs, from the notoriously dangerous ten o'clock high position. Simpkins had never seen anything like it. Few men who did lived to relate the experience. During a short break in the action, some fighters refueled while others formed up and regained altitude for another pass. Almost immediately, a Messerschmitt 100 barreled down from the left, again from ten o'clock, and Burkart blew it out of the sky 800 yards out. Minutes later he shot down a Messerschmitt 109 and saw the pilot parachute out.

At the tail gunner's position, Simpkins found Buske unconscious and bleeding badly. His shredded flight suit revealed a sucking wound in his right chest that exposed a heaving lung, his diaphragm, and another huge gaping stomach wound. The shell had driven large fragments of Buske's own machine gun and exploding bullets deep into his belly, solar plexus, and chest in what appeared to be an enormous connected eighteen-inch gaping wound through which multiple organs were poking out or exposed. It was as if he had been unzipped from his sternum to his groin. The hot fragments still sizzled as they roasted Buske's torn organs. "A dead man," thought Simpkins. With great difficulty, he pulled Buske out of the mangled tail gunner's seat and dragged him forward to the waist guns, which were firing nonstop. He was afraid Buske would rip in half at the belly as he tugged him forward by the armpits in the lurching, swerving plane. Only the flight suit was holding Buske together, as far as Simpkins could tell.

Burkart, who had been ordered to come up from the belly turret during the melee, was firing Simpkins's waist gun. Simpkins grabbed two morphine syrettes, but in the −40 degree plane, both were frozen solid. He popped them into his mouth and thawed them over agonizingly slow minutes as Buske writhed on the deck. After injecting both syrettes, thinking Buske would die soon anyway, Simpkins lay him on the floor atop a life preserver to try to insulate him from the cold steel. The compress bandages he applied did little to stem the torrent hemorrhaging from Buske's multiple wounds, but they hid the hideous jagged void in his chest and abdomen from the other crewmen's eyes.

Simpkins then took over the left waist gun and almost immediately downed a fighter that had also attacked from above. But without a tail gunner, the bomber was dangerously exposed. Simpkins knew the gun was too shot up to be of any use, and all he could do was to shout a warning when a fighter swooped down on *Jersey Bounce*'s dangerously undefended and silent tail.

Vosler's single machine gun, protruding from the radio compartment hatch, responded. The first burst knocked pieces of the fighter's left wing off. Vosler pulled his goggles over his eyes and searched for other threats. He found them, and they found him. The frozen goggles immediately fogged up. Vosler had just shoved them up onto his forehead when an incoming shell exploded into his face and chest.

> I couldn't see very well, but when I moved my hand down to my chest where I'd been hit—I was trying to open my jacket to find out how badly—I noticed that my hand was shaking. I couldn't control it. Then I reached up and dragged my hand across my face to see if there was blood, and when I looked at it my whole hand was covered. . . . the shell fragments had damaged the retina of my right eye, and I was seeing blood streaming down the retina inside my eye, thinking it was on the outside. . . . I had lost the whole side of my face. . . . I thought I only had half a face. . . . I was out of control. . . . Obviously I wasn't going to have a chance to get out of this thing now. I knew I was going to die. . . . The fear was so intense, it's indescribable, the terror you feel when you realize you're

going to die and there's nothing you can do about it. So I started to lose control, and I knew then that I was either going to go completely berserk and be lost or something else.

Vosler relived his life, "day by day, for twenty years." For the first time, he realized "what a wonderful life" he had lived.

There were only a few days in my whole life that were bad, and I asked God to forgive me for those bad days, and thanked Him for all the . . . wonderful days he had given me. I said, "I'm not going to ask you for any more days. It's been too nice." I even reached out my hand and said, "Take me God, I'm ready."

Having made peace with his Maker, Vosler felt "content, very calm, and very collected." He no longer feared death and was determined to make his final moments count. A horrified Ruppel observed Vosler.

He was schrapnel from his forehead to his knees, everywhere. There was blood all over him, coming from all those little shrapnel cuts. There was no place where you could put your hand and stop the blood. I knew he was hit badly in the eyes, too, because I could see the white stuff running down below one eye and onto his cheek.

Vosler, barely able to see, nevertheless started to repair his radio to send an SOS signal to try to save his crewmates; it was clear they were headed for a water crash. "Training took over as he . . . recalled the admonition from Radio School: 'A day will come in combat, when the job of getting home is up to the radio operator.'"

Henderson ordered all equipment jettisoned to reduce weight. Machine guns, ammo boxes, oxygen cylinders, tools—anything that wasn't bolted down went out the hatch, but not the damaged and blood-covered radio, which the nearly blind Vosler adamantly refused to let go of.

"Struggling against his pain and unable to see his radio clearly, Vosler got on the interphone to advise the cockpit that he would transmit an SOS as soon as *Jersey Bounce* reached the water, beyond enemy territory."

Henderson, struggling to keep the shattered bomber in the sky, immediately yelled back, "I think you better send it now!"

Simpkins later recalled:

> As we were throwing things out, [Vosler] said "You're throwing everything else overboard. Well, why don't you throw me overboard? I'm just so much extra pounds. Throw me out, too." And he really meant it, because he asked me more than once to throw him out. I didn't say anything, really, I just sloughed it off. I didn't take him real seriously, even though I knew he was getting serious about it.

Eventually, *Jersey Bounce* reached the North Sea. Vosler, in agony, with blood running out of both eyes and unable to see, repaired his radio by touch; he reattached a damaged wire on the transmitter key and sent out distress signals despite several lapses of consciousness.

He also "clearly instructed the others in finding and inserting the right frequency modules [needed] . . . to contact Search and Rescue. . . . This done, the remaining modules were thrown out the window."

Low over the water, Vosler painfully and repeatedly sent the SOS signal in code and got a response from RAF Search and Rescue asking him "to give a holding signal for 20 or 30 seconds while they shot a true bearing on me. I responded and gave them the signal, and they came back, said they had my course, and asked me to transmit every 10 or 15 minutes so that later they could correct their bearing."

Vosler kept sending out Morse code signals until four British Search and Rescue sea planes met the bomber in midair "to either escort the floundering B-17 to land or to pick up her crew in the sea."

As they approached the English coast, the engines finally gave up the ghost. Henderson and Hungerford, the instructor captain in the copilot's seat, successfully ditched the Fort in the freezing December North Sea. As the plane began to sink, the crew shoved Buske onto the wing. Vosler crawled out unaided and held on to the wounded tail gunner. Buske started slipping into the water and Vosler yelled to the pilot, but he could see he wasn't going to respond fast enough. The men had pulled a life raft out, and it floated on top of the wing. Henderson desperately tried to cut the cord on the raft so it wouldn't be dragged into the deep by the plane. Vosler knew that the helpless and doped-up Buske would be in the deadly water and gone forever in a fraction of a second:

> I jumped and held out my hand at the same time. I grabbed the antenna wire that runs from the top of the tail to just forward of the starboard radio compartment window. I prayed that it would hold, and was able to grab Buske around his waist just as he was going into the water.

For long moments the two wounded men hung on to each other as Vosler, weak, blind, and wounded from head to toe, struggled to keep his grip on the wire. Other crew members finally loaded the gravely wounded men, still clinging to each other and life itself, into dinghies. Thanks to Vosler's SOS signals, the crew was quickly hauled out by a Norwegian ship and then transferred to a PT boat that took them on a rough, fast trip to Great Yarmouth, where they were hospitalized.

Action reports said that in addition to antiaircraft fire, about 125 German fighters had repeatedly attacked the formation in what proved to be a very costly mission for the Eighth Air Force; a total of twenty-seven bombers were lost, including *Jersey Bounce Jr.*

The crew returned to Molesworth the next day, except for Vosler and Buske, who were both facing another long battle, one of survival.

27

THE BATTLE TO LIVE

Ivan W. Brown Jr., M.D., a cardiovascular surgeon and the former James B. Duke Professor of Surgery at Duke University, was a captain in the Sixty-fifth General Hospital, a Duke army reserve unit where Brown treated Buske, whom everyone had assumed was a dead man.

Brown found a large, sucking wound in Buske's right chest that exposed his right lung and "continued through a disrupted diaphragm as a single gaping wound into the right upper abdomen." The tail gunner's liver was torn open, as were both his upper and lower intestines. Ribs were visible in another wound on his left side. In addition, X-rays revealed shell fragments in his right thigh, abdominal wall, and both lungs, perilously close to his heart. The bullet that penetrated his upper abdomen was lodged deep in his back.

> "Because of his extremely critical condition . . . surgeons could only control the bleeding from his torn liver, reattach the disrupted diaphragm, and close the sucking wound of the right chest," wrote Brown. The gaping left chest wound was dusted with an antibiotic powder and stuffed with gauze and left open, as was the stomach wound. Buske needed continual transfusions and was in such bad shape he couldn't be moved for days. Later, at the 231st Station hospital the abdominal wound was found to be grossly infected. It drained "a foul, bile-stained fluid containing digestive juices and bubbles of intestinal gas. Dead tissue was removed and a pocket of pus over Buske's

liver was drained. "An empyema [an accumulation of pus] in . . . his right chest cavity was drained of a large amount of infected, bloody fluid. A few days later, another empyema of his left chest was drained as well." Buske, unable to take fluids or food by mouth "because of the total drainage of upper intestinal contents, which were slowly digesting and enlarging the abdominal wound, was sustained entirely on intravenous fluids."

Buske just didn't want to die, and the medical team marveled at his resilience and stamina. Brown continued:

Often, as a nurse changed his position, he would arouse from his semi-comatose state and exclaim, "Damn it, can't anybody get any sleep around here?" then lapse back into coma. His weight fell to 88 pounds. In an attempt to improve his nutrition, and to provide a source of protein, daily units of reconstituted dried human plasma were added to his intravenous fluids. This proved successful in stemming his increasing emaciation, and improved the healing of his wounds. We later found that many . . . wartime dried plasma units contained the hepatitis B virus, which caused a delayed, serious, and sometimes fatal hepatitis. Fortunately, in spite of receiving over 100 units, Buske escaped this complication. Three months after he was wounded, "the gradually decreasing drainage from his large abdominal" wound allowed Buske to retain some fluids and nutrients taken orally. His nutrition was further improved by eggnog made with fresh eggs—a rare commodity in wartime Britain—brought to him by the vicar of the local Anglican Church. His abdominal and lower chest wounds gradually healed. In May, he underwent further operations to close his wounds, including skin grafts to cover the still unhealed wounds of his right thigh.

By mid-June 1944, Buske was strong enough to be evacuated to the States for additional surgery; he arrived home on June 24, 1944, and was admitted to the army's Halloran General Hospital on Staten Island, where he convalesced until October. Following a three-week leave in November 1944, he requested to return to active duty at Langley Field, Virginia, where he served for almost a year until being honorably discharged from the air force on September 3, 1945.

Like Buske, Forrest Vosler endured a series of surgeries. His heroic story was picked up by the press, and Americans everywhere, including in the White House, prayed for his recovery. Vosler was nominated for the Medal of Honor, but President Roosevelt delayed the presentation, which he insisted on doing personally, pending additional surgery. By then, Vosler had become totally blind in both eyes.

In California, a twenty-five-year-old university student offered to donate one of her own eyes to Vosler. The media was all over the story, and Roosevelt called Vosler's surgeon to ask if there was any chance that he could regain his vision. Told there was some chance, Roosevelt replied, "When he does, you let me know." Surgeons removed Vosler's dead right eye and a cataract on his left. For the first time in six months Vosler saw a faint, blurry light. "God was sure good to me," was his comment as he emerged from months of painful total darkness. Vosler personally received the Medal of Honor from President Roosevelt at the White House. Afterward he was quoted as saying, "I guess I won't see any more fighting and I wish the war was ended, but I've got to help them out with their war bonds drives and so on. I don't like being touted around as a hero, but if it helps the war, I guess that's the only thing left that I can do."

Honorably discharged from the army on October 12, 1944, Vosler said he felt "like a heel. I'm getting out but other guys are staying in." In addition to the Medal of Honor, Vosler also received the Silver Star, the Purple Heart, and the Air Medal. After his death in 1992 at age sixty-eight, his Medal of Honor was donated by his family to the Mighty Eighth War Museum near Savannah, Georgia, where it can be seen today.

28

GONE WITH THE WATER

German fighters, flak, and deadly waters claimed military aircrew and civilians alike. The Flying Fortress *Lady Fairweather,* piloted by Lt. Arthur Reddig, ditched in the Bay of Biscay. All ten crewmen were lost, becoming the Hell's Angels's first casualties at sea.

While returning from a mission to Romily, France, Lt. Orville Witt's bomber also ditched into the English Channel. Again, every man was lost.

On December 15, 1944, the popular bandleader and radio star Glenn Miller, an air force major, died mysteriously when his tiny single-engine plane, in military colors, vanished over the English Channel en route to a Christmas recording and worldwide broadcast from recently liberated Paris. Fred Atkinson, a member of the 320th Transport Wing based in Paris recalled the terrible weather on the day Miller left London in a small aircraft which crashed on the flight to Paris.

His band performed without him. Already thirty-eight when the war broke out, Miller was rebuffed by the navy when he attempted to enlist in 1942. The USAAF took him in, and Miller created the hugely popular Army Air Force Orchestra, which entertained troops throughout the European theater. Less well known was that Miller made propaganda broadcasts at London's Abbey Road studios, where the Beatles recorded albums just twenty years later. Following Miller's death, Gen. Jimmy Doolittle said, "Next to a letter from home, [Miller's Army Air Force Orchestra] was the greatest morale builder in the European Theater of Operations." Bob Hope's reaction to the comment is unknown.

Survivors of water landings became instant members of the Goldfish

Club, established in 1942 by an employee of P. B. Cow & Company, manufacturers of air-sea rescue equipment. The club's membership was exclusively for those who survived wartime aircraft water ditching, many of whom owed their lives to the "Mae West" life preserver or other flotation devices made by the company. By the end of the war, the club had more than 9,000 members.

It was not just warplanes that were shot down over European waters; Allied civilian flights were at risk from the Luftwaffe as well. On June 1, 1943, Leslie Howard, the world-famous British actor of Hungarian Jewish origin, who portrayed the languid Southern aristocrat Ashley Wilkes in the 1939 blockbuster film *Gone with the Wind*, became a victim, shot down over the Bay of Biscay. Though he was ostensibly on a goodwill tour, Howard's famous face and alleged intelligence-gathering activities attracted German attention. Coincidently, the starring role in *Gone with Wind*, which received ten Oscars, a record that stood for twenty years, went to Capt. Clark Gable, who was serving in combat with the Hell's Angels, officially as a photographer but manning a machine gun whenever possible, including on a mission just weeks prior to Howard's death.

Howard, active in anti-Nazi propaganda efforts, reputedly was involved with British intelligence, and his death led to numerous conspiracy theories. He was among seventeen who died, including four aircrew, British executives, civil servants, and several children of Allied military personnel. They were flying to England from Portugal aboard a regularly scheduled civilian Dutch-British passenger plane, a Douglas DC-3, which closely resembled its military cousin, the C-47 Dakota Skytrain transport, and were shot down by a Luftwaffe maritime fighter squadron flying far from its normal patrol area.

It was the third such attack on a civilian airliner in a year. A Luftwaffe pilot involved in the attack, Herbert Hintze, said after the war that his squad shot down the DC-3 carrying Howard in a case of mistaken identity and claimed German pilots were angry that Göring's staff "had not informed them of that scheduled flight between Lisbon and the UK, and that had they known, they could easily have escorted the DC-3 to Bordeaux and captured it and all aboard."

The day after the attack, the British searched the bay with an RAF Short Sunderland flying boat squadron. Near the spot where the DC-3 had radioed it was under attack, the squad was itself attacked by eight

German fighters, and during the subsequent battle, the RAF managed to shoot down at least three German interceptors before crash-landing near Cornwall, England. All British flights from Lisbon were subsequently rerouted farther from the French coast and thereafter flew only at night.

Not coincidentally, it seems, news of Howard's death was published in the same issue of the *London Times*, on June 4, 1943, that reported the "death" of Maj. William Martin, the corpse and red herring used for the intelligence ruse involved in Operation Mincemeat. British intelligence had deliberately attached fake documents to a corpse, which was left to wash up on the Spanish coast, knowing that these would be passed to the Germans.

There has been speculation that the Germans believed that Winston Churchill, who had been in Algiers, was on board. In his autobiography, Churchill expressed regret that his travel schedule might have inadvertently cost Howard his life. According to *Churchill's Bodyguard,* a 2006 BBC television production, Abwehr spies were alleged to have been tipped off about Churchill's departure from Algiers, and the route he took home passed close to where Howard was shot down. The film suggested a case of mistaken identity. Howard's manager, Alfred Chenhalls, who also died on the flight, physically resembled Churchill, while Howard may have been mistaken for Churchill's bodyguard, Detective Walter Thompson, who, like Howard, was tall and thin.

Speculation also centered on whether British code breakers at Bletchley Park had decrypted top-secret Enigma signals that detailed the purported assassination plan and, if so, whether Churchill, who wanted to protect the information to ensure that the Germans would not suspect that their Enigma codes were cracked, allowed the flight to proceed as scheduled despite the known threat. Books written about the episode include *Flight 777,* by Ian Colvin, and *In Search of My Father: A Portrait of Leslie Howard,* by Howard's son, Ronald. Both suggest that Howard was indeed the target.

British historian James Oglethorpe concluded that the Germans were aware of Churchill's whereabouts at the time and were not so naïve as to believe he would fly in an unescorted civilian airliner. Ronald Howard alleged that the order to shoot down the airliner came from Goebbels, "who had been ridiculed in one of Howard's films and who believed Howard to be the most dangerous British propagandist. The *British Film*

Yearbook for 1945 described his work as 'one of the most valuable facets of British propaganda.'"

The 2010 book *Leslie Howard: The Lost Actor,* by Estel Eforgan, concluded that Howard was not specifically targeted and the incident was simply "an error in judgment."

29

THE HELL'S ANGELS

By 1944, the Eighth Air Force was commanded by the legendary Jimmy Doolittle, the highest-ranking reserve officer in WWII. Doolittle had already received a Medal of Honor for having famously bombed Tokyo in April 1942: he led a squadron of B-25 medium bombers that were launched from aircraft carriers; this was one of FDR's pet war projects. Doolittle was promoted two ranks from lieutenant colonel to brigadier general for the raid that is forever associated with his name.

The 303rd was already world-famous as the Hell's Angels, the unit in which "the king of Hollywood," Capt. Clark Gable, first flew as a photographer and waist gunner on May 4, 1943. Gable, playing a B-17 pilot, starred alongside Spencer Tracy, Myrna Loy, and Lionel Barrymore in the 1938 movie *Test Pilot*. In early 1943, Gable was still grieving over the death of his wife, actress Carole Lombard, who less than six weeks after Pearl Harbor was killed returning to Hollywood from a war bond rally in her home state of Indiana. On January 16, 1942, the thirty-three-year-old Lombard and her mother died when their TWA DC-3 crashed in the desert between Las Vegas and Los Angeles. The grief-stricken Gable enlisted in the Eighth Army Air Corps. Lombard's final film, in postproduction when she died, was 1942's *To Be or Not to Be,* a satire about the Nazis in which the script had her character asking, "What can happen on a plane?" It wound up on the cutting-room floor.

Gable had been personally recruited by air force chief Gen. Henry "Hap" Arnold to make a training film for flight crews, but Gable wanted to fight as well and first flew in the B-17 *The 8 Ball.* German fighters attacked the plane while Gable manned a machine gun. When comedian and actor Bob Hope entertained the troops he asked for "Rhett Butler" to take a bow. Gable refused and remained seated among his buddies. Wartime strain was beginning to show. Donald Miller recounts that "even Clark Gable, who flew only occasionally, came close to breaking down. He would drink himself to sleep, and every now and then disappear from the base for a day or two to find refuge" with his friend, actor David Niven. From international press accounts, Hitler and Göring both knew Gable was in England. Hitler considered Gable to be one of the world's best actors, and Göring "offered his fliers a reward equaling $5,000 to bring him down. Gable, fearing Hitler would put him in a cage 'like a gorilla' and exhibit him all over Germany, told [crew member] Jack Mahin he would never bail out of his plane if it got into trouble. 'How could I hide this face? If the plane goes, I'll just go with the son of a bitch.'"

The film Gable made and narrated, *Combat America,* was used for American propaganda, war bond fundraising, and as a training film. Following the war, in 1948, Gable starred in another B-17-related film, *Command Decision,* costarring Walter Pidgeon and Van Johnson. Portraying the strategic bombing of Germany, the film depicted the political infighting involved in conducting a major war effort and the emotional toll it took on commanders who ordered missions that resulted in high casualties; the effects of sustained combat on all concerned; and the nature of accountability for its consequences.

Walter Cronkite, a United Press reporter, also flew with the 303rd and wrote about his experience on a February 26, 1943, mission attacking U-boat pens in Wilhelmshaven, Germany. He reported being "escorted" by FW-190s and ME-109s. "The flak was so thick you could walk on it," he said, he was "too excited to be afraid."

The 303rd got its nickname, the Hell's Angels, from one of its planes, the first B-17 in the Eighth to complete twenty-five missions against the Third Reich, on May 13, 1943. The better-known *Memphis Belle* completed its twenty-fifth mission just six days later, but Hollywood director William Wyler, a commissioned USAAF officer who flew with and filmed the more wholesome-looking *Belle*'s crew for a documentary designed to raise morale and money for the war bond drive, made sure the spotlight fell on that plane. *Memphis Belle* was thereafter described as the first crew to complete twenty-five missions *and return home.* The Hell's Angels shrugged off the slight and continued the fight, while the crew of the *Belle* were lionized in a glitzy stateside film premier and toured the nation raising cash for the war effort.

After completing forty-eight missions, *Hell's Angels* returned to the United States on January 20, 1944, for its own publicity tour. The misleading tale, well known within the 303rd, made *Memphis Belle* the best-known B-17 of the war and not only fueled Werner's distaste for the press in general but for the propaganda machinery of war in particular. He decided never to talk to the press again. The 303rd had the last laugh by becoming the Eighth's most fabled unit and was destined to become the first bomb group to fly 300 missions. By war's end they had completed 364 missions, more than any other Flying Fortress squad in the Eighth Army.

30

AERO MEDICINE

On June 28, 1941, by executive order, FDR created the Office of Scientific Research and Development to coordinate research for the military. OSRD, with almost unlimited access to funds, was directed by MIT's former dean of engineering, Vannevar Bush, who reported only to Roosevelt.

Military airplanes were flying much faster and higher than ever before, creating unprecedented physical and psychological problems for aircrews. Recognizing the medical problems presented by high-altitude flight in planes like the B-17, Bush quickly established and funded the Committee on Aviation Medicine, chaired by E. F. Dubois, a Cornell Medical College physiologist. Dubois oversaw a crash program of thirty-seven aero-medical research projects at twenty-two leading universities and laboratories, including the Aeromedical Laboratory at Wright Field, Ohio; the army air force's School of Aviation Medicine at Randolph Field, Texas; the navy's School of Aviation Medicine in Pensacola, Florida; and the Mayo Clinic in Rochester, Minnesota. Dubois also set up six subcommittees to examine acceleration, oxygen deprivation, decompression sickness, visual problems, flight clothing, and motion sickness.

For three years, OSRD used conscientious objector "volunteers" culled from Civilian Public Service projects as test subjects for research. For tests deemed too dangerous for conscientious objectors or even draft dodgers, scientists turned to man's best friend; a 145-pound Saint Bernard named Major was enlisted for high-altitude parachute test jumps wearing protective clothing and a custom-fitted oxygen mask. In a test to determine the strength of parachute straps, Major was tossed from a plane five miles up—26,000 feet; he furiously dog-paddled all the way down to a safe, and surely bewildering, landing.

U.S. aircraft industries and outdoor clothing manufacturers, including the Eddie Bauer Company, cooperated to develop protective procedures and custom flight gear for high-altitude combat. Since neither the B-17 nor the B-24 was pressurized or centrally heated, and both often flew at 25,000 to 30,000 feet, Mount Everest altitudes, crews suffered hypoxia from the lack of oxygen, decompression illness on descent, and prolonged exposure to extreme cold. The last was especially problematic on longer missions late in the war that lasted for up to ten hours during which temperatures plummeted to −60 degrees Fahrenheit, killing cold. "In the air, every 1,000 feet of altitude was like moving 500 miles closer to the North Pole." In those conditions, oil became as thick "as caramel." Brian Garfield notes:

> The worst difficulty, to which no real solution was found, was the problem of expansion differential—with changing temperatures, steel and copper and aluminum contracted and expanded at different rates. Parts fitted to close tolerances became loose; highly tuned, supercharged engines rated at thousands of horsepower began to make noises like asthmatic outboard boat motors.

Early in the war, fewer than one-quarter of the Eighth air force crews arriving in Great Britain knew how to prevent frostbite at high altitudes. Even as late as 1944, the army treated 46,000 frostbite cases. Wounded men suffering from blood loss and shock were highly susceptible to hypothermia. A ball-turret gunner recalled one incident:

> At 26,000 feet the tail gunner had both cheeks of his buttocks torn by a 20-mm shell. We had him lie face down and put a dressing on as well as possible. Bleeding continued so we put a 140-pound ammunition box directly over the wound. The pressure seemed to stop the bleeding. He rested comfortably but was almost frozen because his heated suit was torn and we had no blankets available.

The tail gunner's blood froze solid and cemented him to the metal flight deck as he died. The moisture in men's nostrils "froze up." If the bombers' hydraulic systems were perforated by flak and the fluid soaked a man's clothing, it would freeze to his skin.

The intense cold was a deadly threat to airmen beyond the obvious severe frostbite cases that were almost epidemic early in the war. Hypothermia's onset and symptoms reduced the crew's effectiveness in any number of ways with often fatal consequences for all. What started with simple shivering led to clumsiness, lack of coordination, slurred speech, mumbling, stumbling, confusion, poor decision making, drowsiness, very low energy, apathy, weak pulse, shallow breathing, and finally loss of consciousness. "Fliers . . . went woozy or even passed out from hypoxia when moisture froze in the tubes of their oxygen masks or when airsickness or fear caused them to vomit into their mouthpieces."

Those who had alcohol in their systems from the night before were particularly susceptible to hypothermia since it took up to fifteen hours to metabolize a big night out. As former air force flight surgeon David R. Jones observed:

> The social role of alcohol in the ambiance of combat fliers deserves brief consideration. The drinking habits of aircrew are the stuff of legends. The stories, the songs, the customs, the superstitions, the very social fabric of the squadrons of old are celebrated . . . and are reasonably accurately presented in plays, movies, books, television, and folklore. For more than 30 years, from the 1940s to the 1970s, flight surgeons in training have been urged to go to the bar with "their" fliers in order to meet them socially, to learn what's really going on, to find out what makes them tick. From the 1940s through the 1970s, at least, the Officers Club bar was a center of aviation society.

One flier recalled that the clubs were often so packed that "regardless of how drunk we got, there was never enough room in the place to fall down."

Adopting an RAF tradition, Eighth Army ground crews prepared double shots of booze, usually whiskey or brandy, for each returning flight crewman. Only Werner and Jack steadfastly declined their shots, which the others, including Iron Ass, gladly guzzled. The two quiet, steady loners would go to the debriefing room, where army psychiatrists searched for visible signs of combat stress. When none were found, the pair would usually return to their huts, where they routinely witnessed the sad ritual of orderlies packing up the personal belongings and uniforms of men who had left that morning and would never need them again.

Heller recalled a day in 1943 when half of the twenty men in his hut died. It was during Big Week, when more than 2,000 men went missing. "Before the Graves and Registration guys were allowed into the hut, the lost men's buddies would go through every item, discarding condoms, girlie magazines, love letters, VD ointments, and anything that would distress loved ones at home," he said.

The onset of severe hypothermia was terrifying to behold, as men literally lost their minds and primitive reflexes took over in cramped airplanes full of frightened men. Up to 50 percent of hypothermia deaths were associated with counterintuitive and often deadly behavior known as "paradoxical undressing," which was often followed by brain-stem mammalian reflexes over which the victim had no control.

> This typically occurs during moderate to severe hypothermia, as the person becomes disoriented, confused, and combative. They may begin discarding their clothing, which, in turn, increases the rate of heat loss. . . . In the final stages of hypothermia, the brain stem produces a burrowing-like behavior. Similar to hibernation behavior in animals, individuals with severe hypothermia are often found in small, enclosed spaces, such as under the bed or behind wardrobes.

The field of aviation medicine was so new that in August 1942 the army opened the Provisional Medical Field Service School at High Wycombe, England, to study the medical and psychiatric problems of combat aviators and to educate new crews about high-altitude first aid. According to the army, "In 1942, about two-thirds of the Eighth Air Force medical staff had no aero-medical training." Flying repeated high-risk missions over Germany was one of the most dangerous and physically demanding tasks of the war. Before long-range fighter escorts like the P-51 Mustang became available, sortie and casualty rates were extraordinarily high. The Americans were under pressure to prove themselves and were often sent aloft woefully unprepared.

An average of five men a day suffered psychiatric breakdowns severe enough for hospitalization, and almost half never returned to flight duty. Donald Miller reports:

> There is also strong circumstantial evidence that bomb group commanders suppressed evidence of mental breakdowns. . . . We will never know for many Eighth Air Force fliers suffered emotional problems severe enough to ground them, but the number is surely greater than official statistics indicate.

In 1942 and 1943, about one-fourth of the returning bombers had sustained some form of battle damage. Statistically, the mandated mission tour of twenty-five, and later thirty-five, in a heavy bomber gave crews less than a 50 percent chance of avoiding becoming a casualty. Only a quarter of bomber crews completed twenty-five missions. The slaughter was so fearsome that the army greatly reduced bombing missions in 1943 to await the arrival of new long-range fighter escort, the P-51 Mustang. Conventionally accepted wisdom, expressed in the 1930s by British prime minister Stanley Baldwin, that the "bomber will always get through" was proven correct, yet more costly than anyone imagined.

Grim, essential research continued throughout the war. Air fatalities were studied by the army's medical Operational Research Section (ORS) in the Office of the Chief Surgeon of the European Theater of Operations. Records showed that for the first eight months of 1944, two out of five missing personnel were possibly dead and three out of five were known to be wounded, prisoners of war, or evaders.

ORS investigated and autopsied aircrew casualties to measure the wounding power of various weapons and the effectiveness of protective measures. Flak injuries were the cause of more than 80 percent of the deaths. Fatalities were caused by as little as ten to twenty grams of steel flak fragments. One ounce equals about twenty-eight grams, about the weight of five nickels.

ORS conducted a survey of battle casualties sustained by the B-17s and B-24s. Headed by Brig. Gen. Malcolm C. Grow, the U.S. Strategic Air Forces chief flight surgeon, a three-month-long study was undertaken in England from June through August 1944 to study combat injury and fatality data for 69,682 bomber sorties corresponding to 657,096 man-combat missions during that single ninety-day period. During just those three months, which included the period when Werner and Jack started flying missions, 693 aircraft and 6,540 aircrew personnel were missing in action. The study focused solely on battle casualties resulting from enemy gunfire.

By quiet arrangement, all dead airmen who were returned to the United Kingdom in heavy bombers, as well as all those who died within twenty-four hours of their wounds, were brought for examination to the ORS morgue on the grounds of the Cambridge American Military Cemetery. The Graves Registration Service of the Quartermaster Corps at the cemetery notified ORS when aircrew battle casualties arrived so that corpses could be examined immediately.

The disparity of wounds was stunning. Some men died from slivers of flak as small as a couple of quarters; others were decapitated, dismembered, or disemboweled. Some fatal wounds appeared as little more than a deep, two-inch scratch. A Medical Corps photo shows a navigator with a groove 3.5 inches wide by 3 inches deep, from his forehead through to the back of his cranium, matching the diameter of an 88 mm shell. Fortunately for his crewmates and tragically for him, an unexploded twenty-pound shell scooped his brains right out of his head. His steel helmet's damage mirrors his fatal injury in the gruesome photo.

The doctors studied the circumstances of the fatalities including munitions involved crew position and altitude. Of the 110 killed in action during the three-month period, 89 were examined. Of the 21 not examined, 7 were casualties who died in a hospital more than a day after being wounded. Daily admission reports were received from twelve primary hospitals serving the Eighth Air Force. There were also 1,007 wounded in action during the study period, but since ORS consisted of only one medical officer and one enlisted man during the first two months of the survey, it was impossible to visit and interrogate all the wounded. During the third month, ORS conducted interviews with the help of additional enlisted men, and a total of 434, or 43 percent, of the wounded were seen. X-ray records of the majority of wounded casualties were examined.

A medical officer visited each of the forty heavy bomber stations to verify the battle casualty status of aircrew members from a perusal of Care of Flyer reports of those patients missed in hospitals and also to obtain information on battle casualties whose injuries were so slight as not to require hospitalization. The Care of Flyer reports also provided more accurate information on the final disposition of the wounded and on the time lost from flying status. Missiles and fragments found inside the corpses were identified from British and U.S. ordnance publications and by consultation with a member of the army's Ordnance Office. Photographic records of the autopsies were made by an army photographer. In addition to flak, surgeons found that bodies contained secondary "miscellaneous missiles," including

> a bearing from an aircraft's engine, parts of electrical apparatus, clothing, personal equipment, oxygen line, rubber, zipper, and "dog tag" chain. With the exception of the bearing, which by itself produced a fatal head wound, all of these were found in aircrew personnel along the fatal wound tracks caused by primary missiles.

The army never supplied an X-ray machine for examination of the dead since they were in great demand for the living. One flight surgeon wrote in complaint to his superiors:

> It is a sad reflection upon the imaginative foresight of the responsible officers to see this reluctance to furnish essential equipment. One of the most important aspects of any casualty survey is the photographic and X-ray record of the casualties. For the immediate purpose of the survey and to furnish a permanent record for future study and teaching, photographs of the external wounds and internal wound track with X-rays of the body regions involved are of paramount interest and value.

31

THE WRITING 69TH

In the spring of 1943, arguably the most dangerous period for bomber crews, an informal group of prominent journalists who called themselves the Writing 69th received permission to fly on heavy bombers as observers. They included Andy Rooney of *Stars and Stripes,* Walter Cronkite of the United Press, Homer Bigart of the *New York Herald Tribune,* Bob Post of *The New York Times,* Gladwin Hill of the Associated Press, Paul Manning of CBS Radio, William Wade of the International News Service, and Denton Scott of *Yank* magazine.

Contrary to the Geneva Convention, the journalists were taught to recognize enemy planes and learned how to shoot and clear machine guns. Cronkite was sent to Molesworth to fly with the 303rd. On February 26, 1943, most of the writers went aloft with various squads scattered around East Anglia, and it was agreed they'd meet at Molesworth afterward for a celebration.

A few days earlier, Bob Post "stunned two friends with a startling admission: he thought he was going to die." Post, a thirty-two-year-old Harvard graduate, told Walter Cronkite, "There are ten of us here now. It kind of makes you think that according to the highest proportion of losses supposedly standable by the air corps, which is ten percent—that one of us will not be here after the first mission." Post flew the next day on a B-24 mission to Wilhelmshaven. The other five reporters were in the air with B-17 crews. Also in the air that day was Hollywood director William Wyler, who was filming scenes for his documentary *Memphis Belle.*

Post flew with a unit on a B-24 Liberator called the *Flying Eight Balls,* and considered itself a hard-luck outfit, and on this day, they were absolutely and tragically correct. Their Liberator was shot down and Post was killed. "Ironically, the Writing 69th proved something to the public that the 8th Air Force would just as soon not have advertised," writes Jim Hamilton, "that is, the extreme risk faced by airmen who participated in these missions."

Post, one of thirty-six Allied war correspondents who died during WWII, was buried in Belgium. William Wyler's film crew shot footage of the downing of *Flying Eight Balls*. This "further diminished the status of the B-24, which was already overshadowed by the B-17 as far as the Allied press corps was concerned."

In the book *Air Gunner,* coauthored by Oram C. Hutton and Andy Rooney, they wrote:

> Newspapers often neglected to mention the fact that the B-24s went out at all, and raid stories read with tiresome regularity for the Lib man "Flying Fortresses Attack Sub Pens in Daylight,"—no mention of the Liberators, which did a good job, took a beating, and returned home with little but official credit for the raid.

And when Jimmy Stewart died in 1997, several obituaries misstated he had been a B-17 pilot, again disappointing the B-24 veterans.

In 1943, Rooney was hanging around a control tower when word spread that a ball-turret gunner was trapped in the Plexiglas bubble hanging from the belly of a B-17 because the gears controlling the rotation of the bubble had jammed, preventing it from moving into the only position in which the hatch could be opened. The hydraulic system, shot full of holes, also failed, making it impossible to lower the landing gear:

> There were eight minutes of gut-wrenching talk among the tower, the pilot, and the man trapped in the ball turret. He knew what comes down first when there are no wheels. We all watched in horror as it happened. We watched as this man's

life ended, mashed between the concrete pavement of the runway and the belly of the bomber.

The year 1943 was the nadir of the Eighth Air Force's war, with two-thirds of U.S. aircrew not completing a twenty-five-mission tour. Losses piled up and morale was driven as low as it could be driven by tragic stories like that of two Hell's Angels brothers from Texas, Mark and Jack Mathis.

Jack Mathis was at Molesworth flying B-17 missions, including the unit's first U.S. raid on Germany. Mark arrived at Molesworth on St. Patrick's Day after having flown in North Africa. His surprise arrival almost exempted Jack from the next day's mission because they had not seen each other since the previous summer.

After a reunion in the officer's club, Jack requested permission for Mark to fly with him the next day on a mission to bomb U-boat pens at Vegesack, Germany. The request was denied. Military regulations prohibited brothers from serving together, the result of a tragic incident on November 13, 1942, in which five brothers from the Sullivan family died when their navy vessel was sunk. Thereafter, siblings were rigidly separated in all combat theaters. The regulation was a key plot device in Steven Spielberg's film *Saving Private Ryan*. Instead, Jack Mathis was promised a three-day leave after the mission, and the brothers planned a wild time in London. The following dawn, Mark accompanied Jack to the flight line. It would be their final moment together.

Lead bombardier Jack Mathis

was just starting his bomb run, upon which the entire squadron depended for accurate bombing, when he was hit by the enemy antiaircraft fire. His right arm was shattered above the elbow, a large wound was torn in his side and abdomen, and he was knocked from his bomb sight to the rear of the bombardier's compartment. Realizing that the success of the mission depended upon him, 1st Lt. Mathis, by sheer determination and willpower, though mortally wounded, dragged himself back to his sights, released his bombs, then died at his post of duty. As the result of this action the airplanes of his bombardment squadron placed their bombs directly upon the assigned target for a perfect attack against the enemy. 1st Lt. Mathis' undaunted bravery has been a great inspiration to the officers and men of his unit.

Moncur writes, "His last word, as he triggered the bomb release was 'Bombs . . .' [but] Jack Mathis died over his bombsight before he could complete the interphone message with 'away.'"

Mathis was the first recipient of the Medal of Honor in the European theater and only one of two (along with Sgt. Forest Vosler) Hell's Angels Medal of Honor recipients. Only seventeen Medals of Honor were awarded to Mighty Eighth airmen during the war.

Compounding the tragedy on May 14, Mark Mathis, having transferred to the 303rd, flew his fourth mission with the group as navigator of *FDR's Potato Peeler Kids* to attack a naval installation at Kiel, Germany. The formation was attacked by more than 100 German fighters, and Mark Mathis died when the plane crashed into the North Sea. Mathis's commanding officer, Capt. William Calhoun, who only one month earlier had written to Mrs. Avis Mathis in San Angelo, Texas, advising her of the loss of her son Jack, left his cockpit to observe the falling Fortress. Calhoun would now prepare a second letter to Mrs. Mathis. San Angelo Airport was renamed Mathis Field to honor these two brothers.

The attrition rate accelerated on August 17, when General Eaker sent 376 Fortresses to bomb Schweinfurt's ball-bearing plant and an aircraft factory in Regensburg, both targets well beyond fighter escort range. Newly promoted Col. Curtis LeMay commanded the Regensburg contingent with 146 bombers and Brig. Gen. Robert Williams led 230 Schweinfurt attackers. That day, one of the worst in Eighth history, 17 percent of the planes never returned. Sixty planes, carrying 600 men, were lost, and another four were so shot up they never flew again. One participant in the "double strike" was lead navigator Harry Crosby of the "Bloody 100th" bomb group, who wrote about the horrors he witnessed that day:

When a plane blew up, we saw their parts all over the sky. We smashed into some of the pieces. One plane hit a body which tumbled out of a plane ahead. A crewman went out the front hatch of a plane and hit the tail assembly of his own plane. No chute . . . A German pilot came out of his plane, drew his legs into a ball, head down. Papers flew out of his pockets. He did a triple somersault through our formation. No chute.

32

MEIER'S TRUMPETS

When Werner's crew went on active bomber duty in August 1944, Allied operations in the European theater were entering the climactic phase. Three-fourths of all bombs dropped by the Allies in the European theater fell in the last year of the war. Of the 364 missions flown by the 303rd, 270 were in 1944 and 1945.

The Allied air war began with Göring's flawed execution of the Battle of Britain, which lasted from late summer to early fall of 1940. It was the first significant military setback for Nazi Germany and, not coincidentally, the first in a long series of setbacks for the Luftwaffe and Hermann Göring.

As Hitler's official heir, Göring was the only German officer to hold the rank of Reich Marshal. Yet he disappointed Hitler when Operation Eagle Day, during the Battle of Britain, failed to achieve German air supremacy, thus preventing Operation Sea Lion, the invasion of Britain.

The Battle of Britain marked a turning point in air war strategy, tactics, and technology. The Luftwaffe, which had been designed as an offensive military arm, was increasingly forced into a defensive posture by the Allies. Britain had developed and then deployed radar to great effect in the Battle of Britain. Even though Germany started the war with the best equipped air force in the world Hitler, incredibly, never ordered a heavy bomber like the Allies produced in the tens of thousands. Instead, he insisted that all German bombers be capable of dive-bombing, which limited German designers since the airframes of a 62,500-pound bomber, like the Fortress or the Liberator, simply could not perform dive-bomber tactics and then pull out. Germany depended on outdated medium bombers throughout the war.

The loss of the Battle of Britain and the pounding Germany took from Allied heavy bombers involved a series of blows to Göring's prestige and influence, although he remained Hitler's designated successor. Early in the war, the Reich Marshal vowed, "If an enemy bomber reaches the Ruhr [Germany's heartland and industrial center], you can call me Meyer." The idiomatic expression's use of the name Meier, one of the most common in Germany, was not specifically anti-Semitic but a way of signifying that someone had become an unimportant nobody. When he later had to make public visits to bombed-out German cities, the Reich Marshal was taunted with "Mr. Meier." And the slang term for air raid sirens became "Meier's trumpets."

In using bombing to take the war to Germany, the RAF followed Bomber Command's Air Chief Marshal Sir Arthur "Bomber" Harris's hotly disputed strategy, supported by Churchill, of so-called area bombing. German civilians considered this practice indiscriminate enough to constitute "terror bombing." The RAF itself used this term internally, but never in public statements.

For their part, Hitler and Göring had initially ordered the Luftwaffe to limit civilian casualties for fear of making the British populace more resistant to an invasion. But during the Battle of Britain, German planes bombed parts of London in error, and Churchill retaliated with a minor air raid on Berlin. Soon area or "terror" bombing became standard operating procedure on both sides.

When the United States entered the war, the USAAF uneasily and gradually adopted the strategy by default after Roosevelt formally endorsed it when he met Churchill at the Casablanca Conference in January 1943. There the two leaders decided that the war in western Europe would begin in the air with round-the-clock bombing of Germany's military, oil, industrial, and transportation infrastructure. It was the only way to strike at Germany until the Allies could mount a land invasion. The British air command took the night shift and the United States would bomb by day. The official orders issued at Casablanca, largely to placate Josef Stalin's anger at the ongoing delay of the invasion of France, included a demand for "unconditional surrender."

After D-day, as Werner and Jack joined the fight, the U.S. Air Force targeted Germany's oil production and transportation network in a plan championed by Air Marshal Arthur Tedder and Sir Charles Portal of the RAF and Generals Hap Arnold and Carl Spaatz of the USAAF. They were also subject to one more change in U.S. air combat policy, an increase in the number of missions needed to complete a bomber crew's combat tour, from twenty-five for lead planes and thirty for other planes to thirty and thirty-five, respectively. (The same increase in mission requirements figures in the plot of Joseph Heller's *Catch-22,* whose bomber crew characters are members of the 15th army air force stationed in the Mediterranean.)

33

SQUEEZING THE NAZIS DRY

Without doubt, the Allies' Oil and Transportation Plan shortened the war in Europe by denying the Nazis fuel they needed for tanks, planes, and submarines. Among other things, this had a decisive impact on pilot training: the Luftwaffe had only enough fuel to give teenaged replacement pilots a few hours in the air before rushing them into active service. Despite the directive, the RAF's bomber command targeted only 20 percent of its attacks on oil installations during October and November of 1944; the remainder targeted city centers. Even by December, despite inquiries from RAF Air Chief Sir Charles Portal, Sir Arthur "Bomber" Harris devoted only half of all missions to oil targets.

German fighter strength had been building throughout 1944, thanks to the efforts of Albert Speer, Hitler's armaments minister. For the first time since D-day, Luftwaffe fighters emerged in strength when 100 fighters, including the new Messerschmitt 262 jet fighter, attacked a squadron of Fortresses near Magdeburg, Germany. Within minutes, twenty bombers from the 445th bomb group disappeared. The next day, another fifty-five bombers were lost to the swarming fighters. A staggering 750 men were lost within forty-eight hours. Allied intelligence was stunned to realize that Speer had performed "a production miracle" by quadrupling fighter production in 1944 alone while simultaneously introducing jet fighters and rockets to warfare.

The impact was immediate. When twenty-five of twenty-nine B-24 Liberators were destroyed by fighters within six minutes over Göttingen, "it was the highest loss for a single group in any Eighth air force operation." Lt. Col. Jimmy Stewart was sent from combat wing headquarters to "settle down the mostly stunned and speechless survivors."

On September 9, when the 303rd returned to Ludwigshafen for the fourth consecutive time, the Germans were ready. One of the Liberators took direct flak into the cockpit and the number one engine. The entire nose section, left wing, and engine fell off. A burst of flame came out of the nose as it fell, and Lt. John Hobgood, bombardier, was seen falling out of the nose compartment, without a chute, at 12,000 feet. The plane crashed, seven men went to their graves, and two went into captivity. One survivor, tail gunner Sgt. Jim Reeves, recalled:

> The ground fire blew the nose off and the left wing along with the No. 1 engine. It was like hitting a brick wall, and I wound up against the tail wheel trying to get out of my flak suit. Luckily, I had seen the flak overtaking us and reached for my parachute an instant before we were hit. I started for the escape hatch in the tail and looked forward to see what the rest of the crew was doing. John Hobgood was lying on his back very still. So I went forward to him. This was very easy because we were in a dive. When I got to him I shook him and asked if he was OK. He nodded his head and I motioned him to follow me. Radio Operator Sgt. J. A. O'Leary had joined us by this time, after finding that Sgt. A. W. Bricker, the ball turret gunner, was dead. Getting back to the waist door was tough because of the dive and when I pulled the emergency handle nothing happened. So I hung on to the side of the ship and kicked the door until it let go. I then waved the radioman out, then John and I went out. That was the last time that I saw him. I saw Sgt. O'Leary in a prison camp about two months later in Poland. He returned home in typical poor prison condition. He enjoyed seven weeks of fun and then died of a heart attack. The German report said that John Hobgood was "killed in fall." At that time civilians were killing the crews they caught, but I came down in the center of town where German soldiers were waiting for me. Our ship also came down in the city.

That day, the Eighth suffered another 200 men killed, wounded, or missing in action. In another plane, flak tore into the compartment occupied by 2nd Lt. Frederic T. Kiesel, a bombardier from Los Angeles, as he bent over his equipment. It knocked out two engines, shattered the Plexiglas nose, nearly severed Kiesel's right arm, pierced his hip, and threw him into a corner of the Fort's nose, unconscious and bleeding severely. But he came to in time to release his bomb load. Aware that the bombardier was wounded, and seeing the rest of the formation dropping their loads, Sgt. Johnnie O. Burcham, engineer and top-turret gunner from Sand Springs, Oklahoma, shouted "Salvo" into the interphone so the plane's bombs could be dropped on the target. Lt. Benjamin Starr, the navigator from Los Angeles, grasped the emergency bomb release used when the bombardier's switch was damaged. But before the navigator could operate the emergency release, Kiesel regained consciousness, dragged himself back to his station, released the bombs, and then collapsed with the fingers of his left hand locked in a viselike grip around the bomb lever. Lt. Richard E. McGilvray, pilot, from Coarsegold, California, went below to check on Kiesel. In the nose, he found quite a mess. McGilvray always carried a very sharp knife and he stripped Kiesel of all his upper-body gear. There was just enough of an arm stump left to apply a tourniquet. The pilot shot him with a morphine syrette and made him as comfortable as possible. Back on the flight deck things weren't much better. The bomber was losing about 1,000 feet a minute and it was "a big sweat" whether they would make it to the front lines or to a Stalag Luft. During the last minutes, they took small-arms fire from the ground:

> It began to get terrifying all over again. We made the front lines by about a quarter of a mile and McCutcheon took over and landed us in a cow pasture. The red flares were shot off and brought an ambulance out of the brush and got Kiesel to an aid station where Kiesel's right arm was amputated and he was awarded the Silver Star.

Jack and Werner flew again the very next day, September 10, bombing the Daimler-Benz motor works near Stuttgart without serious opposition and no casualties. But on their next mission, on September 19, while bombing rail yards at Osnabruck and Hamm, Germany, things got hotter. The 303rd was scheduled to be the last group to bomb that day, which meant all flak batteries were fully alert. After the other two squadrons had completed their part in the mission, they took off for home, which was standard practice to limit losses. Crews had been constantly briefed not to hang back in an attempt to protect slower, disabled aircraft since that practice usually resulted in greater losses. The Hell's Angels were on their own since the fighter escort had also disappeared. The squadron, consisting of twelve or thirteen aircraft, eventually bombed the town of Osnabruck. Because of a navigational error after bombs away, the squadron found itself in the Ruhr Valley, one of the most heavily defended areas of Germany. At least one aircraft was shot down and all were subjected to extremely intense flak. "The aircraft flown by [1st Lt. Robert Akers's] crew sustained something like 400 holes in the fuselage [. Its] radio operator, T/Sgt. Gerald E. Meyer of Mill Valley, Calif., was wounded and all other crew members miraculously escaped being hit, although there were chunks of flak throughout the aircraft."

The ammunition track of tail gunner Sgt. Cletus H. Vogel sustained a hit, which caused several rounds of .50 caliber ammunition to "cook off," luckily pointed out of the aircraft, thereby missing Vogel. Meanwhile, as Aker's plane returned over the North Sea, it was discovered that one of the 500-pound bombs had not dropped because of a bent triggering mechanism. The safety cotter pins had been removed from the bomb, which was the first step toward creating a "live" bomb. Akers directed armament specialist Sgt. Fulton "Pop" Meyer to kick the bomb out of the plane.

Sgt. Donald E. Vanlier was flying with another crew on *Bouncing Betty III* alongside Werner's plane. The target was the synthetic oil plant at Wesseling, Germany:

> We were flying tail end charley, I think. As we went over the target, the sky opened up and the flak was very accurate. We lost the two wing men, Lt. Price and Lt. Lord. We were hit in the right inboard engine. At the same time, the cable to release the three 1,000 pound General Purpose Bombs on that side was cut. We were losing altitude fast and it was my job, as radio man, to get those bombs out of the bomb bay, some way or other. So with a screw driver to release the bombs and a

walk around oxygen bottle, I had to lay on my stomach, on the catwalk, and release the lower of the three bombs. Then I had to get back into the radio room, change to a full oxygen bottle and go back in the bomb bay, and release the other two bombs. We limped home a few hundred feet over the English Channel, on three engines and all alone.

Akers's white-knuckle ride was not yet over.

The weather was so bad when we arrived over England that most of our formation landed at a fighter base, Boxted, home of the famed 56th Fighter Group, in completely zero visibility weather. The Akers aircraft had to go around for a second and successful pass when it was discovered that the left flap had been damaged by flak. The landing called for exceptional skill by Lt. Akers and Co-pilot Lt. Leslie W. Giddings to land a "hot" aircraft with non-existent visibility and on a strange field

Although Goering's crew was unharmed, the Eighth suffered about 100 more casualties that day.

The success of the oil campaign was confirmed after the war by Germany's fighter commanding general and ace, Adolf Galland:*

In my opinion, it was the Allied bombing of our oil industries that had the greatest effect on the German war potential. . . . We had plenty of planes from the autumn of 1944 on, and there were enough pilots up to the end of the year, but lack of petrol didn't permit the expansion of proper training.

---

*Adolf Galland, famed Luftwaffe fighter commander, and Iron Ass Heller became good friends following the war when Heller was a senior pilot for Lufthansa, Germany's national airline. They would sit for hours trying to piece together air battles where they had faced each other as combatants. Heller, who befriended many former German fighter pilots while flying for the airline once overseen by Hermann Göring, found them all to be "remarkable pilots and gentlemen to a man."

During 1944, fuel available to Germany dropped by 70 percent, from a million tons a month to 300,000 tons. In a postwar interview, Galland summarized his views of Göring by stating he had "many problems," and was consistently weak in the face of Hitler, "where he made his greatest mistakes." Galland also mentioned the effects of Göring's drug addiction, which reduced the Reich Marshal "until he was nothing," adding that he thought that Hitler should have replaced Göring as head of the Luftwaffe early in the war.

34

PISS ON THE GENERAL

On September 21, 1944, Werner's crew attacked rail yards in Mainz, Germany. Brig. Gen. Robert F. Travis, Iron Ass Heller's mentor, was flying on his last mission to complete his operational tour and led the 41st Combat Wing to bomb Mainz as the primary visual target. The last-resort target was the Schneider Boot and Shoe Factory two and a half miles west of central Frankfurt. Two aircraft were forced to return early owing to mechanical problems.

Werner and Jack had a lucky break when a shell passed clean through one of their wings and failed to detonate. Amazingly, the wing remained intact, and Werner coolly ordered the remaining fuel to be pumped into the other wing's fuel tank.

Twenty-five bombers dropped cluster bombs on the primary target. The plane *Queen of Hearts* failed to bomb because of yet another bomb rack snafu. Two aircraft dropped leaflets. Seventeen aircraft sustained battle damage.

The Hell's Angels's archives recorded a comedic episode that day. Capt. William E. Eisenhart, the operations officer who flew that mission with General Travis, became something of a folk hero after the mission. The squadron had instituted a new rule that pilots would no longer be allowed to leave the cockpit to urinate during a mission; instead they were ordered to use their sliding window and not the bomb bay. The pilot was required to clean the window area after landing. Moncur records that during the mission

Captain William E. Eisenhart, 359BS Operations Officer who flew with B/Gen. Travis, became somewhat of a folk hero after the mission. Several months previous the 359BS had instituted a policy that pilots should not leave the cockpit area during a mission to urinate in the bomb bay. Pilots were advised to crack their cockpit slide window, get up on their haunches and let the slipstream carry their urine outside. This effective technique was done on a strict condition that the pilot would personally clean the window area immediately after landing. During the 21 September mission Captain Eisenhart used this method to relieve himself, only to discover that General Travis was smoking and had cracked his window, which created a cross draft. Some of the urine swirled in the cockpit and hit the General full in his face. Upon landing General Travis chewed out Captain Eisenhart for a full half hour, threatened him with court-martial, ordered him to immediately take down the bulletin board notice letter on the suggested urination method, advised him that he was going to award the DFC to 1st Lts. Smith and Counts, but was "damned if he would award a DFC" to him. Later Captain Eisenhart was known as the only Captain who had urinated in the face of a General and got away with it. Such is how folk heroes are born."

Eisenhart became known as the only captain who had pissed in the face of a general and got away with it.

Iron Ass's mentor, General Travis, was killed on August 5, 1950, during a B-29 Superfortress mission. The B-29, the plane that dropped atomic bombs on Japan, had a long history of mechanical glitches; Travis's plane developed two runaway propellers, as well as landing-gear problems fifteen minutes after takeoff from Fairfield-Suisun Air Force Base in California. The official accident report stated:

Just prior to liftoff, the number two engine propeller malfunctioned. . . . After liftoff, the pilot actuated the gear switch to the up position, and the gear did not retract. Due to the increased drag (feathered number two engine and the lowered gear), the rising terrain ahead and to the left, and the inability of the aircraft to climb, the aircraft commander elected to make a 180-degree turn to the right back toward the base. Upon completion of the turn, the left wing became difficult to hold up. The aircraft commander allowed the aircraft to slide to the left to avoid a trailer court. A crash landing was imminent as the altitude of the aircraft was only a few feet above the ground. The aircraft struck the ground with the left wing down at approximately 120mph. All ten people in the rear compartment were fatally injured. General Travis and one passenger in the forward compartment received fatal injuries; all other crewmembers and passengers escaped with only minor injuries . . . after twenty minutes . . . the blast, felt and heard over 30 miles away, caused severe damage to the nearby trailer park on base.

What the report did not say was that Travis's bomber carried an atom bomb—a fact kept secret for nearly half a century. The cover story, which mentioned "5000 pounds of high explosive" bombs, was misleading; they were not bombs, they were shaped charges designed to trigger an atomic explosion. The capsule containing the nuclear material was not on board. Over the next half century at least eighteen other atomic weapons were lost in crashes or mishaps. The explosion created a radioactive crater sixty feet across. Eighteen people died, including Travis and seven civilians in the trailer park where the plane crashed. Sixty others, mostly civilians, were injured. Fairfield-Suisun Air Force Base was officially renamed Travis Air Force Base on April 20, 1951, in his honor. Travis is buried at Arlington National Cemetery.

Five days later, Werner's crew again attacked the railroad marshaling yards at Osnabruck:

The B-17s went through intense and very accurate flak in the target area to bomb visually. They dropped 177 1,000-lb. M44 bombs from 26,400, 26,000 and 25,200 ft. with fair to good results. Photos showed high squadron hits right on the assigned main point of impact and numerous bomb craters in the marshalling yards.

Chaff, bunches of aluminum strips thrown from the bombers designed to confuse enemy radar operators, had no effect in curtailing the intense and accurate flak. Six aircraft suffered major battle damage, and six minor. One aircraft returned early when its oxygen failed. Friendly fighter support by 134 P-51s was excellent.

A B-17 piloted by Lt. Paul K. Bennett was hit between the number three and number four engines. Returning crewmen reported that it slid down under the formation, peeled off, went down in a glide, and blew up at about 5,000 to 6,000 feet. Lt. Lloyd E. Goff, who survived the incident, later reported that the aircraft caught fire immediately. He landed with holes in his parachute caused by ground fire and thought his pilot, navigator, and ball-turret gunner were shot hanging from their parachutes.

On September 26, Werner's crew fought in one of the deadliest battles of the entire war. Unbeknown to the pilots, "photo reconnaissance planes had recently been reporting alarming evidence of a resurgence of German fighter strength." For the first time since D-day, Luftwaffe fighters emerged in strength when 100 fighters, including the new Messerschmitt 262 jet fighter, attacked a squadron of Fortresses near Magdeburg, Germany. They gave the heavies the worst shellacking they ever experienced. The jets were so fast that even with power-assisted swivel mounts, waist gunners simply could not get them into their sights. There was no outrunning them, either, since the jets had twice the air speed of the heavies and, over home turf, could quickly refuel, rearm, and catch up to the running dogfight.

The next day, September 27, another fifty-five bombers were lost to the swarming fighters; 750 men gone within forty-eight hours. When twenty-five of twenty-nine B-24 Liberators from the 445th Bomb Group strayed from the formation in dense fog; they were jumped by German fighters and destroyed within six minutes over Göttingen. Only four bombers returned to England, representing the highest loss for a single group in any Eighth Air Force operation during the war. Allied intelligence was stunned that Albert Speer had not only tripled conventional fighter production under aerial bombardment in less than a year but also introduced fundamentally new weapons systems: the jets and ballistic missiles that could have been game changers if deployed in strength earlier in the war. After the war, Göring, when asked why the Germans had not made better use of their new but long-delayed jet fighters, replied instantly, "Adolf Hitler's madness."

On September 27, Lt. Frank W. Federici, a navigator in the 445th, flew with a colonel up to Aberdeen, Scotland. When he returned to his base in England, he noticed that a lot of aircraft were not in their parking places. The mission should have returned to base already. After landing, Federici asked the ground crew chief where the rest of the squad was. "We have been wiped out, sir," was the reply. Federici, thinking the man was joking, upbraided him, whereupon the crew chief burst into tears. The stunned Federici reflexively embraced the sobbing enlisted man on the tarmac as he apologized. He then went to his hut, which was empty, and viewed the possessions of more than a dozen officers lost that day.

On October 6, a rare event occurred while Werner and Jack were attacking a power plant at Stralsund, Germany. There were no enemy aircraft and no antiaircraft fire. The squad suffered no battle damage, no casualties. There was a general feeling that in fact the war might be winding down, and some predicted "We'll be home for Christmas." It was not to be, as their next mission sadly proved.

On October 11, Goering's crew was one of forty-seven bombers that attacked an oil plant, again near Cologne. This time all the planes had the 1,000-pound bombs aboard. Six men were killed and twelve went missing, including Lt. Arvid Anderson, who recalled the event that happened on his seventh mission, which was about the average that air crewmen completed. His plane had been hit, went into a sharp spin, and blew up. Anderson was "blown out of the nose." And the frigid air, like a slap in the face, revived the officer just in time for him to deploy his chute before landing in a farmer's field.

Within the Nazi hierarchy, Göring's star continued to fall and he withdrew more and more into an opiate haze. Hitler had not revoked the formal designation of Göring as his successor, but the indispensable man became Speer, the efficient technocrat who kept the Nazi war machine from sputtering to a halt. As Speer's memoirs would eventually reveal, he saw the American bombing of synthetic oil production as Germany's greatest immediate problem:

> I shall never forget the date, May 12 [1944]. On that day the technological war was decided. Until then we had managed to produce approximately as many weapons as the armed forces needed, in spite of their considerable losses. But with the attack of nine hundred and thirty-five daylight bombers of the American Eighth Air Force upon several fuel plants in central and eastern Germany, a new era in the air war began. It meant the end of German armaments production.

The Luftwaffe's pilot corps had become a shadow of its former self, but antiaircraft flak had not slackened. In fact, with the transfer of artillery from the collapsing Eastern Front, the skies over targets in Germany were well nigh as dangerous as they were when the Luftwaffe was at full strength.

The next day, another tragedy occurred when *Miss Nashville,* a B-25 Mitchell medium bomber used for routine courier flights, the only such plane in the Eighth Air Force other than Eisenhower's personal transport, approached an Allied airfield in occupied France. American antiaircraft gunners failed to recognize the aircraft as friendly and blasted it out of the sky.

Counting down the missions they still had to fly to complete their tours, the crew focused much of their frustration on Werner. But they had come to appreciate him as a courageous officer. They accepted his almost obsessive motivations and had a grudging respect for him as a pilot who kept bringing them back alive.

35

END OF THE CONTRACT

Shortly after the November 21 mission, Jack was alone in the Quonset hut he shared with Werner, studying a German fighter pilot's training manual and trying to ignore the razor blades in his stomach. Major Mackin knocked and walked in.

"What do you think of Goering?" Mackin asked.

"He's a real good pilot," Jack replied.

"No, that's not it. What do you think of his loyalty?"

"Major, he is as loyal as I am."

"That's good. I'm short of crews, and I can't afford to have two first pilots on one plane all the time. So I'm going to give you your own crew."

"Major, if you're going to do that I'd like to have the enlisted crew I'm flying with now. They're the best."

"All right, you got them."

Jack was soon promoted to first lieutenant and assigned a crew. The major didn't or couldn't keep his promise, however, and Jack did not get the sergeants he'd been flying with. From then on, Werner and Jack sometimes flew on the same missions but usually in different B-17s.

As he knew he would, Jack hated commanding a B-17 and being responsible for its crew. First, he didn't like being the boss; second, he missed the quiet, reassuring camaraderie of Werner's presence; third, he had the misfortune of not being able to keep his crew. Most stayed with Werner, who as the more senior pilot naturally didn't want to let his well-trained and familiar crew go. Jack was commander of a plane largely full of strangers. Some, having just arrived from the States, were as foolishly green as they were gung-ho.

Capt. Robert J. Lynch sometimes asked Rencher to fly with new pilots on their first mission to check them out. One time he went up with a newly commissioned regular army officer who was something of a martinet. It was the lousiest crew Jack had ever seen. He later told Lynch "it was a terrible crew and should not go on a mission yet, since the navigator, the bombardier, and the gunner were not up to par." On the next mission, Jack was again assigned to fly with the new man. As they were climbing to altitude to form up over a radio tower on a foggy day, Jack ordered the tail gunner to shine a light out the back in Morse code so the next plane could line up in the fog. The sergeant replied, "Sure thing, Jack," and did as instructed.

Hearing the exchange, the new man, whose name Jack could not recollect, hit the roof. "How the hell can you, an officer and a pilot, allow an enlisted man to call you by your first name?" he demanded, red as a beet. "You damn reservists are all the same, no damn good."

Jack, seeing the man's woefully inept flying skills, said, "You've got to learn to fly better formation because if you get off alone that's what the Germans are looking for and sure as I'm sitting here, you'll get shot down." Jack helpfully suggested that before he flew another mission, "We'll get three planes together and go up for a practice flight and I'll teach you how to fly formation. We'll get someone to slow down an engine and I'll teach you how to recognize it and then teach you how to stay with him in formation." The new man bellowed, "The hell you will— there is nothing you damn reservists can teach me." Sadly and quietly Jack replied, "I can teach you to stay alive." But the new man would not do the training flight Jack offered, so Jack told Lynch that he should not be piloting the plane. "Sure enough, not long after, that pilot strayed from formation and was shot down, captured, and spent the rest of the war as a POW."

The next day, Jack was promoted to first lieutenant and was soon given his own plane and crew to command. Jack completed his thirty-five-mission tour as a commander by Christmas 1944 and was done with combat. Werner volunteered for another thirty-five-mission tour and his offer was immediately accepted. As soon as he could, Jack transferred out of combat and started ferrying planes stateside. As fate had it, the

November 21 Leuna mission, when Jack came closest to having to kill Werner, was one of their last flights together. Military intelligence and Werner's commanders, with Jack's assurances, had at long last come to trust Werner's loyalty to the United States and his proven skills as a flight commander.

On December 6, Werner again flew a mission to Merseburg, his first without Jack at his side. Four planes and thirty-seven men went missing and another ninety-one bombers were damaged. The very next day, Werner volunteered his pissed-off crew to lead a training mission for green pilots when the rest of the squadron was standing down. On December 7, after the "volunteer" training flight, Werner was landing at Molesworth, piloting *Mercy's Madhouse,* when the right landing gear collapsed as he touched down. Since the Hell's Angels had no missions aloft that day, the air station was jammed with planes. With extensive damage to the number four propeller and engine, as well as to the wing, Werner man-handled the skidding bomber, at ninety miles an hour, amid a shower of sparks and smoke, to a wild yet safe landing on the dangerously over-crowded airfield. His men considered it a needless risk and a wasted rest day. Werner considered it duty. Since it was not a combat flight, it didn't even count toward his crew's mission total. They'd almost lost their lives for a mission that never was.

36

DRESDEN

Behold, your house is left unto you desolate.

—Matthew 23:38

Werner flew as squadron leader for the firebombing of Dresden, Germany, on February 14, 1945, one of the most controversial Allied bombings of the war because of the number of civilian casualties. "Up till then," noted historian Martin Gilbert, "Dresden, a city of baroque palaces, art galleries and opera houses—where Schiller once lived, Wagner composed and Dostoevsky gambled—had not been the target of a British or American bombing raid." The number of deaths has been much disputed, but even at the lowest figures it represents an overwhelming loss of life. The attack on the ancient capital city of Saxony in the eastern part of Germany had been demanded by the Soviets, who saw Dresden's untouched rail hubs as a threat to the Red Army's invasion of Germany from the east. "Dresden had been smashed to smithereens as a Valentine's Day present to the Red Army," observed British historian Giles MacDonogh. The Russians made urgent requests for the bombing of Dresden at the Yalta summit, which ended only two days prior to the attack.

In a pitiless twist of fate, Ash Wednesday and Saint Valentine's fell on the same day in 1945. "An inharmonious combination," observed Winston Churchill's private secretary, Jock Colville in his diary. Colville knew that Churchill supported the attack on Dresden, a city crowded with civilians fleeing the Soviet slaughter and rape then under way in the eastern regions of Germany.

As the sun rose over a still-flaming Dresden, it revealed a city laid to waste from the previous evening's two high-explosive and incendiary bomb attacks by Britain's RAF Bomber Command, spaced three hours apart. The resulting firestorm turned the ancient city into an inferno that incinerated thousands of civilians and their homes and destroyed baroque churches, ancient palaces, historic museums, and art galleries. Fifteen square miles around the city center were destroyed. "People who were blocks from the flames and thought themselves safe were suddenly picked up by hurricane-force winds and pulled into the inferno; their corpses were reduced to ash," writes historian and author Marshall De Bruhl, a self-described pacifist, who nevertheless considers Dresden "a legitimate war target."

Yet the raid was not over. "It was left to the Americans . . . to deliver the coup de grâce to the mortally wounded Florence of the Elbe." At midday, a third wave of heavy bombers, this time from the U.S. Eighth Air Force, appeared over the stricken city and unleashed fresh hell on the heads of emergency workers and rescuers who had been struggling to put out the fires and extricate victims.

Werner flew as the lead pathfinder of Hell's Angels Group C that day. In the USAAF and RAF, "Pathfinders were the *corps d'élite* . . . and consisted of specially selected crews identifying and marking targets." Directly behind Werner flew Lt. Col. Harry D. Gobrecht, who later became the 303rd Bomb Group's official historian and wrote about Werner's relationship to Göring.

The first responders in the city once known as "Florence on the Elbe" were killed; caught in the open as planned, they died in droves. Nine-year-old Lothar Metzger was a child during the Dresden firestorm:

> We saw terrible things: cremated adults shrunk to the size of small children, pieces of arms and legs, dead people, whole families burnt to death, burning people ran to and fro, burnt coaches filled with civilian refugees, dead rescuers and soldiers, many were calling and looking for their children and families, and fire everywhere, everywhere fire, and all the time the hot wind of the firestorm threw people back into the

burning houses they were trying to escape from. So intense was the heat that many corpses were reduced to the size of dolls, small enough to be removed in buckets.

It struck some as being morally akin to targeting medics on a battle-field. The third U.S. attack, in which Werner was again a pathfinder, was regarded as the cruelest of the triple blows to hit Dresden during eighteen hours of firebombing. De Bruhl, a self-described pacifist, said he "had once subscribed to the conventional view that the firebombing of Dresden was unnecessary" but came to accept it as a legitimate act of war. Yet "the Dresden attack immediately became a symbol to many of the horror of a war waged on civilian populations."

After the Dresden raid, Goebbels, the odious minister of propaganda, first wept, then swung into action. Nazi-controlled press circulated a grossly inflated casualty figure of up to 200,000 dead in Dresden. In other countries, including Switzerland and Sweden, the propaganda was swallowed whole by the "neutral" press, which published the figure to world-wide outrage.

Dresden, the Third Reich's seventh-largest urban center and the second largest city in eastern Germany, had, according to OSS reports, 110 known armament and chemical manufacturing sites and 50,000 laborers, including slaves working in critical war industries. It had a re-gional Gestapo headquarters and thousands of troops at Dresden's rail hubs preparing to deploy east to stem the Russian advance on Prussia. Flowing westward, panicked civilians fled the Red Army. Stalin put pressure on the Allies, and all agreed Dresden was a valid and vital war target.

Most current accounts maintain that the actual numbers of dead in Dresden were between 25,000 and 50,000, a fraction of what was com-monly reported during and after the war. In 2005, historian John Keegan wrote:

By the time the raids finished . . . 35,000 people, mostly civil-ians, had been killed . . . the casualty figure was inflated . . . while the name of Dresden was used to brand Air Marshall [Sir Arthur "Bomber"] Harris, head of RAF Bomber Command, a war criminal.

Discredited author, historian, once-jailed Nazi apologist, and, most recently Holocaust denier turned Auschwitz tour guide David Irving published *The Destruction of Dresden* in 1963, in which he claimed 135,000 died. Author Kurt Vonnegut, an infantryman captured at the Battle of the Bulge in December 1944, was a prisoner of war and witnessed the firebombing and used the inflated data from Irving's book in his classic *Slaughterhouse-Five,* in which the firebombing is the defining event. Calling Vonnegut's book "science fiction," not history, De Bruhl blames Vonnegut for sharing "with David Irving the distinction of being one of the two best known sources of disinformation about the destruction of Dresden." De Bruhl does state, however:

> During the war and after, the Americans insisted that their unchanging and official policy throughout was always their precision bombing of military targets, and that civilians were never purposely targeted. It is clear, however, from the Casablanca directive that terror bombing of civilians was an official, albeit unannounced, policy of both the RAF and the Eighth Air Force.

Given the technology of the era, "when only 34 percent of bombs dropped . . . fell within a thousand feet of their target," virtually all bombing was area bombing, and everyone, including Churchill and Roosevelt, knew it. While viewing a film of an urban bombardment's aftermath, Churchill once asked his military advisers, "Are we beasts?" Up to 650,000 civilians died in about seventy German cities and towns during the war. In France, 70,000 civilians died; in Italy 50,000 more. The UK death toll was about 60,000.

Winston Churchill, in his multivolume history of WWII was even more succinct, "disposing of the issue in one sentence," reported De Bruhl. Air Marshall Harris, the head of the RAF's Bomber Command.

Churchill, heretofore an enthusiastic supporter of terror bombing, did a politically expedient about-face after the international outcry regarding Dresden. Despite his February 1942 directive to Bomber Command "to primarily focus on civilian morale, particularly industrial workers," after Dresden, he nimbly distanced himself from the very policy of area and terror bombing he had personally approved and advocated. By referring to the Dresden raids "as an act of terror and wanton destruction . . . he was criticizing Bomber Command for carrying out a policy he had repeatedly endorsed. . . . Churchill . . . used the opportunity to pose as having moral qualms [he] had repeatedly urged on Harris." Following an Associated Press article claiming "terror bombing" had been approved by Allied leaders, Henry L. Stimson, U.S. secretary of war, was compelled to issue a statement that American policy "has never been to inflict terror bombings on civilian populations, it has been and remains, targeted against military installations."

In February 1944, Churchill addressed the issue of terror bombing in the House of Commons. "I shall not moralize further than to say that there is a strange, stern justice in the long swing of events."

Yet after the international outcry, on March 28, 1945, Churchill forwarded this message to the Chiefs of Staff, including the Chief of the Air Staff:

> It seems to me that the moment has come when the question of bombing of German cities simply for the sake of increasing the terror, though under other pretexts, should be reviewed. . . . The destruction of Dresden remains a serious query against the conduct of Allied bombing. . . . I feel the need for more precise concentration upon military objectives . . . rather than on mere acts of terror and wanton destruction, however impressive.

"Churchill's minute" sent "a thunderbolt down the corridors of Whitehall." Sir Arthur Harris was incandescent with rage at what he saw as a disgraceful, hypocritical maneuver by Churchill to distance himself from Dresden's political firestorm. Allied leaders simply wanted to look away from the "amoral blemish" of terror bombing and just get "this ghastly bloodbath over," observed historian Sir Max Hastings.

It is perhaps revealing that there was no mention of Bomber Command in Churchill's victory address after Germany's surrender and that neither Göring nor any Nazi would ever be charged for German terror attacks over England, which killed 60,000 British civilians, or for similar attacks on Holland and Poland. The victors' judges presiding at Göring's Nuremberg trial knew a legal and moral can of worms when they saw one.

Incredibly, Sir Arthur Harris's request for a campaign medal for Bomber Command, as had been struck by her majesty's government for Fighter Command, was ignored following the war, and as recently as 2008, petitions for the medal fell on deaf ears.

It was embarrassingly clear, even before the atomic era, that a new age of maddeningly amoral—yet arguably essential and effective—civilian targeting had dawned. Industrial war engaged industrial populations in total war. Civilian attacks have not faded from history. Today, despite advances in smart-bomb technology, civilian targeting remains with us—moral equivalency aside—as the preferred weapon of terrorists worldwide. That the terrorists learned the concept of targeting civilians and the various justifications for it from the "civilized" industrial powers is one legacy of WWII that is beyond question.

When Werner reflected on the Valentine's Day Dresden raid years later he called it "a hell of a deal, nothing to be proud of. It was murder, but it wasn't. I didn't talk about it ever afterwards. We were five miles up and through the smoke and haze could not see much. You see, air war is such an impersonal thing." In historian Niall Ferguson's opinion,

> [It] was possible to pulverize a city without looking into the eyes of those [women and children] being visibly consigned to hell below. Allied bombing was as indiscriminate as Nazi racial policy was meticulously discriminating. The moral difference . . . is that the crews of Bomber Command were flying their missions in order to defeat Nazi Germany and end the war . . . Hatred filled the minds of the SS men . . . ; it was absent from the thoughts of Allied airmen.

Bomber reports said pilots could smell human flesh in the smoke that rose tens of thousands of feet above the city. One RAF pilot reported the nighttime raid illuminated the sky so brightly that he could read his logs at 18,000 feet in a blacked-out bomber without having to turn on the overhead light. "Reading the log by the light of an inferno . . . is a vivid summation of the bomber's disconnection from the indiscriminate death and destruction he [was] causing."

Records from the 303rd Bomb Group state that visual bombing was impossible. There was no fight left in what the Allies termed the "dead city." Only one aircraft in Goering's group sustained minor battle damage that day.

37

FOG AND FIRE

On the next day, February 15, 1945, as the story was sweeping the globe, Werner was ordered to lead yet another attack on the "dead city." By this time, Werner had thirty-seven completed combat missions; he regularly flew squadron lead and was considered an excellent formation commander. The paperwork for his promotion to captain had been filed before his twenty-first birthday. Jack called Werner "the best damn formation pilot in the army, hands down." Privately, however, Jack was concerned about Werner's instrument flight skills, which did not meet Jack's exacting level of excellence. "Goering had a habit that I thought would kill him. He could not take off on instruments although he had no fear." Werner, not surprisingly, hotly disputes Jack's assertion in this regard.

The brutal 1944–1945 winter was interrupted by an early February thaw. With the warmer air came fog. Solid cloud cover resulted, and instrument takeoffs and landings were the norm.

On February 15, just a few weeks after Jack left Werner's side, East Anglian air stations were blanketed in perfect pea soup. As squadron leader, Werner was the first to take off, with thirty-eight other B-17s behind him. The long line of idling B-17s wrapped around onto the taxiway to the left of the main runway. A steady, strong crosswind buffeted the stationary Forts. The wind pushed against the enormous tail rudders, which offered a flat surface the size of a barn door twenty-five feet off the ground.

To avoid the jarring gusts, idling planes were positioned nose to the wind, which also meant ass to the runway. This meant that the dozens of idling 1200-horsepower motors created an invisible prop wash on top of the already dangerous crosswinds. In the fog, Werner saw neither the plane's ass-end toward him nor the end of the 1.3-mile-long runway.

Next to Werner sat a new West Pointer, Lt. Donald R. Walter, flying his maiden combat mission. Ready for takeoff, Werner applied power to his four engines and released the brakes. As the Fortress gathered speed and just before liftoff, long past the abort point, it was slammed broadside by the blast of prop wash crossing the runway from the left.

The B-17 lifted off too soon. Walter's headset was turned off, and inside the roaring plane Walter didn't hear Goering's command for full flaps. "All this is happening in a matter of seconds clicking by, click, click, and click. The next thing I felt was the plane pulling out from under me," recalled Werner years later. Flight Engineer Raymond C. Eckert reached over Walter's head and pulled up the flaps, but it was too late. Rapidly losing speed—and loaded with fuel, ammo, bombs, and men—the Fort fell from the sky 300 yards past the runway. Because of the fog, Molesworth's control tower didn't even immediately notice the crash. The bomber broke into three sections. Eugene J. O'Brien, a Hell's Angels aircraft mechanic, reported:

> I was standing approximately 30–40 feet from our craft when I heard a roar of engines. The plane was coming down fast. . . . A long scraping sound was heard when they crashed. My first thought was to rush to the scene and see if we could save the men. . . . I heard the 50 caliber machine gun bullets exploding indicating the plane was on fire.

It was at that point that the bombs exploded and O'Brien was blown off his feet.

O'Brien claimed in his memoirs he had previously mentioned to Werner that he was taking off "from only half the runway" and was concerned. O'Brien said Werner "thought it was quite a feat" to get the plane aloft as quickly as possible and speculated that extra weight and a premature liftoff caused the crash.

Lt. Bill Condor, the bombardier, suffered a broken arm, and three other crewmen sustained lesser injuries, but Lt. James C. Buckner was trapped in the crushed radio compartment with a shattered kneecap. The field in which they crashed was a sea of mud created by the late winter thaw. The plane's 100-mile-per hour momentum caused its bottom half, which held the high-explosive bombs, to plow deep into the mud.

Machine gunner Sgt. Joseph Blinebury recalled what happened next:

> I was in the waist section which broke off from the forward fuselage portion just behind the Radio Compartment. I must have been unconscious for a brief time, and when I came to . . . I was lying in a muddy field. Getting to my feet I noticed a bright glare in the fog and I slogged through the muddy terrain in the direction of the light . . . the area around it broke into a clear circle of vision, showing the wings on fire and the .50 caliber shells popping off from the top turret guns.

The engineer, Sergeant Eckert, and radio operator Sgt. P. B. Johnson Jr. tried to get to the radio compartment area of the fuselage, which was tilted up seven feet off the ground. To get to the navigator, Buckner, whose knee was wedged into the wreckage, Blinebury recalled:

> The Engineer and myself boosted the Radio Operator up so he was able to get the [navigator] freed and lowered him to us below. We did not know it at the time but [learned later that Lt.] Buckner had suffered a crushed knee cap. The three of us carried Lt Buckner away from the burning fuselage. After struggling for a time through the field, we came to rest against a hay stack. Shortly thereafter we heard the bomb load explode and felt the ground beneath us shudder.

Once free of the plane, Werner couldn't lift his legs, which were stuck knee-deep in the mud. Knowing the flaming bomber would explode any second, he clawed the mud away from his feet just enough to unlace his boots and pull free. In socks, he clambered through the mud to the nose of the plane but saw nothing in the smoky fog that blanketed both sight and sound. Werner heard some small explosions: the oxygen canisters were blowing up. "I thought to myself, it's really going to blow—it was all fog and fire." Werner turtled like mad through the muck until he was about fifty feet away from the wreck; the main bomb load exploded just minutes after impact.

The enormous fireball blew open a crater that after-incident photos showed was deep enough to bury a three-story house. The control tower was still unaware of the event and remained so for what seemed to be a lifetime to the injured, concussed, and shocked aircrew. Ironically, the sucking mud that almost trapped Werner saved his life and that of his crew. The mud absorbed much of the force when the bombs in the plane's belly blew up. Werner was blown over by the concussive force of the blast and knocked unconscious, flat on his back. "It was a hell of a concussion, of course, and the next thing I knew there was a terrible hissing sound right next to my left ear." A flaming 1200-horsepower half-ton engine was blown skyward by the blast and crashed to earth inches from Werner's head.

Flight surgeons told Werner that if he didn't resume flying quickly, the incident would increasingly haunt him. A week later, he was back in the air.

On March 22, Werner was flying as the squadron leader over Bauer, Germany, when severe flak hit the cockpit right next to him and knocked out the onboard oxygen system, the number one engine, and the interphone. An electrical fire in the cockpit's fuse box broke out and filled the cockpit with toxic smoke. Werner calmly donned a portable oxygen canister, grabbed a fire extinguisher, vented the cockpit, dropped his altitude, and completed the bomb run manually. It was all in a day's work.

On another mission, an .88 millimeter flak shell passed clean through the port-side wing and failed to explode. Werner pumped fuel into the starboard fuel tank and continued the mission. He marveled for the rest of his life that the wing remained intact and the shell failed to detonate. "It was the Lord's work," he said.

Slave laborers in German armament factories were known to sabotage ammunition. It occurred to Werner that this was why the shell hadn't exploded, and that the unknown hero might well have been one of his victims in the numerous raids he'd led against such facilities in Germany. "The Lord works in mysterious ways," he concluded.

From January to May Werner commanded fifteen missions and by war's end he had completed forty-nine, fourteen of them as the lead crew pilot. Had he not crashed, it would have been a nice, round fifty. But Werner had a lot of missions to come in the next decade as a jet bomber commander carrying hydrogen bombs in the Strategic Air Command.

After Jack's promotion and departure, Werner realized how much he benefited from Jack's skills—and how much he missed Jack's company. Werner had not fully realized how dangerously worn-down and ill his stoic best friend had become.

Adjusting to postwar life had its difficulties. After Jack returned to the States, he was hospitalized with battle fatigue and stress-related ulcerative colitis. Gastrointestinal disorders were epidemic in both combat and noncombat soldiers; these were termed "gastrointestinal neurosis." He had been in constant agony for months, with severe rectal bleeding; his guts were literally ripping themselves apart. He underwent a series of grueling surgeries that resulted in the removal of ever larger portions of his intestines and colon. At 24, Jack was forced to use a colostomy bag for the rest of his life.

38

GÖTTERDÄMMERUNG: TWILIGHT
OF THE GODS

As the Red Army hammered its way into Germany, raping, looting, and killing civilians en masse, Göring fled with his stolen art, gold, and loot after destroying his beloved and ornate hunting estate, Carinhall. Following a perfunctory visit to "celebrate" Hitler's birthday in the infamous Berlin bunker, Göring fled to the Tyrol.

As the Red Army closed in on Berlin in April 1945, the last hope of Hitler, Goebbels, Himmler, and Göring was that the Allies would finally find common cause with the Third Reich and unite against the Communist threat enveloping Eastern, and possibly Western, Europe. Himmler and Göring both secretly proposed a joint German, British, and American anti-Soviet front to Swiss and Swedish diplomats. Toward the end, Himmler was brazen or deluded enough to negotiate directly with Jewish leaders.

In Moscow, Josef Stalin was whipping his commanders, Generals Koniev, Chuikov, and Zhukov, to deliver the German capital by May Day, the "holiest" day on the Communist calendar.

In London, Churchill was aghast at the prospect of a Communist-dominated Eastern Europe. The Soviets had already made it plain that Poland's government in exile in Scotland was unlikely to be welcomed to return. Poland, the final trigger that launched England into war, was effectively handed from one murderous invading totalitarian dictator to another.

In the Tyrol, top Nazis, including Göring, stashed trainloads of art, gold, and currency in salt mines. Another Nazi general, Reinhard Gehlen, head of Nazi intelligence for the Eastern Front, knew more about the USSR than any foreign spymaster alive; he was sure his files and spy networks would save him from the gallows—unless of course he fell into Soviet hands.

The advent of the atomic era changed forever the way the United States looked at preparation for war and established a mind-set among policy makers that the country and its strategic air arm could never again be caught unprepared. Testifying before the Senate's Military Affairs Committee on November 15, 1945, Gen. Carl Spaatz, later the first chief of staff of the U.S. Air Force, said:

> The blessing of a time lag we enjoyed in two world wars is gone, perhaps forever. As top dog America becomes target number one. There will be no time lag. The airplane will possibly exceed the speed of sound. The possibilities for surprise are thus multiplied beyond measurement . . . Never again could the nation wait for the outbreak of war before under-taking the time-consuming business of building an air force.

Werner watched these developments with keen interest. His expertise, strategic bombing, was at the forefront of national defense policy, and the twenty-one-year-old war hero, who had received the Distinguished Flying Cross just months earlier, after completing forty-nine combat missions without losing a man, wanted to make the transition from a reservist to the regular army, no easy feat during the rapid demobilization of 7 million men.

Although the USSR was the United States' key ally during WWII, the USSR effectively and brutally occupied all of Eastern Europe and was seen by many, including Churchill and U.S. diplomats, as an existential threat to democracy. Few in the Truman administration doubted that the Soviets would develop atomic weapons of their own. Intelligence was needed about Soviet intentions and strategic capabilities. Werner's language skills and bombing technical know-how suddenly became indispensible assets. The former "damn reservist" would become a founding member of the U.S. Air Force in its most sensitive unit: intelligence. The wheel had truly come full circle.

As Nazi Germany imploded, Göring dusted off Hitler's June 29,

1941, decree granting him "total leadership of the Reich" if the führer should die or "lose freedom of action." He cabled Hitler in his Berlin bunker and suggested that he, Göring, should now take command. An outraged Hitler had the SS arrest Göring; he then stripped Göring of all titles and authority but stopped just short of having him executed, as his chief aide and Nazi Party secretary Martin Bormann had urged. Hitler named Grand Admiral Karl Doenitz as his successor before committing suicide, a poisoned chalice Doenitz would bitterly regret having accepted, and one that contributed to his decade-long postwar imprisonment.

Following Hitler's suicide, a relieved and ever-hopeful Göring now fancifully viewed himself as the perfect man to negotiate peace with Eisenhower, "soldier to soldier." Attempting to make contact with Eisenhower, Göring was captured by American soldiers, together with forty pieces of personal luggage, near Kitzbühel, the chic Tyrolean ski resort. For a few days, he was wined and dined in uniform, in luxurious surroundings, by Gen. Robert J. Stack; he even held a press conference with Allied reporters. When Eisenhower saw pictures of Göring regaling Allied reporters in his Reich Marshal's uniform, he blew his notoriously short fuse; sharply reprimanded General Stack; ordered Göring stripped of his uniform and decorations, including his treasured Blue Max; and had him clapped in irons as a prisoner of war. For Göring, the highest-ranking Nazi captured, it was all over except the dying.

Göring's marshal's baton was seized, and today is a prized war trophy on display at West Point, along with Hitler's pistol. Göring told his American captors that they had had a hell of a run during the dozen years that the thousand-year Reich actually lasted. Imprisoned and forcibly weaned from opiates, a surprisingly impressive, and much thinner Hermann Göring had his last flamboyant turn on the world stage. Tried for war crimes at Nuremberg in 1946—but never specifically for aerial attacks against civilians—he put up the most vigorous defense of all the top Nazis. He was sentenced to death on evidence of his personal role in signing the order approving Hitler's Final Solution for the Jews. He requested a firing squad. Told he would hang, he committed suicide, hours before his scheduled execution, with cyanide he had hidden from prison guards for more than a year. A dozen top Nazis were hanged.

On a rainy late autumn morning in 1946, in the countryside outside Munich, "on the bend of an anonymous lane, the charred remains of the lords of the Third Reich, Hermann Göring's among them, were poured into a muddy gutter."

Meanwhile, the Cold War gathered steam. In Switzerland, OSS head and later CIA director Allen Dulles fully shared Churchill's deep mistrust of Stalin and was determined that Nazi intelligence and technical assets survive and wind up in American hands. A deal was cut with Reinhard Gehlen. Within days of his capture in late 1945, Gehlen and his subordinates were living in a safe house near Washington, D.C. He would soon return to Germany with his staff to take over one of Bormann's facilities and begin a three-decades-long fulsome partnership with the CIA. It is now known that Gehlen harbored known Nazi war criminals, and that he often gave incorrect intelligence to the United States to maintain his importance, especially about the so-called missile gap, which played such a large role in the Cold War and in Richard Nixon's 1960 defeat by John F. Kennedy. The notoriously thorough Nazi intelligence apparatus was quickly and quietly integrated into military intelligence and the Office of Strategic Services, which became the CIA in 1947. From its inception, Reinhard Gehlen was the crown jewel of American foreign intelligence.

The United States and West Germany were allies, united against the red menace, as Hitler had always predicted they would be. Amazingly, Karl Wolff, once Himmler's chief of staff and an SS general, was released after only a week's detention after the war and worked openly for the next fifteen years in public relations of all things:

> Key to his evasion of justice was his role in "Operation Sunrise"—negotiations conducted by high-ranking American, Swiss, and British officials in violation of the Western Allies' agreements with the Soviet Union—for the surrender of German forces in Italy. After 1945, these officials, including [most notably OSS head and future CIA chief] Allen W. Dulles, shielded Wolff from prosecution in order to prevent information about the negotiations from coming out. The details had to be kept secret, they believed, in order to avoid a confrontation with Stalin as the Cold War took shape. New evidence suggests that the Western Allies not only failed to ensure cooperation between their respective national war crimes prosecution

organizations, but in certain cases even obstructed justice by withholding evidence.

Despite minor inconveniences, including a few years in prison during the 1960s, Wolff spoke openly to the media in several documentaries filmed during the 1970s and died peacefully in his bed at age eighty-four in 1984. Gehlen, who served as West Germany's official spy chief for decades, lived comfortably until 1974.

From December 1941 to August 1945, U.S. aircraft losses totaled 65,164, with 43,581 lost overseas and 21,583 in the United States, 18,418 in the European theater and 4,530 in the Pacific. Estimates of aircraft-related expenditures range from a quarter to a third of the war's $350 billion cost.

With the defeat of Japan, the U.S. military immediately began a drastic demobilization, as it had at the end of WWI. The USAAF was hit hard. Officers and crew were discharged, installations closed, and aircraft stored or sold off. "Between August 1945 and April 1946, its strength fell from 2.25 million men to just 485,000, and a year later to 304,000. Aircraft inventory dropped from 79,000 to less than 30,000, many in storage. Permanent installations were reduced from 783 to 177, just 21 more than before war broke out."

By July 1946, the U.S. Army Air Force only had two combat-ready groups. An air force of seventy groups, the authorized peacetime strength, was anticipated, with reserve and National Guard forces available for active duty in an emergency. Considerable opposition to a large peacetime military establishment, and the financial cost, resulted in cuts to forty-eight groups.

39

CLOAK, DAGGER, AND CAMERA

After Germany's surrender, Werner went home on leave. He met a former high school classmate, German-born immigrant June Schott, and a romance developed; on August 15, 1946, they married. Werner was selected to continue on active duty in the U.S. Army Air Force and, in 1947, with its successor, the U.S. Air Force, an unusual honor for a reservist during the U.S. military's postwar multimillion reduction in force. He still wanted to distinguish himself in his country's service, and the dawn of the Cold War presented him with an entirely new and unexpected career opportunity as an intelligence officer. He used his fluent German as an American spy in East Germany.

As an experienced, decorated, and, finally, trusted strategic bomber commander, Werner was in the right place at the right time, with the nerve, knowledge, and language skills needed to penetrate East Germany and spy on and photograph the latest Soviet military aircraft and hardware.

Werner served in Potsdam, in the Soviet zone of occupation, under the cover of his official job as an air force liaison officer to the fearsome "steel-toothed" Soviet general Vasily Chuikov, the Soviet commander of East Germany. Chuikov was one of the very few men to be twice decorated with the USSR's highest military decoration, Hero of the Soviet Union, once for his defense of Stalingrad and once as conqueror of Berlin. At Stalingrad, Chuikov crossed the frozen Volga River on foot to prove it could be done; he promptly fell through the ice and nearly drowned. Only five men in the history of the Soviet Union were more highly decorated;

some were politicians like Leonid Brezhnev, who served as both president of the USSR and head of the Communist Party between 1964 and 1982.

Initially, Werner was told to make note of Soviet military assets and memorize all warplane tail numbers he saw. "I thought why the hell don't we just photograph the airfields?" Werner raised the question with military intelligence and the newly created CIA.

U.S. Air Force historian Lawrence Aronsen observed that "air force intelligence (A-2) was, more than any other agency . . . convinced of the Soviet willingness to wage war." However, even though "A-2 came to be possessed by a rigidly anti-communist ideology, it established a progressive-minded reputation for introducing new ideas, techniques, and technological innovations."

Despite some resistance from the State Department and military intelligence, who were concerned about blowback if Werner was caught, the air force and the CIA loved the idea. Werner was supplied with "all kinds of new gadgets and miniature spy cameras." He was one of the first agents to smuggle pictures out of the Soviet zone routinely; he "had become a somebody." In a dangerous game of cat and mouse that went on for three years, Werner would hide camouflaged in ditches, snowfields, and wooded areas of East Germany, risking his life to take the invaluable photos. He impressed his spymasters with his unique, highly classified photos and was frequently called into intelligence headquarters to elaborate on what he had seen.

Werner photographed the latest jets, including the Ilyushin Il-28, the Soviet Union's first jet bomber in the immediate postwar period, and the Mikoyan-Gurevich MiG-17, an early Soviet jet fighter. He also photographed radar installations and troop formations. He was the first spy to take detailed pictures of several new Soviet weapons systems, including jet fighters, jet bombers, and new radar arrays. As airplanes came in to land, Werner lay on his back along the flight path he knew they must take and snapped high-resolution photos of their undercarriages and armaments. The highly classified photos were devoured by army intelligence and the CIA. "They went crazy over the pictures," which showed details of new Soviet warplanes, many of which had never previously been seen in the West. The CIA began to request specific photos of certain Soviet assets and facilities, and Werner was able to deliver them, despite almost being captured several times. In one photo, a line of new Soviet jet fighters, with tail markings visible, form the background. In the foreground, guards can be seen scrambling onto a truck while others run directly toward Werner's hideout. In the extremely sensitive and dangerous job, Werner was hailed as a courageous innovator. He put his life on the line each time he hid in the forest near thirteen different Soviet airbases, snapping away with his spy camera. One day, he was hiding just off a logging road in a thick forest near a particularly heavily defended airfield when the sun glinted off his camera lens and he was spotted. Machine gunners opened up and shredded the tree limbs just above his hideout, showering him with branches, bark, and leaves. Werner, nose to the ground, quietly slipped away into the undergrowth.

The combination of Werner's courage and results was noticed by the brass and his star seemed on the rise.

40

STRATEGIC AIR COMMAND

When Douglas MacArthur learned of the development of the atomic bomb, he said, almost wistfully, "Well, that changes warfare." It would also change the United States military structure, and nowhere would that be felt more than in the U.S. Army Air Force.

The "bomber mafia," a group of air force officers who believed that heavy bombers were the essential and primary weapon of modern warfare, began to plan for a separate and independent military air force. This triggered a bitter debate between the U.S. Army and its own air corps; the air corps was hell-bent on creating its own command to develop tactics and strategy, unhindered by the army's brass hats, who preferred to keep air power as an instrument in support of the army's traditional "boots on the ground."

This led to the creation of the Strategic Air Command within the army to ensure global bombing capability. In June 1946, the Eighth Air Force was assigned to SAC, but because of the massive postwar demobilization, for its first two years SAC existed primarily on paper. Eventually the bomber mafia won their independence, and the U.S. Air Force was established in September 1947. On October 19, 1948, former Eighth Air Force colonel and now lieutenant general Curtis LeMay took command of SAC, a position he would hold until June 1957, "the longest tenure for any U.S. Armed Forces commander since Winfield Scott, who served as General of the Army from 1841 to 1861."

Soon after taking over, LeMay established SAC headquarters at an air base in Omaha. His goal was to create a force of atomic-armed long-range bombers capable of devastating the Soviet Union quickly. Under his leadership, SAC eventually developed the technical capabilities, strategic plans, and operational readiness to carry out its mission: being able to deliver a nuclear attack quickly anywhere in the world. But at the beginning of the Cold War, SAC was effectively powerless in shaping American nuclear strategy.

From 1946 to 1948, the United States had only twelve atomic bombs and between five and twenty-seven B-29s, then the only plane capable of dropping them. The new strategic thinking was spelled out in the Joint Emergency War Plan, code-named Halfmoon, which envisioned dropping fifty atomic bombs on twenty cities in the Soviet Union. President Harry S. Truman initially rejected Halfmoon and ordered the development of a nonnuclear option, only to change his mind during the Berlin blockade.

LeMay and SAC planners unilaterally attempted to form American nuclear strategy. Shortly after his arrival at SAC, planners drew up Emergency War Plan 1-49, which envisioned striking seventy Soviet cities with 133 atomic bombs within a month. After 1949, when the Soviets unveiled their own atomic weapons, "SAC's goals were to inhibit Soviet nuclear capabilities and advances in Eastern Europe and to be prepared to demolish Soviet industrial capabilities." The redefinition and expansion of its mission would help SAC formalize and consolidate its control over nuclear planning and strategy. This was done by LeMay in a 1951 meeting when he convinced the Joint Chiefs that unreasonable operational demands were being placed on SAC, and in order to alleviate the issue, SAC—meaning LeMay personally—should be allowed to approve final target selections.

SAC's near complete control of nuclear weapons led to the adoption of a strategy based on "counterforce." SAC planners understood that as the Soviet Union increased its nuclear capacity, destroying or "countering" those forces (bombers, missiles, etc.) became of greater strategic importance than simply destroying industrial capacity.

The Eisenhower administration concurred with the new strategy, and in 1954 Eisenhower expressed a preference for military over civilian targets. With Eisenhower's approval, LeMay continued to increase SAC's independence by refusing to submit SAC war plans for review, believing that operational plans should be closely guarded, a view even the Joint Chiefs eventually came to accept.

The concentration of power in SAC was unprecedented. In the twenty years from 1946 to 1976, the SAC budget and personnel roster rose from 37,000 to 146,000 personnel. In 1946, the unit started with 279 bombers. Twenty years later its complement included 1,136 aircraft, 1,046 Minuteman missiles, and 29 bases. It controlled more than $18 billion in assets; it had annual operating expenses of more than $2.5 billion and an operational and maintenance budget of almost $600 million. During the two-term Eisenhower administration, the U.S. Air Force received about half of the nation's defense budget, compared with about a third under Truman. Mutual assured destruction—MAD—had arrived as national policy. Film director Stanley Kubrick took perfect aim at this insanity in his satirical 1964 film *Dr. Strangelove,* which featured a fictional SAC general named Jack Ripper.

Returning from his Potsdam spying missions in the early 1950s, Werner joined SAC and flew under LeMay, piloting nuclear-armed, six-engine B-47 Stratojet bombers on routine patrols from Tucson, Arizona, to the northern tip of Greenland and into the Arctic Circle. The development of the jet bomber, specifically the B-47 Stratojet, was the key to fulfilling LeMay's vision.

The grueling eighteen- to twenty-hour-long SAC patrols, which re-quired refueling twice in midair, a new innovation, were the heart of the indispensible 24-hours-a-day, 365-days-a-year security blanket that pro-tected the nation against surprise attack by the Soviet Union. SAC inte-grated new technological developments—radar early-warning systems, midair refueling, jet engines, and, by the late 1950s, ballistic missiles—into its operations.

The B-47 Stratojet, with its swept wings and sleek, aggressive design, was considered one of the most beautiful airplanes ever built. "Although it was often admired, respected, cursed, or even feared," wrote former SAC chief of staff Maj. Earl G. Peck, "it was almost never loved." Werner, who would later admit to being "arrogant," said he finally "learned humility" in the B-47 and recalled how dangerous the early refueling missions were.

Having seen and photographed Soviet jet bombers and fighters, Werner knew as much about the enemy's capabilities as probably any man of his rank in the military. He quickly trained and qualified as a

B-47 commander and carried top-secret atomic and, later, hydrogen bombs from his post at Davis-Monthan Air Force Base in Tucson, the city that became his home. In 1955, then only thirty-one years old, Lt. Col. Werner Goering had the nation's highest security clearance and was again flying the world's most sophisticated strategic bomber. By 1958, Werner was a squadron commander and a training commander, and by 1959 he was chief of combat operations for the 43rd Bomb Wing.

The key factor that allowed the B-47 to become the backbone of SAC was the development of midair refueling. Before this, bases in Morocco, Spain, and Turkey provided infrastructure for the bombers, as would later famously come to light during the Cuban missile crisis, when John F. Kennedy came to a secret agreement with Nikita Khrushchev to quietly dismantle the already obsolete Turkish bases in exchange for the Soviet Union's public withdrawal of nuclear weapons from Cuba.

Midair refueling of jet bombers became a reality in 1954 with the introduction of the KC-135 Stratotanker, which effectively meant that the B-47 could remain flying for extended periods, rendering foreign bases in hotspots near Russia less essential. The new capability was not so subtly demonstrated to the USSR by several highly publicized nonstop round-the-world flights. As the Stratotanker transferred fuel to the B-47, it got lighter and the bomber got heavier. It was a delicate and dangerous midair duet with continual adjustments of power, positioning, and altitude. As always, aerial accidents were not uncommon, but with nuclear materials involved, they became much more politically sensitive as well as potentially catastrophic. In one incident, the tanker unexpectedly slowed down and a prop hit a vertical stabilizer on one of Werner's squad planes. Werner, as squad commander, received a chewing out from LeMay, which he passed down to the flight commander, in classic shit-flows-downhill military fashion.

In 1956, Werner was also appointed chief intelligence officer for the 43rd Bomb Wing. His primary concern was the security of nuclear weapons and he had plenty to be concerned about. In 1968, the government admitted there were thirteen "serious nuclear weapon accidents" between 1950 and 1968, the first occurring in February 1950, when an American bomber jettisoned an atom bomb into the Pacific Ocean.

In another famous accident, on February 5, 1958, the air force lost a 7,600-pound Mark 15 hydrogen bomb in the waters off Tybee Island near

Savannah, Georgia, during a practice exercise when a Stratojet collided with an F-86 fighter. This was neither the first nor the last accident involving nuclear weapons. Current research documents nineteen incidents of planes carrying nuclear weapons catching fire, crashing, or dropping nuclear bombs in emergency situations, both inside the United States, including in North Carolina, in Georgia, and off the shores of New Jersey, and abroad, in Spain and North Africa. To prevent a possible detonation in the event of a crash and to save the aircrew, the Tybee Island bomb was allowed to be jettisoned over the Atlantic and the crew landed safely. The bomb was presumed lost in relatively shallow water somewhere off Georgia. In a 1966 congressional inquiry, then assistant secretary of defense W. J. Howard said the Tybee Island bomb was a "complete weapon, a bomb with a nuclear capsule," and was one of two weapons lost up to that time that contained a trigger device. The military subsequently changed its tune and said the bomb did not have the trigger needed to detonate a nuclear explosion, but doubts remain and conflicting testimony exists. To this day, the bomb has not been found. What is still in doubt is whether the bomb contained plutonium. Col. Howard Richardson, who flew thirty-five B-17 missions in the Eighth Air Force during the war, piloted the Tybee B-47 and received the DFC for getting his crew home alive after the midair collision.

In 1962, the Atomic Energy Commission and the Department of Defense concluded a study that did little to calm fears:

> Weapons are designed with great care to explode only when deliberately armed and fired. Nevertheless, there is always a possibility that, as a result of accidental circumstances, an explosion will take place inadvertently. Although all conceivable precautions are taken to prevent them, such accidents might occur in areas where weapons are assembled and stored, during the course of loading and transportation on the ground, or when actually in the delivery vehicle, e.g., an airplane or a missile.
>
> Abroad, the balance of power is shifting. There are new and more terrible weapons. . . . The world has been close to war before—but now man, who has survived all previous threats

to his existence, has taken into his mortal hands the power to exterminate his species some seven times over.

Despite the rhetoric in 1960, Kennedy had run to the right of Nixon on the missile gap and national security issues, knowing full well that Nixon, the ultimate cold warrior, could not refute Kennedy's overblown allegations without breaching national security. JFK effectively hoisted Nixon on his own petard. After peering into the abyss during the Cuban crisis, JFK became the first of all succeeding presidents to call for agreements with the USSR in an ongoing effort to limit nuclear proliferation and, in JFK's time, specifically aboveground detonations. JFK memorably addressed the issue at the 1963 commencement of American University.

I speak of peace because of the new face of war. Total war makes no sense in an age when great powers can maintain large and relatively invulnerable nuclear forces and refuse to surrender without resort to those forces. It makes no sense in an age when a single nuclear weapon contains almost ten times the explosive force delivered by all the allied air forces in the Second World War. It makes no sense in an age when the deadly poisons produced by a nuclear exchange would be carried by wind and water and soil and seed to the far corners of the globe and to generations yet unborn. . . . For, in the final analysis, our most basic common link is that we all inhabit this small planet. We all breathe the same air. We all cherish our children's future. And we are all mortal.

41

AFRICA

It seemed that the printers of the African maps had a slightly malicious habit of including, in large letters, the names of towns, junctions, and villages which, while most of them did exist in fact, as a group of thatched huts may exist or a water hole, they were usually so inconsequential as completely to escape discovery from the cockpit.

—Beryl Markham, *West with the Night*

In 1962, after seven years of SAC patrols and command, Werner was offered his choice of two posts. He could be the assistant U.S. Air Force attaché in Paris, a cushy posting if ever there was one. Or he could take the top attaché job for all of East Africa, based in Addis Ababa, Ethiopia, with responsibility for Somalia, Kenya, Sudan, Uganda, Tanganyika, and Zanzibar (today's Tanzania). As usual, Werner chose the hotspot, the tip of the spear, the Horn of Africa.

The top job and the chance to fly almost continually, in some of the world's most primitive and dangerous airstrips and diplomatic postings, was an easy choice for Werner. He'd rather fly in and out of the desert, mountains, and bush—across 2 million square miles of land, nearly 60 percent of the size of the continental United States—than sip champagne in Parisian embassies and diplomatic salons with bureaucrats and desk jockeys. Africa offered more far more danger, adventure, independence, and opportunity for flying and espionage for the now thirty-six-year-old lieutenant colonel.

Flying over the rainbow of deserts, savannahs, highlands, and mountains of East Africa was an almost religious experience for Werner. Far from an organized military command structure, he felt free, and the wonders of the lands and animal herds he saw below filled him with a quiet grace. The majestic African dawn reminded him how grateful he was to have come home from the war not only intact but sane. He crossed numerous torrents that swept too many others away in death or insanity, but somehow he'd always found a firm stepping stone.

Yet Werner knew that "a great evil" remained loose in the world. He'd seen it, and at some level he knew he had contributed to it. How can the Almighty, he wondered, who created all this beauty, allow his children to slaughter one another by the millions? For what, he couldn't say. He knew his life had been a solitary one and was comforted by his family. He thought about his crew, his "kids," and especially about Jack. Were they doing well and living good lives in the knowledge that their numerous prayers during combat were indeed answered? Did they appreciate that they were given a second chance at life after a new baptism by fire? He was filled with pride that every soul he ever took aloft during training, and war, had survived. He knew he could not have done it without his Creator, the Boeing Corporation, and Jack.

The vast expanses of Africa he saw from the air reminded Werner of the Almighty's grand design, and he realized that he had been protected, for some reason, all his life. Yet even as he winged peacefully across the brilliant African skies, he knew it was an illusion. Bad things were happening in Africa. Evil was at work there and gaining a terrible momentum. Portions of Africa slid into postcolonial boiling cauldrons of ethnic slaughter.

By the time Werner took up his African post in 1962, independence movements were gaining momentum as the European colonial powers, bankrupt after two world wars, shed themselves of expensive and messy colonies on a wholesale basis. Virtually the entire continent was up for grabs. The Soviet Union, Cuba, and the Warsaw Pact allies were eager to fill the power vacuum and lucrative arms markets left behind by Western Europeans, and began to smuggle weapons and Marxist "technical advisers" into the region, undermining fragile independent states that were emerging from a century or more of colonialism. When a country gained independence, it was financially pressured to align with one of the two superpowers. Many countries in northern Africa received Soviet military aid, while many in central and southern Africa got aid from the World Bank—that is, from the United States. Africa was a hotbed of espionage, intrigue, and proxy wars between the superpowers at the very pinnacle of Cold War madness: 1962 to 1964.

During the Cold War, Africa experienced more than seventy coups and thirteen presidential assassinations. Border and natural resource disputes were frequent and the colonial borders were contested through brutal, ethnically fueled armed conflicts, including genocide and famine, which continue in the twenty-first century. The wholesale chaos and slaughter, however, first arrived more than a century earlier with European colonialists, whose governments were all monarchies or empires except France.

42
REICHSKOMMISSAR GÖRING

Werner was not the first person in his family to serve in an African diplomatic post. In the late 1800s, Hermann's father, Heinrich Ernst Göring, played a major role in German Africa. He was appointed second Reichskommissar of German South West Africa, today's Namibia, in 1885, by the "iron chancellor" Otto von Bismarck. The first chancellor of the newly amalgamated German Empire proclaimed that the immense swath of territory from the Orange River in the south to the Kunene River in the north was German soil. The 319,000-square-mile territory was more than twice the size of Mother Germany.

Germany, although somewhat late in the game, joined the British, French, Belgian, Spanish, Portuguese, Dutch, and Italian colonialists in the great African land grab that began in the seventeenth century. By the end of the nineteenth century, German colonial possession in Africa included Togoland, now the nation of Togo, Cameroon, German East Africa, which included parts of Burundi, Rwanda, Tanganyika, and German Southwest Africa, today's Namibia. The land seized by Germany was home to two indigenous tribes, the Herero and the Nama, and both resisted colonization. In 1893, the commander of German colonial troops, Curt von François, concluded that "nothing but relentless severity will lead to success." The Germans unleashed forced subjugation and approved an attack by François on a remote Nama village, quaintly named Hornkranz by the Germans. The raiders killed ninety men, women, and children.

By 1904, the policies initiated by Göring had metastasized into an ugly, all-out colonial war. The Herero revolted and slaughtered German colonialists and farmers, although showing restraint, which the Germans had not, largely sparing white women and children. German officials "opted for ruthlessness without restraint . . . and soon began 'indiscriminate killing of the wounded, male prisoners, women and children.' Herero casualties quickly reached 5,000 killed and 20,000 wounded."

The war escalated in savagery, with German troops seizing watering holes and forcing 50,000 African men, women, and children into a barren desert. On October 2, 1904, General Lothar von Trotha issued an extermination order, and the officially sanctioned genocide ensued. Native prisoners were deported to German-occupied zones, used as slave labor, and died like flies. The rest were swept into concentration camps.

Lt. Fred C. Cornell, OBE, a British officer and diamond prospector, found himself in Luderitz in German South West Africa in the first decade of the twentieth century, and there he witnessed the brutal conditions on Shark Island, the century's first concentration camp, which had been established on a barren, windswept granite island by the German colonial administration. Cornell recorded the conditions on the tiny, wind-scoured South Atlantic outcrop. "Cold—for the nights are often bitterly cold there—hunger, thirst, exposure, disease, and madness claimed scores of victims every day, and cart loads of their bodies were every day carted over to the back beach, buried in a few inches of sand at low tide, and as the tide came in the bodies went out, food for the sharks."

In 1905 the German language adopted the word *Konzentrationslager* from German South West Africa, "where [Heinrich] Göring's colleagues carried out medical experiments on the Herero in the interests of racial research." As historian Norman Davies observed, "His son Hermann was to introduce similar practices into Germany thirty years later."

Also, the concepts of legally institutionalized racism and ethnic cleansing and even the terms *Lebensraum* (room for living), *Endlösung* (final solution), and *Lebensunwerte Leben* (lives unworthy of life) emerged from Germany's dark experiments in the "Dark Continent," the pejorative name of the unknown and underexplored region of the world coined by eighteenth-century European colonialists. The extermination of the Herero "proved to be the opening genocide of the twentieth century . . . totaling 125,000 people . . . at a cost of 676 German dead, 907 wounded, and 97 missing."

In Germany, the study of racial "sciences" emerged with Africa as its first laboratory. In 1912, a study of the racial anatomy of 17 Hottentot heads was published in a German morphology and anthropology journal. Dr. Eugen Fischer, later a Nazi racial theorist, was invited to German South West Africa, as an anthropologist and geneticist from the University in Freiburg in Germany, to elaborate upon the science of racial superiority and warned the colonists against the "dangers of race mixing." In 1921, Fischer coauthored, with Edwin Bauer and Fritz Lentz, a book entitled *Human Hereditary Teaching and Racial Hygiene,* in which he claimed that the Herero were "animals." Fischer had numerous international supporters. "Socially beneficial" eugenic selection and sterilization was practiced in numerous countries, including the United States, during the early twentieth century.

The Germans were ousted from all of Africa by the British at the end of WWI, but their ill treatment of Africans was later mimicked by the Nazis in the racial persecution of the *Untermenschen:* Jews, Slavs, Gypsies, and other so-called inferior races.

The fact that Hermann Göring grew up in an environment heavily influenced by his father's "heroic" achievements in German West Africa can not be underestimated. "Yet it was Göring's father's experience in the colony that most likely predisposed Hermann Göring toward colonialism and empire building."

Nazi concentration camps, including Dachau, were initially ordered opened by Göring when he became the first head of the Gestapo. The Gestapo was subsequently taken over by SS chief Heinrich Himmler, in 1934. Nevertheless, Göring not only oversaw the early establishment of the Nazi camps but was a driving force in transforming fuzzy Nazi racial philosophy into genocidal reality, on a scale previously unknown to humanity. Hitler was said to have studied Fischer's book while in Landsberg Prison after the failed beer hall putsch of 1923. Once in power, Hitler appointed Dr. Fischer rector of the Friedrich Wilhelm University in Berlin, where one of his brightest medical students was Josef Mengele, the notorious and never-captured war criminal who conducted unspeakable medical experiments in Auschwitz.

Göring told Nuremberg interrogators and psychiatrists that "the position of my father as first Governor of Southwest Africa" was one of the key "points which are significant with relation to my later development." As he prepared to die for his crimes, Göring stared at an old photo of his father in the uniform of the German South West African Reichskommissar on his flimsy prison desk. Other than a hidden cyanide capsule, it was his greatest and last treasure.

43

ADDIS ABABA

In 1962, Werner decided that he'd take his family along for the two-year posting. So he and June packed up their two-bedroom ranch-style home in Tucson and moved to Addis Ababa with their two children, eleven-year-old Scott and fourteen-year-old Carlinda. The move from a 1950s Arizona suburban home to one of the poorest nations on earth could not have been more of a shock. On his first day in Addis Ababa, Scott witnessed a man hanged in a public square. Flies, spiders, and parasitic insects abounded, and eventually the whole family contracted malaria and dysentery. But it was not all bad: their new home was an elegant villa, complete with five servants. Werner had a huge official USAF staff car, complete with chauffer and an American flag mounted on the grill. More important, he had a "personal" C-47 Dakota Skytrain, a very hardy military transport aircraft that was developed from the Douglas DC-3 airliner. It was a medium-sized twin-engine plane used extensively during WWII, particularly in the Pacific campaign, on the remote, rough airstrips of Guadalcanal, New Guinea, and Burma. The Dakota's main claim to fame was for flying "the hump" over the Himalayas from Burma and India to supply Chinese troops fighting the Japanese. C-47s were used for ferrying soldiers back from the Pacific theater to the United States and later were widely used during the Berlin airlift, earning its reputation as a reliable, can-do transport plane.

Werner's Skytrain was outfitted by the CIA with the latest photographic and communications equipment so he could record and photograph Communist shipping and monitor communications in the coastal regions surrounding the vital Horn of Africa. The plane, which accommodated twenty-five passengers, was the primary lifeline to civilization for American ambassadors, soldiers, spies, consular officials, and sick or injured Americans in the enormous region. In Africa, Werner flew nonstop since he addressed the needs for food, medicine, ammunition, and weapons between the various U.S. embassies, missions, and consular offices and associated military units in the huge, godforsaken region.

Mogadishu, Khartoum, Kampala, and Nairobi were regular stops, as were remote desert and jungle airstrips when needed. The government gave Werner a $5,000 monthly no-questions-asked slush fund for whatever local bureaucratic wheels needed greasing or special permits needed buying in the graft-ridden and poverty-stricken region. When cholera broke out in Mogadishu, Werner repeatedly flew in medical teams. The outbreak coincided with flooding, and Werner recalled having "to land on runways that looked like lakes. I had no real idea how deep the water covering the runway was." After landing, as the medical team unloaded supplies, Werner saw "a mass of desperate, sick, and starving Africans rushing the plane." He barely managed to take off, saving the plane from ruin, and then repeated the dangerous exercise several times over the coming days. He was constantly on the lookout for mobs, bandits, and hijackers, who, like today, were epidemic in the region and wouldn't think twice about seizing Werner and everything he carried in the Dakota, especially weapons, medicine, and money. He became expert in dangerous landings with a very low approach, taxiing to a point as far from the "airport" as possible, unloading immediately as he kept the engines running, and then taking off over the heads of howling, onrushing mobs.

44

THE LION OF JUDAH

In his official capacity, Werner was befriended by the last emperor of a dynasty that traced its direct origins to the thirteenth century and, by tradition, back to King Solomon and the Queen of Sheba in biblical times: his royal highness Emperor Haile Selassie I, the Conquering Lion of the Tribe of Judah, the King of Kings, and the Elect of God. On October 14, 1954, Queen Elizabeth II made the emperor a Stranger Knight of the Order of the Garter, making Selassie "the first, and to date only, member of The Order from Africa." Becoming the 914th member of the order, which was founded in 1348, was a rare distinction, personally chosen by the sovereign of the United Kingdom, and was the pinnacle of the honors system as the most senior British order of chivalry. In 2008, the queen's grandson and heir presumptive, Prince William, became the 1,000th member of the ancient order.

At the League of Nations in 1936, the diminutive emperor famously humiliated Mussolini by publicly condemning Italy's use of chemical weapons and airpower against his primitive army. After the brutal Italian occupation of Ethiopia, Selassie spent five years in a fourteen-room Georgian manor, Fairfield House, which he purchased in Bath, England. Following the war, he returned home after donating the estate to the city of Bath as a residence for the elderly, which it remains to this day. He led Ethiopia into the United Nations as a founding member, as he had done with the League of Nations. Selassie, a Christian, was revered as Jesus incarnate among the Jamaican-born Rastafarian movement. Werner was a favored guest at the emperor's various palaces and was given special permission to hunt on the emperor's royal hunting preserves. In a photo from the period, Werner is shown in full-dress black-tie uniform with gold braid, playing with a full-grown pet royal cheetah on a leash.

Like Göring, former Reich master of forestry and game, Werner was an avid and skilled big-game hunter and often led remote, dangerous safaris. The Awash River, where the human species is thought to have arisen, was only charted in 1933, when a British explorer and travel writer, Sir Wilfred Patrick Thesiger, traced the course of the Awash to the Aussa oasis near Eritrea and Djibouti.

During one safari, Werner trekked with a companion, USAF crew chief Sergeant Landis, as well as two U.S. embassy staff from Cairo and several royal porters and guides, into the remote Awash river basin. The 1,200-kilometer-long Awash River, one of the longest in Ethiopia, was nearly 200 feet wide during the dry season. In the rainy season, the river rose 60 feet above its low-water mark and inundated plains along its banks for thousands of square miles, both giving and taking life.

Werner reveled in the desolate, unique paradise and tracked oryx, antelopes with long, straight horns; Soemmerring's gazelle; wild pig; and waterbuck, reddish brown antelopes that weighed up to 530 pounds and stood four and a half feet tall at the shoulder. He watched them watering in the late afternoon and spotted the unique white bib under their throats and the white ring surrounding their tails, like a Lucky Strike bull's-eye on their butts. He knew the feeling. One morning, he took down a charging wild boar with a single clean shot through the animal's shoulder and heart. In T-shirt and jeans, Werner sat atop the beast and posed holding his gun as Landis snapped a trophy photo—good bush meat that the porters cleaned and dressed for dinner.

Moving on, Werner saw a tiny dik-dik antelope and watched zebra graze while cheetah, serval—a medium-sized African wildcat—and leopards crouched in the dappled grass targeting young, old, or infirmed who strayed from the herd. It reminded Werner of a bomber out of formation. He heard the eerie howls of baboons and spotted kudus with their distinctive and devilish curlicued horns, like giant drill bits. There were also giant tortoises; hippos; reedbuck; aardvark; and caracal, the desert lynx; as well as Klipspringer, or "rock jumper," small African antelope, at higher altitudes. Scurrying around on the rocky ground were the curiously brave or foolish hyrax, a small, thickset herbivore. In the gorge's bottom he spotted the elegant black and white colobus monkey with its trademark white beard.

The Awash river basin was home to more than 400 species of birds, including great ostriches, the secretary bird, and the Abyssinian ground hornbill. He saw flashes of bright pink carmine bee-eaters and turquoise and purple Abyssinian rollers. In this unique paradise he found birds of the river and of the forest, migratory birds, birds of prey, and birds of the savannah. Their dazzling colored wings flitted across Africa's cloudless, deep blue skies.

Werner carried his cherished European walnut Husqvarna M38 Swedish Mauser, one of the most beautiful bolt-action hunting rifles made. Fording the swollen Awash with Landis and a few other men in a small raft, they pulled themselves across by a rope secured to both banks. Suddenly a tree flowing in the torrent hit the raft and tossed the men into the foaming deluge. An Ethiopian officer who couldn't swim seized Werner from behind. Werner instantly dropped his prized rifle, snagged the rope with one hand, and quickly tried to grab Landis with the other, but to no avail. Landis vanished in an instant. The capsized raft quickly disappeared around a bend. Seconds later, it was as if Landis had never existed. After a stunned silence, monkeys hollered in the distance and birds screeched while native porters on both sides of the river raised the alarm and ran along both sodden riverbanks. The porters were frightened. These American officials were imperial guests. Meanwhile, Werner slowly dragged himself, with the Ethiopian still hanging on to him, up to his chin in foaming water, hand over hand to the far riverbank and then searched for hours for any sign of Landis—but it was hopeless. The crew chief had simply disappeared in the raging, rust-colored African water. His body was recovered days later, far downstream. Werner was devastated, but he knew he did everything he could to save Landis.

The fatality of an active-duty American serviceman was investigated by both local authorities and the U.S. ambassador to Ethiopia, Arthur L. Richards, who, as it happened, was no fan of Werner's.

Before President Eisenhower appointed him to Ethiopia in 1960, Richards had been a career foreign service officer for three decades. He served in Mexico, Iran, Palestine, and South Africa; after WWII, he was the assistant chief of the State Department's British Commonwealth division.

As ambassador, he was the senior American in Ethiopia, and nominally Werner's superior. Richards treated Werner's Dakota like his personal plane and Werner like his personal pilot. But Werner had several other ambassadors, as well as military and intelligence officials, in the region who frequently needed the plane and his services. Often intelligence-related activities were purposefully not reported to the ambassador so he could maintain a tissue of deniability regarding things he'd rather not be "officially" aware of. In any event, Richards demanded the plane on several occasions when Werner was unable to oblige him, including during the cholera outbreak in Somalia when he was ferrying medicine and, as it happened, a German medical unit to the victims. Richards blew his stack each time Werner was unavailable, and the relationship quickly soured. Although he was popular with the emperor, who saw Werner as an honorable man of action, a hunter, and a war hero, and although all witnesses absolved Werner of any blame in Landis's drowning, his situation—serving several masters—was impossible. He had never lost a man in two decades of service, and although he nearly died trying to save the crew chief, he berated himself for Landis's death.

Richards left his post in Addis Ababa soon thereafter and Werner finished his two-year tour fifteen months later, but Richards's reports to Washington ensured that Werner's Ethiopian tour as a diplomatic attaché would be his last. It's likely that Richards's black mark on Werner's record effectively ended any hope Werner had for promotion to full colonel, much less to general, despite his nearly twenty-two years of dedicated and heroic service, two combat tours, and eight years in grade as a lieutenant colonel. Werner was never enough of a politician to navigate his way through the staff and bureaucratic niceties—kissing ass, in other words—that were needed to become a general officer. He was a pilot, plain and simple, and his towering disdain for desk jockeys who never had to put it all on the line was not only palpable; it had become his badge of honor. He had done his best and it was damn good, better than most, for two decades. He never shied away from a dangerous mission; indeed, he sought them out. He wondered if the bloodstain on his family name, which he had tried all his life to wash away, was also a factor in the sudden stall in his military career.

Before leaving Addis Ababa, Werner bade farewell to the emperor, who would suffer an ignominious death as a prisoner in his own palace dungeon under mysterious circumstances eleven years later, in August 1975, after a Soviet-supported coup by the Derg, a rabble of low-ranking officers and enlisted men toppled the throne.

The Cold War proved deadlier to the emperor than did invasion by Italy, a WWII Axis power. The imperial family was imprisoned in the Addis Ababa prison of Kerchele, nicknamed "Alem Bekagne," or "Goodbye, cruel world!" Sixty former imperial officials were executed without trial, including Selassie's grandson and two former prime ministers. Ethiopians today refer to the killings as "Bloody Saturday"; they marked the end of the Solomonic dynasty, which stood, in one form or another, for at least three millennia, from about the tenth century B.C.

Torn by bloody coups, uprisings, widescale drought, and massive refugee problems, the Derg regime was toppled in 1991, the same year its sponsor in mayhem, the USSR, collapsed. Ethiopia was toppled by a coalition of rebel forces called the Ethiopian People's Revolutionary Democratic Front. In 1992, the emperor's bones were found under a concrete slab on the palace grounds. A new constitution was adopted in 1994, and Ethiopia's first multiparty elections were held in 1995. A border war with Eritrea late in the 1990s ended with a peace treaty in 2000. In November 2000, Selassie, honored in death despite some abuses of power during his reign, was disinterred and given an "unofficial" imperial funeral by the Ethiopian Orthodox Church.

Unique among African countries, the ancient Ethiopian monarchy remained free from colonial rule, with the exception of the short-lived Italian occupation from 1936 to 1941. Today, despite crushing poverty, with average per capita income averaging $900 per year, Ethiopia remains the oldest independent country in Africa and one of the oldest in the world.

The Lion of Judah's legacy was largely one of international cooperation, multiculturalism, and religious tolerance in an intolerant, violent region. During his life, the Lion served as an inspiration to, among others, Nelson Mandela, Dr. Martin Luther King Jr., and Malcom X, each of who corresponded with him.

By the 1960s, vast portions of Africa descended into madness, rapine, murder, and genocide. Factional leaders fanned ethnic conflicts and, in many countries, presented themselves as the only "strongmen" who could effectively maintain order. Most of the countries they headed were initially Cold War client states of either the Soviet Union or the United States. Even democratically elected leaders like Robert Mugabe of Zimbabwe have tended to choose life presidencies rather than face their often starving and brutalized citizens again at the polling booth. South Africa's Nelson Mandela is the shining exception to the long, sorry list of African despots, which includes Mengistu Haile Mariam of Ethiopia, who ousted Haile Selassie; Muammar al-Gaddafi of Libya; Idi Amin Dada of Uganda; Siad Barre and Mohamed Farrah Aidid of Somalia; Omar Al Bashir of Sudan; Joseph Désiré Mobutu of Zaire; Isaias Afewerki of Eritrea; Jean-Bédel Bokassa of the Central African Republic (who adopted the title of "Emperor" after a $30 million coronation ceremony); Hissène Habré of Chad; Sékou Touré of Guinea; and most recently Hosni Mubarak of Egypt. These men, among many others, looted billions and cumulatively killed millions as the race for Africa's riches accelerated in the postcolonial Cold War era. Slaughter, official looting, and famine continue largely unabated today in portions of the continent from which humanity first emerged on the long road toward enlightenment.

45

WHIZ KIDS AND CIVILIAN LIFE

After his tour in Africa, Werner was assigned to a desk job in the Pentagon just as Secretary of Defense Robert McNamara's "whiz kids" were ginning up the rationale for the escalation in Vietnam. "We played war games," he said. "It was a damn farce with these civilians developing military tactics, as well as strategy." Despite his sterling record, he lacked the political drive and skill to make his way up the career military ladder in peacetime. He was viewed as an outspoken relic with no real power base in the Pentagon. And he hated staff work. At forty-four, stalled in rank and no longer an active pilot, Werner had seen enough. In 1964, after twenty-two years of active service, he retired as a lieutenant colonel to Tucson, Arizona, never achieving the high rank he had dreamed of as a teenager.

The day after his retirement he threw out his many medals and citations and burned his uniforms and service records. In the following years, he attended one, and only one, SAC reunion. He very rarely attended Eighth Air Force or 303rd Bomb Group reunions, as Jack did religiously. For Werner, the military was the past; and in civilian life he never referred to himself as "Colonel." He was simply Mr. Werner G. Goering. "I thought that using the title was unfair to my business competitors, who for no fault of their own hadn't been able to serve," he said.

Although he never experienced the acute disturbances that Jack did in the immediate postwar years, Werner carried difficult memories from the war. The thoughts and images that troubled him most were the bombing raids that set aflame civilian areas of Dresden and Cologne, where his own grandmother was still living during the war.

He returned to Tucson, earned his real estate license, and started a highly successful career as a Realtor and speculator in the booming southern Arizona land market. He sold the largest ranch in the state and purchased cotton futures. He invested in cattle ranches and subdivided lots on Tucson's Old Mission Trail. He managed a 78,000-acre ranch for the Imperial Valley Cattle Company, and "it all took off like gangbusters."

By the 1970s, Werner and June were definitively well-to-do. They built a home on a hilltop in Tucson's most expensive zip code. He devoted the next two decades to charitable works and Christian philanthropy, often as not anonymously. He rejected his Mormon upbringing and became a fundamentalist Christian. He got burned for $120,000 in a Ponzi scheme sponsored by a crooked preacher but continues giving money to far-flung Christian missionaries to this day

46

JACK'S POSTWAR YEARS

In war, neuroses [and] psychosomatic untitled troubles are
frequent. The normal visceral concomitants of intense emotion are universal. Men are afraid and can't eat; they vomit,
or suffer from diarrhea, rapid heart rate or breathlessness, or
from all of these symptoms at the same time. It is when
these are prolonged and intensified, without full conscious
expression of the basic feeling, that the pathological psychosomatic syndromes develop.

—from WWII Army Air Force medical journal

From January 1 to May 1, 1945, Jack was either in military hospitals or on
recuperative leave. When he arrived back in the States after his bombing
tour, "Jack looked like death," recalled his sister, Gladys. He never told
anyone outside his family about the seriousness of his "gastrointestinal
neuroses," as it was called at the time by the military, and wanted to continue to fly. On August 1, 1945, he was ferrying a new plane from Seattle's Boeing plant to Love Field in Dallas when the shooting pains in his
stomach suddenly reappeared. The next day, he was admitted to a hospital for more surgery and remained in bed until late September. Upon
release, he resumed duties as a ferry pilot, shuttling bombers and fighters, including his beloved P-51 Mustang, around the United States. Jack's
sister, Gladys, who married one of Jack's fellow bomber commanders,

Roger Ashton, recalled that Jack would fly the Mustang under bridges regularly, and once even buzzed the Ashton family home in Oregon.

No longer worried about the fate of others, Jack demonstrated his love of flying and gambling, as well as his nerve and skill. One day, on a bet, "I flew the Mustang through an open airplane hangar upside down, ten feet off the ground at 200 miles per hour." Reprimanded and fined, an unchastened, grinning Jack more than covered the fine by collecting the bet from the astounded ground crew. He always regretted never having been a fighter pilot in combat, but he proved to all that he could indeed thread a needle with a plane. Werner doubts the veracity of this account.

During yet another hospitalization, in San Antonio, Jack met Louise Schlotterbeck, a German American dietician who tended to Jack's delicate gastric system, as well as his heart. They married on October 10, 1947, and over the years had three sons and five grandchildren. They started married life with a huge financial stake, thanks to Jack's skill at cards. He had been so good at poker that by the end of the war he returned home with $32,000 in cash duct-taped to his body. In today's dollars the money was worth at least ten times that amount. The poverty-stricken homeless youth who joined the army for the free clothes and food eventually went home a very ill but quite rich officer and gentleman.

When Jack ferried new planes from Boeing's Seattle plant to Dallas, he repeatedly flew over Idaho and fell in love the state's majestic scenery; he and his family settled in Boise in 1948. In the following years, Jack opened an aircraft refurbishment and machine shop, peddled vacuum cleaners door-to-door, and sold real estate. The constant change wasn't driven by economic need—Jack did well in each job—but by a restlessness that harkened back to his succession of jobs before the war and stemmed partly from his experiences in it. About once every decade, as snowbirds, Jack and Louise visited Werner and June in Arizona. They always met for a quiet dinner and never discussed the war.

In 1968, Jack founded a small industrial cleaning products company called Technichem in Boise, Idaho. He remained vice president of sales until 2010, and his son Brian runs the company today. In 1999, fate struck Jack a cruel triple blow. His eldest son, Jack Q. Rencher, died of cancer in his early fifties. Weeks later, Louise was admitted to the same Boise hospital where Jack Jr. had died, diagnosed with cancer herself; within weeks,

Jack suffered a heart attack and was admitted to the hospital where Louise lay dying. Jack underwent heart surgery and his first request—his first demand—in the recovery room was to see Louise. Against all hospital protocol, Jack was wheeled on a gurney from the recovery room to Louise's room on another floor and held her hand as she died.

By 2005, as an eighty-five-year-old widower, Jack began to tell a few people, including Idaho-based educator, history buff, and writer Rob Morris, author of *Untold Valor: Forgotten Stories of American Bomber Crews over Europe in WWII,* about his amazing war experiences. Chapter 9, "Goering Bombs Germany," reveals that Werner Goering was the nephew of Reich Marshal Hermann Göring. Morris cites an interview with Jack in which he stated that the FBI had "recruited [Jack Rencher] to watch . . . and kill [Werner Goering], should he turn out to be a traitor or a spy." Jack later said that at eighty-five, with Louise gone, he figured he was too old for the FBI to come after him, and he didn't want to carry the secret to his grave. He expected his comments would make their way to Werner and trigger a conversation between the two of them. But Werner, who once spoke briefly with Morris on the phone, never saw the book. He never owned a computer and never visited the 303rd Bomb Group's Web site. And he continued to avoid any discussion of the war when he talked to Jack on the phone, less and less frequently as the years passed and age set in. Every now and again a curious historian or reporter would call Werner, but he ignored them, usually in a huff. His own children often asked him about the war and he always changed the subject.

By 2009, the two men had not seen each other in the decade since Jack's wife, Louise, died at age seventy-six, and as fate would have it, they never saw each other again. I met them both during the summer of that year.

47

2009

After getting Jack's phone number from Gary Moncur, the 303rd Bomb Group's historian, I called Jack in Boise and had the first of many personal and telephone conversations with him, thanks to the assistance of his son Brian. The flak shell from the Merseburg raid permanently damaged Jack's hearing, and even with hearing aids he needed to have someone repeat what had just been said to him. His mental faculties remained sharp, however, and in retirement he amused himself very successfully playing the stock market.

Eager to probe beyond his vague statements in *Untold Valor,* I asked Jack point-blank if the FBI had given him kill orders for Werner. The question echoed back at me as Brian repeated it into his father's ear. After a moment's silence Jack said loud and clear, "They told me to shoot Werner in the head if we were going down over Nazi territory." I decided then and there to visit both men.

As our conversation continued, Jack revealed that he had kept in touch with Werner and felt a special bond with him. "I was always a loner, still am," Jack said. "The only male friend I've ever had was out of that war, and that's Werner."

"In that case," I asked, "how did Werner react when you told him about your FBI orders?"

"I never did tell him, or even thank him for getting me home alive," Jack said. "But he deserves to know."

When the two men met now and then over the years for dinner with their wives, or when they spoke on the phone every few months,

Werner never wanted to talk about the war. That made it difficult for Jack to disclose an oppressive secret, especially since the dynamic between them remained very much that of pilot in command and copilot, respectively. Sometimes, Jack said, he figured Werner must have guessed the secret during the war or after. There was always scuttlebutt about Werner and "Uncle Hermann" during their training and combat tour. At the very least, Werner knew that many people questioned his loyalty, and he must have suspected that the authorities were keeping an eye on him. When I later spoke to crew member Gus Gustafson, he told me much the same thing.

Werner said he refused to meet or talk substantively to Rob Morris for *Untold Valor,* and over the years he has given other writers and reporters the cold shoulder or, in the case of pushy ones, a hot blast. He stonewalled me after I contacted his son, Scott, a Tucson defense attorney. Following two months of telephoning and emailing Scott to ask for a little of his father's time, he got Werner to take my call. Hearing that I had spoken to Jack and wanted to fly to Arizona to meet him, Werner said icily, "Send me some of your published material."

A few weeks later I called again. Werner agreed to a meeting but warned, "You're wasting your time and money. I didn't do anything a lot of other men didn't do, and I left the war behind me a long time ago."

48

TUCSON

It was blazing hot the first week in July 2009. Tucson's dead season. I stepped out of my hotel at 8:35 A.M. and walked toward my hideous maroon rental, the kind of low-end model shaped like a sneaker. It felt like 120 degrees inside that car. I loosened my tie and stuck the suction cup mount of my Magellan GPS to the windshield. By the time the tiny Chevy began to ascend the Catalina foothills of Tucson, its engine and air conditioner both whining, I was sweaty but making good time. At the behest of my robotic female guide, I turned right after 500 feet, and a steel gate manned by a security guard came into view. All visitors must be announced.

The private road took me up the hillside past several recently built, hacienda-style houses whose vast size declared their owners' importance to passersby. Without the alert from my GPS locator, I might have missed Werner's driveway. On an expansive lot at the top of the hill, a modest, single-story ranch-style house sat discreetly back from the road, obscured by mature plantings.

Werner's diminutive wife, June, greeted me at the door with a smile, showed me into a simply furnished living room, and invited me to sit down. "Werner's working in the backyard," she said. "I'll just go and fetch him."

As I stood waiting, my eyes darted to the large picture window's spectacular view of the valley below, the portrait of Jesus over a brick fireplace, Meissen porcelain figurines on the fireplace mantle, Black Forest carvings on the wall, and 1970s furniture so clean and neat it might have come that morning from a retro-chic store in Tucson's hippest shopping district. Hip young homeowners don't put lace doilies on their coffee tables, however.

I heard the back door open and close, firm footsteps on a linoleum floor, and the sound of hands being washed and dried. A few seconds later, a tall, muscular man strode into the room, head up, shoulders back, and looking decades younger than his eighty-five years. He stretched out his right hand and fastened mine in a powerful grip.

The bigger shock to my composure, however, was my host's face. A good face, lined I could now see by age and exposure to the harsh sun of the Southwest, but with strong, regular features, a friendly, tooth-filled smile, bright clear eyes—and an uncanny resemblance to the young Hermann Göring.

A devout fundamentalist Christian, Werner does not own a computer and has attended military reunions very rarely. Although Werner and June could live quite lavishly, thanks to his successful real estate investments, they have kept the same simple house with its immaculately maintained original appliances and furnishings, since they built it in 1971. Instead they give significant sums to various Christian charities.

My first sight of Werner convinced me I wasn't wasting my time. A lifelong teetotaler and nonsmoker and always physically active, Werner hardly resembled the morphine-addicted Göring who indulged wantonly in every luxury and grew grotesquely fat during the Nazis' reign over Germany. Werner works out daily with weights in a small gym he has in his toolshed. Yet when I looked at him, I saw an image of the young Göring, the dashing WWI fighter pilot, in my mind's eye.

As a young man himself, the tall, blond, blue-eyed Werner was movie-star handsome and looked like he could have stepped out of a Nazi recruiting poster. He cut the sort of figure that Marlon Brando did, with his hair dyed blond, in *The Young Lions,* playing a heroic German officer who comes to hate what the Nazis have done to his country.

Before Werner even released my hand, he underlined the importance of the portrait of Jesus over his fireplace by saying that God played the leading role in his life. Unsure how to respond, I said I hoped the Almighty would guide our conversations.

"Excellent idea," Werner said. He called to the kitchen, "June, come back in here." At his direction, the three of us held hands in a circle, and I prayed aloud, ad-libbing for "divine guidance in our quest for the truth."

For the next four days, Werner and I sat and talked about the war, family, and life from midmorning to evening. June was always within earshot, a cheerful, birdlike presence flitting in regularly to check on us and refill our glasses with lemonade and calling us into the kitchen for ham and cheese sandwiches promptly at 12:30 P.M. It was obvious that Werner was the center of her universe, and that he could not get along without her. When they graciously let me take their picture together, Werner stooped down to bring his head closer to hers. Their mutual affection shone in their happy eyes and smiles.

Toward the end of the second day, I asked to see any documents or photos related to his father, Karl, and his uncle Hermann. "Hey, June!" Werner sang out, as if she were a hundred yards away rather than in the next room. "Where's that scrapbook?" A few minutes later June brought in a photo album. Werner quickly flipped to a small passport photograph of his father, whom he described affectionately as "quite corpulent." Then he walked over to the couch against the wall and reached behind it. He lifted something up, and turned around to show me a two-by-three-foot framed portrait photograph of Reich Marshal Hermann Göring wearing a Luftwaffe uniform with his WWI medals, the Iron Cross and the Blue Max, and carrying his marshal's baton.

"I haven't shown this to many people," Werner said ruefully. "We keep Uncle Hermann hidden, especially when we have Jewish friends over."

The portrait dated from relatively early in WWII, before Göring's dissipation told on him, and Werner's facial resemblance to him was striking. Before he secreted the portrait back behind the couch, Werner allowed me to take a photograph of him holding it. But as he stood there, shoulder to shoulder with the image of the Reich Marshal, there was no trace of a smile on his face. Instead there was a mixture of embarrassment, shame, wounded pride, and anger.

It was like a knife twisted in Werner. He began to wish me a good trip home to Rhode Island, but I said, "I have something to share with you, too." I took *Untold Valor* out of my briefcase and asked if he'd ever seen it. He hadn't.

"Chapter nine is about you, Werner. It's titled, 'Goering Bombs Germany.'"

Voice quavering, I read the brief chapter aloud. When I finished, Werner was leaning back in his chair with his arms folded loosely. He seemed a little bewildered. "Well, Stephen," he said, "that's an interesting story."

"There's more," I said. And then I explained how less than twenty-four hours before their first meeting, Jack had accepted the FBI's contingent orders to kill him.

Werner stared at me as if I had two heads. Finally he said calmly, "That doesn't surprise me. It makes sense." He looked down at his hands and thought some more. "Jack said this?" he asked, not making eye contact. "You're sure Jack said this?"

"Yes, I'm sure."

Werner's initial calm bespoke his commander's instinct to remain cool under fire. But his questions about Jack signaled that he could not immediately accept what I was telling him. Over the next two days he betrayed little outward distress, but the set of his jaw and the look in his eye as he lapsed into long silences showed that he was going through a gamut of emotions.

On my last afternoon in Tucson, Werner signed and mailed the FBI's Freedom of Information Act request form I'd printed out for him. When his older brother, Karl Jr., and he entered the U.S. military, they learned from family friends of investigations into their loyalty. Through all the years since then, Werner had never cared to learn what was in his file. Now he wanted to know exactly what it said. I flew to Boise to meet Jack.

Months later, when we did receive a response to the request, the government released only Werner's "Army-originated records." Werner's FBI file, and perhaps other documents, remain classified on the grounds that "release of some of the information would result in an unwarranted invasion of the privacy rights of the individual concerned." An appeal of the decision made directly to the secretary of the army was ignored, a circumstance that itself constitutes indirect proof of the contingent kill order against Werner.

After weeks on the road, I returned home with nearly forty hours of audiotape. I ordered dozens of books. Göring biographies and related nonfiction works trickled in over the next month. I began to look closely at the books.

Comparing my notes and dates from my conversations with Werner, I couldn't match the Karl Goering that Werner described to the Karl Goering documented as the Reich Marshal's elder brother. Werner had made reference to his father's correspondence with Göring in the 1930s but said his father's attitude toward the Nazis changed after 1939. "After they invaded Poland, that ripped it for him," Werner said, referring to Hitler's repudiation of the Munich agreement. "He and Uncle Hermann never communicated again."

Werner gave me no reason to doubt that I was in fact speaking to Göring's nephew, but I needed to confirm all the facts regarding his relationship, and as I continued my research I discovered discrepancies.

Werner said his father, Karl Frederich Goering, was born in 1875 and immigrated to the United States after WWI. According to published sources, Hermann Göring's father, Heinrich Ernst Göring, a German diplomat who was a favorite of the great Bismarck, had four children by his first wife and five children by his second wife, including Hermann, born in 1893.

One of the children from the first marriage was Heinrich Karl, born in 1879, and one from the second marriage was Karl Ernst, born in Africa in 1885. There were three Karls, all about the same age, yet none of their birthdates matched. My first thought was that the Mormon Church, Karl Goering's employer for decades and the holder of a vast repository of European genealogical information, could clear things up. The church informed me that it could not legally release Karl's personnel records, but a church archivist recommended a German researcher I could hire to confirm the birth dates, places, and names in German public records.

The researcher reported that Werner's father, Karl Frederich Goering, had indeed been born in 1875. There was no mistake there. Equally important, Karl hailed from Thuringia, Germany, whereas the Heinrich Karl Goering with a birth date of 1879 had been born in Metz, near the German-French border. There was also no mistake about the third Karl; he had been born in 1885 in German South West Africa, today's Namibia, when his father was colonial governor.

Revisiting biographies of Hermann Göring, I read that he attended the funeral of his first wife in Sweden in 1931 with his brother Karl, who died the next year in Germany. This was long after Werner's father came to the United States and settled in Salt Lake City.

Convinced Werner's resemblance to the Reich Marshal surely had some genetic basis, given Werner's own belief and his family's oral history, I searched for older blood ties, perhaps in the 1800s or even earlier. Were Karl and Hermann half-brothers or second cousins? I had no idea, but by then I knew for a fact they were not brothers, which also meant Werner was not a nephew of "Uncle Hermann," despite what he thought and the remarkable resemblance he bore to the young Göring.

In 2010, in commemoration of the sixty-fifth anniversary of the end of WWII, Jack was featured in a photograph crisply saluting the flag on the cover of the Memorial Day edition of *The Idaho Statesman*. He was planning to meet Werner and me at the Eighth Air Force's July 21, 2010, reunion celebrating the anniversary. Arrangements are made with a film company to record the event, and special permission was granted by the air force for the aging comrades-in-arms to visit a pristine B-17 on display at Pima Air Force Base in Tucson.

Just before leaving for Arizona, Jack's body and mind finally betrayed him and he was unable to go. I got the call from his son, Brian, the day before I was to fly to Tucson. Werner, saddened and disappointed, started making plans for us to visit Jack in Boise instead. But in early August Jack underwent kidney stone surgery in a Boise hospital; he waited for ten hours, in agony, for a urologist to show up late on a Saturday afternoon. Kidney stones had plagued Jack since his intestinal surgeries during the war, and his family believes that the complications from the kidney stone surgery can be traced directly to his war injuries. The emergency surgery was unsuccessful in removing the stone, and a temporary stent was implanted so he could pass water around it.

For two weeks, Jack, on heavy morphine, thought he was back at Molesworth. He repeatedly asked Brian if the plane was ready for take-off.

"Yeah, Dad. It's all set to go."

Jack died in his sleep in a Boise nursing home at four o'clock in the morning on August 20, 2010. The next day, the author offered to *The Idaho Statesman* a complimentary feature about Jack's life, with photos and research obtained during the preparation of this book. They declined. The family paid the paper $480 for a black-bordered box on the obituary page instead. After Jack died, Brian went to Jack's house and found eighty-eight various firearms: pistols, rifles, and shotguns, including a pistol formerly owned by bank robber Breezy Cox.

Each weapon was fully loaded. Some habits never died.

49

"THE DEVIL'S COUNT"
IS RESURRECTED

A few days after Jack's death, the second genealogical study I had requested finally arrived from the Mormon Church. Mrs. Baerbel Johnson,
a German specialist with the Mormon Church's Family Research Library,
traced primary European sources for Werner's family back to 1601, including parish birth, wedding, and death records.

My eyes flew over the pages, at last arriving at her final conclusions:

1. This [Werner's] family resided in Heytersbach (aka Heiters-
   bach) in Goldlauter parish, Thueringen, from at least 1600
   to the 1850s.
2. In today's Germany there are over 1700 Gering/Göring
   families; most of them not related to any [of the] others.
3. The surname Gering/Göring is a patronymic name form
   related to the given name Ger/Gerd/Gers, etc. As such, it
   shows up as a surname in areas where the given name Ger
   in its various forms was used.
4. *A filial relationship between Werner Goering of Salt Lake City
   and Hermann Göring . . . is highly unlikely.* [Italics added]

While Werner's grandfather and Hermann's father were both indeed
named Heinrich Ernst Göring, and lived at about the same time, the two
were totally unrelated. Dumbstruck, I immediately called Werner and
told him that he shared neither blood nor shame with Hermann Göring.

His response was calm, muted, and, I believe, profoundly grateful. The father's exaggerations had been uncovered, and perhaps the truth would wash away a lifetime of shame and opprobrium.

Jack went to his grave not knowing that the best friend he almost shot was a victim of an understandable yet totally mistaken identification by the FBI and the military. The errors about Werner's extended family relationships, accepted and published as fact for a half century, hardly count as the worst of the absurdities and odd chances of life, and especially of war.

Whatever Jack and Werner went through because of mistaken identity, it led not to tragedy but to the great fortune of their lifelong friendship. I hope this book does their story, their honorable service, and their friendship the justice it deserves.

It is certain that the commonly accepted identification of the Utah Karl Goering as Hermann Göring's older brother is mistaken, and numerous history books, Web sites, and military records need correction.

At the bottom of it all are Karl's claims, which represent little more than a struggling immigrant's grasping at a bit of grandeur for himself and his family. This may explain the intensity of Karl's anger at the Nazis after they invaded Poland in 1939 and after they declared war on the United States in 1941. The false glory he'd draped around his family now constituted a social liability, and perhaps worse.

Given the letters that Werner saw as a teenager in the 1930s and given his physical appearance, it seems Karl believed or wanted to believe the Salt Lake City Goerings were indeed distant poor relations of Reich Marshal Göring. But the only things Hermann and Werner had in common were their last name and their high honors and combat medals as pilots. Otherwise, they are as different as angels and demons.

Sometime before his death in 1950, Werner's father typed a thirty-two-page, single-spaced manuscript called "The Devil's Count," a gothic horror story set in the mid-1800s, filled with magic, ghosts, secret treasure, tangled family relationships, and murder.

The manuscript belongs to the Mormon Church. I learned of it while inquiring about the contents of Karl's file in Mormon archives, and after several levels of clearance from Mormon officials, I was given a copyrighted photocopy.

In the novella, nineteenth-century Count Conrad von Felsing of Transylvanian Austro-Hungary has married a widow, Adele (Werner's mother's real name) and adopted her son, Werner, a blond "real German" with every imaginable virtue, as his heir. The fictional Werner is mistakenly thought to have been assassinated in a foreign land, and his brother, Franz, the count's firstborn biological son, a dark-haired scoundrel with every imaginable vice, takes his place.

Franz squanders the family fortune, tries to seduce his brother's fiancée, and searches desperately for a treasure believed buried by his late grandfather, Count Wolf von Felsing. Franz's evil schemes are dashed, and the treasure is found and shared with the poor. Finally, the ghost of Wolf von Felsing appears at the same time as the fictional Werner, who had been declared dead and struggled to return home for years after fighting nobly in the Franco-Prussian war as a highly decorated officer.

The tale reads in part as if Karl knew about the FBI's orders to Jack Rencher. Karl didn't know, of course, but "The Devil's Count" seems the anguished fantasy of a father whose foolishness has endangered his favorite son's life and prospects, a son who does not look like him but like a "real German." In this regard it is surely no coincidence that Wolf was Adolf Hitler's self-chosen code name and that the "devil's count" in the Nazi regime was Hermann Göring, not an aristocrat but the only member of the inner circle with personal connections to the upper reaches of German society.

The fictional count's surname, von Felsing, oddly echoes the name of Dr. von Helsing, the learned scientist determined to defeat the vampire Count Dracula in Bram Stoker's famous novel, suggesting the extent to which Karl continued to have ambivalent feelings about the Nazis.

Two details are particularly telling. The fictional Werner, like the real Hermann Göring, is awarded the *Pour le Mérite* (the Blue Max). Also like Göring, who enjoyed the patronage of the kaiser's eldest son, Crown Prince Wilhelm, the fictional Werner is befriended by an earlier crown prince of Prussia, the future Kaiser Friedrich III.

Although I will avoid chasing after speculative clinical diagnoses, it does seem that Karl's tangled psychology unwittingly influenced his claims about his relationship to Hermann Göring and oddly mirrored the Reich Marshal's own florid megalomania—even shaped Werner's sense of himself. The mistaken belief about his family identity that

Werner has carried throughout his life, first as a point of honor and then as one of shame, is intertwined with the secret knowledge (based on the FBI's same mistaken belief) that Jack likewise carried as a burden of honor and shame for the majority of his life.

Perhaps by virtue of his perceived distant relation to, or because he shared the same last name as, Hermann Göring, a hero of WWI, Karl latched on to a mythical, mystical bond to the fatherland and gained some short-lived recognition in Salt Lake's German community. This proved to be a poisoned chalice that almost cost his younger son's life.

Werner became a knight of the air, risking it all daily, unnecessarily driving himself and his crew to the very brink of hell to exorcize demons that his father had created and that swirled around him for life.

And who was Werner's best pal and ultimate savior? A "hangdog-looking" half-Jewish kid, an assigned assassin who had the power of life and death over Werner, who learned to love him like a brother.

By WWII, Karl was well aware that the FBI had interviewed everybody in town, including the long list of immediate neighbors, employers, and friends documented in the FBI files. He realized his folly and the serious wartime mortal danger he had foolishly placed his favored saintly Germanic warrior son in. Werner was what his father never could become: an aerial warrior and hero.

Tormented by the real possibility of Werner's assassination, he spun a story, "The Devil's Count," in which it seems to have happened. One doesn't have to be a Viennese psychiatrist to figure it out.

The exaggerations of the father took a heavy toll on both Werner and Jack over the years. The price they paid emerged in the look on Werner's face when Werner took out the Reich Marshal's photograph and said, "We keep Uncle Hermann hidden." And Jack hoped to finally tell Werner about his assassination orders but could not bring himself to face Werner with the truth and then to ask for his best friend's understanding and forgiveness. Yet both men bore their burdens with remarkable resilience and lived their lives as friends in war and peace in ways that anyone can admire.

The last time I saw Werner, he said, "War is a nasty, nasty thing. It really made me more aware of the reality of evil in the world." His prayers for survival, he is convinced, were answered by the Almighty. As part of the deal, Werner devoted his life to prayer and charitable works, in part to honor the Lord but also to try to atone for the evil to which his name and, he believed, his blood had bound him.

Werner inspected me with piercing blue eyes, hands clasped as if in prayer, and said quietly, "I didn't ever get emotional about things and never really had a best friend, except for Rencher. It was a hell of a deal we did together, nothing to be proud of. I never talked about it, because afterward, when I thought of it, I realized it was murder." Goering looked down at his hands and paused for a long moment, "Yet, it wasn't," he repeated, "it wasn't. It was war."

The nighttime panorama from Werner's picture window, high above the city's twinkling lights, resembled nothing less than the view from a bomber's cockpit.

50

EPILOGUE: THE MEN I NEVER MET

When I first contacted Gary Moncur, the Hell's Angels bomb group historian, Gary thought some of the Goering crew might still be alive, including Rencher. Jack, then an active member of the 303rd veterans group, lived in Boise, and Moncur quickly found his phone number. When I asked about Lt. Col. Werner Goering, Moncur's reply was, "Good luck. I've never met, corresponded, or spoken with him."

In the sixty-five years since the end of the war, Werner, the unit's legendary, elusive ghost, attended only a few reunions long ago of the 303rd. No one knew if he was dead or alive—no one, that is, except Jack.

After months of trying, I reached Werner in Tucson. He had spoken briefly with Jack and both had agreed to speak with me. Orall G. Gustafson, the top-turret gunner and flight engineer, in Seneca, South Carolina, did likewise. The wife of tail gunner Weldon "Tex" Mahan said he had recently passed away, one of the thousand WWII veterans who die daily.

The other seven crewmen are all dead. Jack was the eighth to go. Gus Gustafson was the ninth, and Werner the last of the Goering crew. William C. "Iron Ass" Heller died on November 16, 2011, in Las Vegas. Heller had gone on to become a senior commercial pilot after the war and flew passenger planes for three and a half colorful decades. Once, while in the Philippines, Iron Ass, who went everywhere armed with a pistol, shot and killed a man who was attempting to kidnap and rob him at gunpoint, then disarmed the robber's accomplice and took him to the police station. After checking the dead man's identity, the local police commander personally thanked Iron Ass for getting known dangerous criminals off the street and, in the one case, off the planet. He flew as a commercial pilot for thirty-five years with, among other airlines, Lufthansa, the German national airline that Göring once oversaw. His younger brother, Lt. Col. Emerson Heller, served in the air force until he died on his final mission during the Vietnam War. Emerson Heller is buried at Arlington National Cemetery, where Iron Ass will be in early 2012.

Werner never met with a writer or spoke about the war, even to his children, but in his mideighties, they convinced him it was time. Days later, winging my way to Arizona, it hit me: I was about to meet the mysterious, reclusive nephew of Adolf Hitler's designated successor.

I never met that man.

The following week I headed to Boise to meet the assassin.

I never met that man, either.

I just met Werner and Jack, two humble old aviators, warriors and friends who hoped but failed to meet for one final shared moment in the summer of 2010 and honored me with an invitation to join them in Arizona at the Eighth Air Force Reunion during its sixty-fifth victory anniversary. They spoke to each other through me in a way men of their "greatest" generation, to borrow Tom Brokaw's famous phrase, often can't seem to do directly. Telling their story was my mission, and my honor.

NOTES

References to Werner George Goering and his relationship to Hermann Wilhelm Göring are drawn from the following sources: Brian D. O'Neill, *303rd Bombardment Group* (Oxford, UK: Osprey Publishing, 2003); the Web site for the Hell's Angels, 303rd Bomb Group, 358th Goering Crew, http://www.303rdbg.com/358goering.html; Rob Morris, *Untold Valor: Forgotten Stories of American Bomber Crews over Europe in WWII* (Sterling, Va: Potomac, 2006); as well as other referenced sources and Web sites.

Dialogue in certain chapters has been reconstructed from firsthand interviews, mission group reports, post-incident reports, airmen's private journals, and wartime letters home.

Interviews were conducted with the three Goering crewmen then alive—pilot Werner Goering, copilot Jack Rencher, and top-turret gunner Orall Gustafson—as well as with wing commander William Heller. The first two were personal interviews conducted in 2009 in Arizona and Idaho respectively. The latter two were telephone interviews; in Gustafson's case, in 2009, 2010, and 2011; and in Heller's case, 2010 and 2011. The passage of sixty-seven years has no doubt left room for omission, error, or lapses. Dialogue is therefore not a verbatim transcript, but it is the way these aviators all seem to remember the war—as if it happened yesterday. Any errors, which I'm sure exist, are strictly my own.

NOTES

258

p. 8 12.3 percent, Donald Miller: 471–72.

p. 8 U.S. Navy suffered 37,000 deaths: 8thafhs.org/ourhistory.htm.

p. 8 "the highest casualty rate," "Army Battle Casualties and Nonbattle Deaths in WWII: Final Report" (Washington, D.C.: Office of the Adjutant General, 1953): 84–88.

p. 8 "Air war, in large part," Oliver, Aldcroft, 114.

2. THE BOTTOM RUNG

p. 10 "the foremost non-interventionist": www.marxists.org/glossary/orgs/a/m.htm.

p. 11 "If I should die tomorrow," Freidel: 323.

p. 15 Managed to keep: Kennedy, *Freedom from Fear:* 68.

p. 15 years when Utah received $7 in federal aid: McCormick: media.utah.edu/UHE/DEPRESSION%2CGREAT.html.

p. 15 Most notorious Nazi, *Third Reich*: Evans, 406.

p. 15 "The annual running costs," Burleigh: 99.

p. 17 "made a much-publicized," Black: 467.

p. 18 A "flabbergasted" Craig: Maiolo, 309.

p. 20 Hermann, obese, morphine-addicted, and happy: Goebbels Diary.

p. 21 "Pilot and navigator error," Hillenbrand: 61.

p. 21 "largest single educational organization," Ambrose, *The Wild Blue:* 52.

3. GERMAN AMERICANS IN WWII

p. 23 Census Bureau, Census Bureau, "S0201. Selected Population Profile in the United States" 2006–2008 data.

p. 24 "Two Americans of German," Burleigh: 506.

p. 24 "Reliable estimates place," "German American Bund," U.S. Holocaust Memorial Museum Encyclopedia: www.ushmm.org/wlc/en/article.php¿ModuleId=10005684.

p. 25 Such events made their way FBI, "Frederick Duquesne Interesting Case Write-up" (Washington, D.C.: Freedom of Information Act, March 12, 1985): www.fbi.gov/about-us/history/famous-cases/the-duquesne-spy-ring.

4. J. EDGAR HOOVER

p. 27 "confidential letter of transmittal," US War Department Military Intelligence Division De-Classified Files of Werner G. Goering": 1.

p. 27 "confidential letter of transmittal," "Declassified Files of Werner G. Goering," U.S. War Department, Military Intelligence Division; hereafter "Goering Files": 1.

p. 29 "All entrances to the building," See description of building at U.S. General Services Administration Web site: www.gsa.gov/portal/ext/html/site/hb/category/25431/actionParameter/exploreBy Building/buildingId/321.

p. 30 "As Secretary of State for War and Air," Ferguson, *War of the World:* 558.

p. 30 "as she was wont to do," Black: 424.

p. 32 variously described as Göring's cousin, Read: 420.

5. A MATTER OF NATIONAL SECURITY

p. 33 "'When we get good and ready,'" Black: 623.

p. 34 "The attached communications," "Goering Files": 2.

p. 36 "During the war, approximately forty B-17s," Sion: 34.

p. 36 Dornier Do 200, Sion: 35.

p. 38 "With a pistol in his hand," Frater telephone interview with Gladys Rencher-Aston, Jack's sister, 2010.

7. BOOTLEGGERS, BODYGUARDS, AND BANK ROBBERS

p. 44 Lionel Bert "Breezy" Cox: for a photo of Cox, see http://tinyurl.com/3p4ffm5.

p. 46 "From the time it was numbered," Rosenblum: 13–14.

p. 47 "sold the ice," Rosenblum: 5.

8. OFFICER, GENTLEMAN, AND PILOT

p. 50 "The Great Depression had taken a physical," Roberts, *Storm of War:* 214.

9. TEX RANKIN

p. 53 "ace of aces": "Richard Ira Bong," AcePilots.com: www.acepilots.com/usaaf_bong.html.

p. 54 "had been known to Americans," Roberts, *Storm of War:* 303.

p. 54 "superstition-defying antics," "Ted Rankin and His Legacy—50 Years Later," Oregon Aviation Museum: www.visi.com/~bsimon/OregonAviationMuseum/Tex.html.

10. FLIGHT TRAINING

p. 58   In the mid-1930s, North American Aviation, "American Aircraft of WWII," Century of Flight: www.century-of-flight.net/Aviation %20history/photo_albums/timeline/ww2/2/T%206%20Texan .htm., 58.

p. 58   North American Aviation's technical representative, "History Rebuilt," *Tora! Tora! Tora!*: www.toratoratora.com/historyrebuilt.html.

11. THE NAZI'S NEPHEW

p. 62   Göring was the last: Irving, *Göring:* 40.

12. TO ARMS

p. 70   *Empress of Ireland,* www.theshipslist.com.

p. 71   These ships formed: Satchell: 9

p. 71   "Ballads and classical works," www.sputnikmusic.com.

p. 71   "Remember you are coming," U.S. Army War Department pamphlet, 1942; www.tircuit.com/bandofbrothers/messages/18/18.html.

p. 72   "But many never did," Nichol and Rennell: 92–93.

p. 72   "The more Stalin pressed," Ferguson, *Second World War:* 39.

p. 72   Neville Chamberlain's 1938 declaration that "Air attacks against civilians are a violation of international law," Garrett, 168.

p. 72   "The progressive destruction," Combined Chiefs of Staff of the Western Allies Communiqué issued following Casablanca Conference: http://en.wikipedia.org/wiki/Casablanca_directive#cite_note-USDS -781-4.

p. 72–73   "bombardment from the air," Kennedy, *Freedom from Fear:* 426.

p. 74   "As bombers flew," "WWII Military Service, Clifton Morris Pyne, 16 April 2002, Orem, Utah": www.orem.org/PDF/Vet/Pyne_Clifton.pdf.

13. FRUIT OF A POISONED TREE

p. 75   The first zeppelin: Untitled, Spartacus Educational; www.spartacus .schoolnet.co.uk/FWWzeppelinraids.htm.

p. 76   "on the blacklist," Pearson.

14. THE BLUE MAX

p. 78   "Technically, he had laid himself," Mosley: 33.

p. 80   "a personal triumph", Manvell and Fraenkel: 84.

p. 80   "From this period, Göring's," Ibid.

15. MOLESWORTH

p. 81–82   in Old English, *mulesword:* www.houseofnames.com/molesworth
-family-crest: 1.

p. 83   Molesworth had the distinction, Smith: NA.

16. INTO THE FRAY

p. 84   "The beginning of 1942," Groom: overleaf, http://en.wikipedia.org/
wiki/RAF_Molesworth.

p. 84   "Among every hundred," Hastings: *Armaggen*, 315.

p. 85   "lost two of its engines," Korda: 359.

p. 85   "Obviously knows nothing," Rick Atkinson, 466.

p. 85   "Monty boasted," Ibid.: 372–3.

17. WHAT FRESH HELL IS THIS?

p. 87   Stricken with Bell's palsy, Donald Miller: 104.

p. 87   "[LeMay] masked this facial paralysis," Budge, "Curtis E. LeMay."
The Pacific War Online Encyclopedia 2007–2009; http://pwencycl.kg
budge.com/L/e/LeMay_Curtis_E.htm.

p. 88   "Directly below us," "303rd BG (H) Combat Mission No. 187: 21
June 1944": www.303rdbg.com/missionreports/187.pdf.

p. 89   "From the ground a formation," Nicholl and Renell: Tail-End Charlies, 98.

p. 89   "big heavy monster," Nichol and Rennell: *Tail-End Charlies*, 99

18. HELL OF A MESS

p. 90   "Two doctors," Nichol and Rennell: 145.

p. 91   "In 1944, 2,835," Carroll: 27–28.

p. 91   "Low morale among the aircrews," Craven and Cate: 306.

p. 93   "Struck poor pilot," Stenbuck: 120–21.

p. 93   "Landing a fortress," Stenbuck: 124.

p. 94   "Approximately 86 percent," Palmer: 607.

p. 94   "The Mighty Eighth," Freeman, 64.

p. 94   "was to be expected," Palmer: 557.

19. ASSASSIN'S DILEMMA

p. 99   "My crew was stellar," Correspondence from Heller, 2011.

20. MURDERSBURG

p. 104   "like half a bloody glove,": Roberts, *Storm of War*: 365.

p. 105   "In a single cloud front," Garfield: 159.

p. 105   "Flak was heavy," Gabay: 2, Mission 15.

p. 105   In the fall and early winter of 1944, Sion: xiv.

p. 108   "Within the vast daily effort," Freeman, Crouchman, and Maslen: 371.

p. 108   On October 25, 1944, *The Second World War: A Day by Day Account*: http://homepage.ntlworld.com/andrew.etherington/1944/10/25.htm.

p. 109   "Like a donkey on ice," Donald Miller: 85.

p. 111   "They came in from nose," Malone (mission report #22, 9-12-44).

21. IRON ASS

p. 114   "with less propriety," Donald Miller: 80.

p. 115   "Lucky Strike Green Has Gone to War," Barbara Mikelson, "Bull's Eye Logo," Snopes.com: www.snopes.com/business/market/luckystrike.asp.

p. 115   "a convenient way": http://en.wikipedia.org/wiki/Lucky_Strike.

p. 116   "prime month of the war," Craven and Cate: 644.

p. 117   "so dark from flak," Donald Miller: 318.

p. 117   An early British analysis, Burleigh: 489.

p. 117   334 Leuna workers, Bowden: 153.

p. 118   "Over [that] period," Miller: 315.

p. 118   "fine esprit de corps," www.303rdbg.com/missionreports/089.pdf.

p. 118   The Eighth Air Force's twenty: Bowden: www.usaaf-noseart.co .uk/mbfo(150-153).pdf.

p. 118   1,412 airmen: Bowden.

p. 120   "utter disregard for his," http://militarytimes.com/citations-medals -awards/recipient.php?recipientid-1582.

p. 120   "For sheer determination," http://en.wikipedia.org/wiki/James_H. _Howard.

p. 120   "The following week," Ibid.

p. 121   the Oscherleben "mission," www.b17queenofthesky.com/mission stories/missionfive.html.

p. 122   "thick belt of haze," www.303rdbg.com/missionreports/275.pdf.

p. 123   "You couldn't get into Germany," "Recollections of the Mission to Merseburg, 21 November 1944: An Interview with Bob Welty,

November 28, 1997," 398th Bomb Group Memorial Association: www.398th.org/History/Veterans/History/Welty/Interview_Welty_Merseburg.html.

p. 124   Speer had "effectively dispersed aircraft production," Craven and Cate: 658.

p. 124   "there had been no corresponding rise," Ibid., 641, 658.

p. 124   "The Nazis were able to reconstruct," Ibid.: 641.

p. 127   "the price the heavies paid," Freeman: 82.

22. THE FORT

p. 129   "They were intended to be flown," Kennedy: 604.

p. 129   Norden bombsights cost, Sion: 21.

p. 129   "grease, stale sweat," Donald Miller: 84.

p. 129   "the pilot and co-pilot," Ibid.

p. 130   The crews were wary of, "Recollections of the Mission to Merseburg, 21 November 1944: An Interview with Bob Welty, November 28, 1997," 398th Bomb Group Memorial Association: www.398th.org/History/Veterans/History/Welty/Interview_Welty_Merseburg.html.

23. BLOODRED SKY

p. 132   "I could see the skipper," Freeman: 207.

p. 132   "Every time I stood up," Ibid.: 208.

p. 132   "I only remember," Ibid.: 208.

p. 136   Whisner was credited with, Frisbee. (After retiring, Colonel Whisner was killed, in 1989, by another type of aerial foe after being stung by a yellow jacket at home in Louisiana.)

24. HEAVING THE MONSTER

p. 138   "Crews often returned with uniforms," Kennedy: 605.

p. 138   "Of course it stayed there," "History of the B-17 Flying Fortress," 91st Bomb Group (H): www.91stbombgroup.com/91st_info/91history.html.

p. 142   "almost half still drowned," The United States Army Air Forces in WWII: Aeromedical Challenges in Mounting an Attack from Great Britain: www.usaaf.net/wwa/medical/mspg7.htm.

p. 142   *The Tweachuous Wabbit,* Freeman: 181.

25. HOMEWARD

p. 145   "Where are the rest?" Allen Ostrom, "Merseberg . . . Dreaded Merseberg: This Target Would Prove Costly to the 398th": 398th Bomb Group Memorial Association: www.398th.org/History/Arti cles/Remembrances/Ostrom_Merseburg.html. (Unknown to Lieutenant Johnson, some of the 398th planes returned safely but were forced to land at other airfields.)

26. THE FINAL FLIGHT OF *JERSEY BOUNCE JR.*

p. 150   "They cut one of his wings off," O'Neill, *Half a Wing*: 258.

p. 150   "Just five months earlier," "Saving Sergeant Buske," Hell's Angels, 303rd Bomb Group (H); www.303rdbg.com/saving-buske.html.

p. 150   "I'm hit," www.homeofheroes.com, Douglas Sterner.

p. 152   "I couldn't see very well," "Technical Sergeant Forest Lee Woody Vosler," *Home of Heroes:* www.homeofheroes.com/wings/part2/13_ vosler.html.

p. 153   "There were only a few days," Ibid.

p. 153   "He was shrapnel from his forehead," Ibid.

p. 153   "A day will come in combat," US Army Air Forces, NA. www .homeofheroes.com/wings/part2/13_vosler.html.

p. 153   "Struggling against his pain," www.homeofheroes.com/wings/ part2/13_vosler.html.

p. 154   "As we were throwing," Ibid.

p. 154   "to give a holding signal," Ibid.

p. 155   "I jumped," Ibid.

27. THE BATTLE TO LIVE

p. 156   Continued through, Brown, 23.

p. 156   "Because of his extremely critical condition," Brown: 23.

p. 157   "Damn it," Ibid., 24.

p. 158   "I guess I won't see," "Technical Sergeant Forest Lee Woody Vosler," *Home of Heroes*: www.homeofheroes.com/wings/part2/13_vo sler.html.

28. GONE WITH THE WATER

p. 159   terrible weather: Fred Atkinson

p. 159   "Next to a letter," Butcher: 203–205.

p. 159-60   the Goldfish Club, "Ditched B-17s & Goldfish Club Members,"
Hell's Angels, 303rd Bomb Group: www.303rdbg.com/goldfish.html.

p. 160   "had not informed them," Goss: 55–56.

p. 161   "who had been ridiculed," Howard: N/A.

p. 162   "an error in judgment," Eforgan: N/A.

29. THE HELL'S ANGELS

p. 164   "even Clark Gable," Donald Miller: 139.

p. 164   Hitler and Göring both knew: Donald Miller: 119.

p. 164   "offered his fliers a reward," Ibid.

p. 164   *Combat America,* www.archive.org/details/combatam1945.

p. 164   "The flak was so thick," "303rd BG(H) Combat Mission No. 17, 26
February 1943": www.303rdbg.com/missionreports/017.pdf.

30. AERO MEDICINE

p. 166   Military airplanes were flying much faster, Nanney: www.airforce
history.hq.af.mil/oldsite/online/nanney.pdf.

p. 166   For tests deemed too dangerous: Whipps.

p. 167   "In the air, every 1,000," Garfield: 161.

p. 167   "The worst difficulty," Ibid.

p. 167   Even as late as 1944: Military Channel, "Future Weapons: Alaska";
aired January 27, 2011.

p. 167   "At 26,000 feet," Klinkowitz: 82.

p. 168   "Fliers . . . went woozy," Kennedy: 605.

p. 168   "The social role of alcohol," Jones: 185.

p. 168   "Regardless of how drunk we got," Garfield: 167.

p. 169   "This typically occurs," "Hypothermia," *Wikipedia*: http://en.wiki-
pedia.org/wiki/Hypothermia#cite_note-pmid7632602-23.

p. 169   Early in the war, Nanney: 19.

p. 170   "There is also strong circumstantial evidence," Donald Miller: 128.

p. 170   In 1942 and 1943, www.usaaf.net/ww2/medical/mspg7.htm.

p. 172   "a bearing from an aircraft's engine," USSTAF; see also photo
section.

p. 172   "It is a sad reflection," Ibid.

31. THE WRITING 69TH

p. 173   "stunned two friends," Hamilton, "Sample Chapter: Bob Post":
greenharbor.com/bobpost.html.

p. 173   "There are ten of us," Hamilton, "Sample Chapter: The Writing 69th": greenharbor.com/wr69chap.html.

p. 174   "Ironically, the Writing 69th," Hamilton, "Sample Chapter: Conclusion": www.greenharbor.com/wr69conc.html.

p. 174   "further diminishing the status," Ibid.

p. 174   "Newspapers often neglected," quoted in Ibid.

p. 174   Jimmy Stewart: Ibid.

p. 174   "There were eight minutes," Rooney: 100.

p. 175   The following dawn, "Mark and Jack Mathis," *Home of Heroes*: www.homeofheroes.com/wings/part2/05_mathis.html.

p. 175   Lead bombardier Jack Mathis, "Medal of Honor Recipients: World War II (M–S): history.army.mil/html/moh/wwII-m-s.html.

p. 176   "His last word," "303rd BG(H) Combat Mission No. 24, 18 March 1943": www.303rdbg.com/missionreports/024.pdf.

p. 176   "When a plane blew up," Crosby: 94–95.

32. MEIER'S TRUMPETS

"If an enemy bomber reaches," Roberts: *Storm of War*, 432.

33. SQUEEZING THE NAZIS DRY

p. 182   "It was the highest loss," 457th Bomb Group Association, "Mission No. 127: Cologne, Germany: 27 September, 1944": www.457th bombgroup.org/narratives/MA127.html.

p. 182   "settle down," Donald Miller: 352

p. 182   "The ground fire blew," "303rd BG (H) Combat Mission No. 238": www.303rdbg.com/missionreports/238.pdf.

p. 183   "It began to get terrifying," Ibid.

p. 184   "The aircraft flown by," "303rd BG (H) Combat Mission No. 244: 19 September 1944": 303rdbg.com/missionreports/244.pdf.

p. 184   "We were flying tail end charley," "303rd BG (H) Combat Mission No. 255": www.303rdbg.com/missionreports/255.pdf.

p. 185   "The weather was so bad," "303rd BG (H) Combat Mission No. 244: 19 September 1944": www.303rdbg.com/missionreports/244.pdf.

p. 185   "In my opinion," *IMPACT,* July 1945, 62: www.au.af.mil/au/awc/ awcgate/ww2/nazis/nazidbrf.htm# 0001–0002.

p. 186   "many problems," "Interview with World War II *Luftwaffe* general and ace pilot Adolf Galland," *HistoryNet*: historynet.com/

interview-with-world-war-ii-luftwaffe-general-and-ace-pilot-adolf-galland.htm.

34. PISS ON THE GENERAL

p. 188 "Capt. Eisenhart used this [method]" www.303rdbg.com/359eisenhart.html.

p. 188 "Just prior to liftoff," "Robert F. Travis": www.arlingtoncemetery.net/rftravis.htm.

p. 189 The cover story, Keeney: 71.

p. 189 "The B-17s went through intense," "303rd BG (H) Combat Mission No. 246": www.303rdbg.com/missionreports/246.pdf.

p. 190 "photo reconnaissance planes," Donald Miller: 349.

p. 190 "Adolf Hitler's madness," Donald Miller: 354.

p. 190 After landing, Federici, Federici: 1.

p. 191 "I shall never forget," Speer: 346.

36. DRESDEN

p. 196 "Up till then," Martin Gilbert: 641.

p. 196 "Dresden had been smashed," MacDonogh: 45.

p. 196 The Russians made urgent requests, Roberts: *Storm of War*: 454.

p. 196 In a pitiless twist of fate, Frater, "Hearts and Ashes," 1.

p. 196 "An inharmonious combination," De Bruhl: xvii.

p. 197 "People who were blocks," Ibid.: 212.

p. 197 "It was left to the Americans," Ibid.: 215.

p. 197 "Pathfinders were the *corps d'élite*," Roberts: 447.

p. 197 "We saw terrible things," Halloway.

p. 198 "had once subscribed," author telephone interview with De Bruhl, 2006.

p. 198 Dresden, the Third Reich's: Angell.

p. 198 "By the time the raids finished," Keegan, "Necessary or Not, Dresden Remains a Topic of Anguish": www.fpp.co.uk/online/05/10/Dresden_011105.html.

p. 199 "During the war and after," De Bruhl: 47.

p. 199 "When only 34 percent," Roberts: Storm of War: 247.

p. 199 "Are we beasts?" Ibid.: 453.

p. 199 "disposing of the issue of Dresden," DeBruhl: *Firestorm*: 271.

p. 200 "as an act of terror" Burleigh: 513.

p. 200   "has never been to inflict terror," "1958 Tybee Island Mid-Air Collision," Wikipedia: http://en.wikipedia.org/wiki/1958_Tybee_Island_mid-air_collision

p. 200   "It seems to me that," Roberts: 457.

p. 200   "Churchill's minute," Ibid.

p. 200   "amoral blemish," "this ghastly bloodbath," *Time Watch*, "Bombing of Germany," London BBC productions, 2001.

p. 201   Incredibly, Sir Arthur Harris's request, "Why Political Correctness Has Denied Wartime Bomber Crews the Honour They Deserve," *Daily Mail,* April 2008.

p. 201   "[It] was possible to pulverize a city," Ferguson, *War of the World:* 571.

p. 201   "Reading the log," Ibid.

37. FOG AND FIRE

p. 204   "I was standing," "Memoirs from Molesworth, England—Eugene J. O'Brien (358) Aircraft Mechanic": www.303rdbg.com/journal-obrien-eugene.pdf.

p. 204   "from only half the runway," Ibid.

p. 205   "I was in the waist section," "303rd BG (H) Combat Mission No. 315: 15. February 1945": www.303rdbg.com/missionreports/315.pdf.

p. 205   "The Engineer and myself," Ibid.

38. GÖTTERDÄMMERUNG: TWILIGHT OF THE GODS

p. 205   "The blessing of a time lag," Moody: 38.

p. 210   "soldier to soldier," Irving: 21.

p. 210   Goering told his American captors, Irving: 22.

p. 210   "on the bend of an anonymous lane," Mosley: 430.

p. 211   "Key to his evasion of justice," Von Lingen.

p. 212 $350 billion cost: Roberts: *Storm of War:* 604.

p. 212   "Between August 1945," Futrell: 156.

39. CLOAK, DAGGER, AND CAMERA

p. 214   "air force intelligence," Aronsen.

40. STRATEGIC AIR COMMAND

p. 216   "Well, that changes warfare," Carter: 27.

p. 216   "on October 19, 1948," Boyne: 99.

p. 217   "SACs goals," Rosenberg

p. 218   "Although it was often admired," Keeney: 101.

p. 220   "complete weapon," Howard: 1–2.

p. 220   "Weapons are designed with great," Tiwari and Gray: 1.

p. 221   "I speak of peace," www.jfklibrary.org/research/ready-reference/
jfk-speeches/commencement-address-at-american-university-june
-10-1963.aspx.

41. AFRICA

p. 222   "African maps" Markham: 35.

42. REICHSKOMMISSAR GÖRING

p. 225   "nothing but relentless severity," Kiernan: 381.

p. 225   "opted for ruthlessness," Ibid.: 382–38.

p. 225   On October 2, 1904: Kiernan: 383.

p. 226   "died like flies," Kiernan: 385.

p. 226   "Cold—for the nights," Silvester and Erichsen.

p. 226   In 1905, the German language adopted: Davies: 325.

p. 226   "His son Hermann," Ibid.: 325.

p. 226   "proved to be,": Kiernan: 386.

p. 226   In 1912, a study of: Fetzer.

p. 227   "Yet it was," Madley: 451.

p. 227   "the position of my father": Ibid.

p. 227   "it was Göring's father's experience,": Ibid.

44. THE LION OF JUDAH

p. 230   On October 14, 1954, www.heraldica.org/topics/orders/garterlist
.htm.

p. 230   "the first and to date," http://en.wikipedia.org/wiki/order_of_the_
garter.

46. JACK'S POSTWAR YEARS

p. 240   "recruited [Jack Rencher] to watch," Morris 143

49. "THE DEVIL'S COUNT" IS RESURRECTED

p. 250   "This [Werner's] family," Johnson

p. 251   Sometime before his death, Goering, "The Devil's Count," circa
1941.

BIBLIOGRAPHY

PRIMARY SOURCES

In addition to declassified files of Werner G. Goering from the U.S. War Department, Military Intelligence Division, under a Freedom of Information Act request, October 7, 2009, I was able to conduct interviews with a number of the principals in this book and others who were close to them.

Werner G. Goering, Lt. Col. USAF (ret.): personal and telephone interviews, Tucson, Arizona, 2009 and 2010 audiotape; personal photographs, U.S. War Department service records. U.S. War Department, Military Intelligence Division, 7 October 2009.

Jack P. Rencher, 1st Lt. USAAF (ret.): personal and telephone interviews, Boise, Idaho, 2009 and 2010 audiotape; personal photographs, U.S. War Department service records; video circa 2003 at 303rd Bomb Group reunion.

Orall G. Gustafson, Sgt. USAAF (ret.): telephone interviews, 2009 and 2010.

William C. Heller, Maj. USAAF (ret.): telephone interviews and correspondence, 2010 and 2011.

Gary Moncur, 303rd Bomb Group historian: telephone interviews and correspondence, 2009, 2010, 2011.

Vivian Rogers Price, Research Center director, Eighth Army Air Force Library and Archives: telephone interviews, 2009, 2010.

Michael P. Faley, 100th Bomb Group historian and member of Eighth Air Force Historian Society Board of Directors, interview and correspondence.

Jean Prescott, reference specialist, Mighty Eighth Air Force Museum, phone interview, 20 June 2011.

John Pyram King, Lt. Pilot: personal interview, Anna Maria, Fla., 2010.

Gladys Ashton, Jack Rencher's sister: telephone interviews, 2010, 2011.

Phyllis Blackwell, Assistant Managing Editor, North Carolina Medical Journal. Telephone interview, 2011.

Scott Goering, Esq., Werner Goering's son: personal and telephone interviews and correspondence, 2009, 2010.

Carlinda Dirks, Werner Goering's daughter: personal interviews and correspondence, 2009, 2010, 2011.

Zoe Dirks, Werner Goering's grandmother: personal interview 2009 and correspondence 2010, 2011.

Fred Preller, 384th Bomb Group historian: correspondence, 2011.

Douglas L. Keeney, author of *15 Minutes: General Curtis LeMay and the Countdown to Nuclear Annihilation:* telephone interview, 2011.

Brian and Monica Rencher, Jack Rencher's son and daughter-in-law: personal and telephone interviews and correspondence, 2009, 2010, 2011.

Kay Johansen, Jack's niece, daughter of Gladys Rencher Ashton and Roger Ashton, USAAF (ret.): telephone interviews and correspondence, 2009, 2010, 2011.

Marshall De Bruhl, Dresden historian: telephone interviews, 2006, 2011.

Bruce G. Sundlun, Governor and Colonel. USAFR (ret.) WWII B-17 commander in the Eighth Airforce, Eighth Air Force Historical Society. Member, board of directors: personal and telephone interviews and correspondence, April–June 2011, Jamestown, and Providence, R.I.

Michael Korda, author and historian: telephone interviews and correspondence, 2006, 2008, 2009, 2010, 2011.

Baerbel Johnson, German genealogy specialist, Church of the Latter-day Saints Family Library Division: telephone interview and correspondence, July and August 2010.

Martin Koepple, German-based genealogy researcher: telephone interview and correspondence, August 2009

George Hoidra, public affairs director, Eighth Air Force Historical Society: telephone interview, 2010.

Manuscript Collections

Air Force Historical Research Agency, Maxwell Air Force Base, Alabama

Eighth Air Force Fighter Command Reports

The Mighty Eighth Air Force Museum, Pooler, Georgia

Oral History Collections

The Mighty Eighth Air Force Museum, Pooler, Georgia

United States Strategic Bombing Survey (European War) www.anesi.com/ussbs 02htm.

Air Force Official History

Craven, Wesley Frank, and James Lea Cate, eds. *The Army Air Forces in WWII.*

Vol. 1: *Plans and Early Operations, January 1939 to August 1942.* Chicago: University of Chicago Press, 1948.

Vol. 2: *Europe: Torch to Pointblank, August 1942 to December 1943.* Chicago: University of Chicago Press, 1949.

Vol. 3: *Europe: Argument to V-E Day, January 1944 to May 1945.* Chicago: University of Chicago Press, 1951.

Vol. 6: *Men and Planes.* Chicago: University of Chicago Press, 1955.

Vol. 7: *Services Around the World.* Chicago: University of Chicago Press, 1958.

SECONDARY SOURCES

Ambrose, Stephen E. *Citizen Soldiers: The U.S. Army from the Normandy Beaches to the Bulge to the Surrender of Germany, June 7, 1944 to May 7, 1945.* New York: Simon & Schuster, 1997.

———. *The Wild Blue: The Men and Boys Who Flew the B-24s over Germany* 1944–45. New York: Simon & Schuster, 2001.

Angell, Joseph W. "Dresden, Germany, City Area, Economic Reports," vol. 2, Headquarters U.S. Strategic Bombing Survey, 10 July 1945; and "OSS" London, No. B-1799/4, 3 March 1945. U.S.A.F., 1953. www.enotes.com/topic /Bombing_of_Dresden_in_World_War_II#cite_note-USAFHD-2.

Aronsen, Lawrence. "Seeing Red: U.S. Air Force Assessments of the Soviet Union, 1945–1949." *Intelligence and National Security* 16, no. 2 (Summer 2002): 103–32.

Astor, Gerald. *The Mighty Eighth: The Air War in Europe as Told by the Men Who Fought It.* New York: Dell, 1997.

Atkinson, Fred. "The Mysterious Disappearance of Glenn Miller"; http://www .mishmash.com/glennmiller/

Atkinson, Rick. *An Army at Dawn: The War in North Africa, 1942–1943.* New York: Henry Holt, 2002.

Beevor, Antony. *The Fall of Berlin 1945.* New York: Viking, 2002.

Bellany, Ian. *Terrorism and Weapons of Mass Destruction: Responding to the Challenge.* New York: Routledge Taylor and Francis, 2007.

Black, Conrad. *Franklin Delano Roosevelt: Champion of Freedom.* New York: Public Affairs Books, 2003.

Bohn, John T. *Strategic Air Command History 1946–1976 Declassified.* Washington, D.C.: USAF Office of the Historian, 1976.

———. Command Historian SAC Office of the Historian, USAF. Declassified and released DOD USAF SAC files.

Bonsor, N. R. P. *North Atlantic Seaway,* vol. 1. Devon, UK: David & Charles, 1975.

Bowden, Ray. *Merseburg: Blood, Flak and Oil—the Eighth Air Force Missions.* Dorsett, UK: Design Oracle Partnership in association with USAAF Nose Art Research Project, 2008.

Bowman, Martin. *B-17 Flying Fortress Units of The Eighth Air Force.* Oxford: Osprey, 2002: http://tinyurl.com/3rr5wbg.

Boyne, Walter J. *Beyond the Wild Blue: A History of the United States Air Force 1947–1997.* New York: St. Martin's Press, 1997.

Brown, Ivan W. "An Account of Remarkable Valor and Amazing Survival from the Records of the 65th General Hospital, a Duke University Army Reserve Unit of WWII." *North Carolina Medical Journal* 60, no. 1 (January–February 1999).

Bullock, Alan. *Hitler: A Study in Tyranny,* abridged ed. New York: HarperCollins, 1971.

Burleigh, Michael. *Moral Combat: Good and Evil in WWII.* New York: HarperCollins, 2011.

Butcher, Geoffrey. *Next to a Letter from Home: Major Glenn Miller's Wartime Band.* Devon: Sphere Books, 1987.

Buttar, Prit. *Battleground Prussia: The Assault on Germany's Eastern Front 1944–45.* Oxford, UK: Osprey, 2010.

Carroll, James J. "Physiological Problems of Bomber Crews in the Eighth Air Force During WWII." Air Command and Staff College, March 1997; http://tinyurl.com/3p2f8co.

Carter, Dale. *The Final Frontier: The Rise and Fall of the American Rocket State.* New York: Verso Books, 1988.

Chant, Chris. *Allied Bombers 1939–45.* London: Zenith, 2008.

———. *The World's Greatest Bombers.* Edison, N.J.: Chartwell, 2005.

Churchill, Winston. *Memories of the Second World War: An Abridgement of the Six Volumes of the Second World War.* London: Houghton, Mifflin Company, 1959.

Combined Chiefs of Staff of the Western Allies, *Casablanca Directive.* February 4, 1943.

Cox, John Stuart, and Athan G. Theoharis. *The Boss: J. Edgar Hoover and the Great American Inquisition.* Philadelphia: Temple University Press, 1988.

Craven, Wesley Frank, and James L. Cate. *The Army Air Forces in WWII*. Chicago: University of Chicago Press, 1953.

Cronkite, Walter. *A Reporter's Life*. New York: Knopf, 1996.

Crosby, Harry H. *A Wing and a Prayer: The "Bloody 100th" Bomb Group of the U.S. Eighth Air Force in Action over Europe in WWII*. New York: HarperCollins, 1993.

Davies, Norman. *No Simple Victory: WWII in Europe 1939–1945*. New York: Viking, 2007.

Dear, I. C. B., and M. R. D. Foot. *The Oxford Companion to World War II*. Oxford, UK: Oxford University Press, 1995.

De Bruhl, Marshall. *Firestorm: Allied Airpower and the Destruction of Dresden*. New York: Random House, 2006.

Eccles, Marriner S. *Beckoning Frontiers*. New York: Knopf, 1951.

Eforgan, Estel. *Leslie Howard: The Lost Actor*. London: Valentine Mitchells Publishers, 2010.

Evans, Richard J. *The Coming of the Third Reich*. London: Penguin, 2004.

———. *The Third Reich in Power*. New York: Penguin, 2005.

Fawcett, Jack B. "Remembering the Big O." *Hell's Angels Newsletter*, July 1991.

Federal Bureau of Investigation. Army-originated records on Werner George Goering. Maryland: Freedom of Information/Privacy Office, 2009.

Federici, Frank W. "A Sequel to a Kassel Mission Disaster, 7 October 1944"; www.docstoc.com/docs/43723643/On-September-27-1944-the-445th-Bomb-Group-flew.

Ferguson, Niall. *The Second World War as an Economic Disaster*. Cambridge, Mass.: Harvard University Press, 2006. http://www.wcfia.harvard.edu/sites/default/files/Ferguson_SecondWorld.pdf.

———. *The War of the World: Twentieth-Century Conflict and the Descent of the West*. New York: Penguin, 2006.

Fetzer, Christian: *Rassenanatomische Untersuchungen an 17 Hottentottenköpfen, Zeitschrift für Morphologie und Anthropologie*, Bd. XVI. 2003.

Frater, Stephen. "Cry Havoc," *Herald Tribune Media Group*. February 24, 2011.

———. "Hearts in Ashes," *Sarasota Herald-Tribune,* December 24, 2006.

Freeman, Roger A., *The Mighty Eighth: A History of the U.S. Eighth Army Air Force: Units, Men and Machines*. London: Doubleday, 1970.

Freeman, Roger A., Alan Crouchman, and Vic Maslen. *Mighty Eighth War Diary*. London: Jane's Publishing Company, 1981.

Freidel, Frank. *Franklin D. Roosevelt: Rendezvous with Destiny.* Boston: Little, Brown, 1990.

Frisbee, John L. "Valor: A Very Special Ace." *Air Force Magazine* 73, no. 6 (June 1990).

Frischauer, Willi. *The Rise and Fall of Hermann Goering.* Boston: Houghton Mifflin, 1951.

Futrell, Robert. USAF Historical Study No. 69: Development of AAF Base Facilities in the United States, 1939–1945. Washington, D.C.: U.S. Air Force Historical Research, 1951.

Gabay, John. *Diary of a Tail Gunner;* www.historyplace.com/specials/personal /gunner-diary1.htm.

Galland, Adolf. "Interview with WWII Luftwaffe General and Ace Pilot Adolf Galland," June 2006; www.historynet.com/interview-with-world-war-ii -luftwaffe-general-and-ace-pilot-adolf-galland.htm

Garfield, Brian. *The Thousand Mile War: World War II in Alaska and the Aleutians.* Garden City, N.Y.: Doubleday, 1969.

Garrett, Stephen A. *Civilian Immunity in War.* Oxford, UK: Oxford University Press, 2007.

Gilbert, G. M. *Nuremberg Diary.* New York: Da Capo Press, 1995.

Gilbert, Martin. *Descent into Barbarism: A History of the 20th Century, 1933–1951,* vol. 2. London: Harper, 1998.

Gobrecht, Harry D. *Might in Flight: Daily Diary of the Eighth Air Force's Hell's Angels, 303rd Bombardment Group (H).* San Clemente, Cali: 303rd Bomb Group Association, 1997.

———. Werner G. Goering's Crew—358th Bomb Squadron, Hell's Angels: Home of the 303rd Bomb Group Association. 2006.

Goering, Karl F. "The Devil's Count." Salt Lake City, Utah: LDS Archives, circa 1941.

Goss, Chris. *Bloody Biscay: The Story of the Luftwaffe's Only Long Range Maritime Fighter Unit, V Gruppe/Kampfgeschwader 40, and Its Adversaries 1942–1944.* London: Crécy Publishing, 2001.

Groom, Winston. *1942: The Year That Tried Men's Souls.* New York: Atlantic Monthly Press, 2005.

Grose, Peter. *Gentleman Spy: The Life of Allen Dulles.* Boston: Houghton Mifflin, 1994.

Halloway, Tom. "Timewitnesses." *The Fire-bombing of Dresden: An Eyewitness Account of Lothar Metzer.* Berlin, recorded May 1999; http://timewitnesses.org /england/~lothar.html.

Hamilton, Jim. *The Writing 69th.* Green Harbor Publications, 2001; http://www .greenharbor.com.

Harmon, Christopher C. "'Are We Beasts?' Churchill and the Moral Question of WWII 'Area Bombing.'" *The Newport Papers*. Newport, R.I.: Naval War College Press, 1991.

Hastings, Max. *Bomber Command: Churchill's Epic Campaign*. New York: Simon & Schuster, 1989.

———*Armageddon: The Battle for Germany, 1944–1945*. New York: Vintage Books, 2004.

———. *Retribution: The Battle for Japan 1944–45*. New York: Knopf, 2007.

Hillenbrand, Laura. *Unbroken: A WWII Story of Survival, Resilience, and Redemption*. New York: Random House, 2010.

Henig, Ruth B. *Versailles and After: 1919–1933*. New York: Routledge, 1985.

Hoover, J. Edgar. *Masters of Deceit: The Story of Communism in America and How to Fight It*. Whitefish, Mont.: Kessinger Publishing, 1958.

Howard, James H. *Roar of the Tiger*. New York: Orion Books, 1991. http://en.wikipedia .org/wiki/james_h_howard.

Howard, Ronald. *In Search of My Father: A Portrait of Leslie Howard*. New York: St. Martin's Press, 1984.

Howard, W. J. Letter Assistant to the Secretary of Defense (Atomic Energy) to the Chairman of the Joint Committee on Atomic Energy, Congress of the United States (22 April 1966). (PDF)

Hutton, Oram C., and Andy Rooney. *Air Gunner*. New York: Farrar & Rinehart, 1944.

Ed/Auth? *IMPACT*: Interview with Office of the Assistant Chief of Air Staff, Intelligence, July 1945. Leesburg, Va. Wider History Group, 1994; http://tinyurl .com/3hou4ml.

Irving, David. *Apocalypse 1945: The Destruction of Dresden*. London: Focal Point, 1995.

———. *Göring: A Biography*. London: Perforce UK Ltd., 2010.

Jablonski, Edward. *Airwar*, vols. 1–4. New York: Doubleday, 1971.

Jenkins, Roy. *Churchill: A Biography*. London: Penguin, 2001.

Johnson, Baerbel. *The Goerings, 1601–1845*. Salt Lake City, Utah: Church of the Latter-day Saints, Family Library Division, 2010.

Johnson, Richard R. *Twenty-five Milk Runs and a Few Others*. Bloomington, Ind.: Trafford Publishing, 2004.

Jones, David R. *War Psychiatry*. Washington, D.C.: Department of War, Office of the Surgeon General, 1995.

Keegan, John. *The Second World War*. New York: Viking, 1989.

Keeney, L. Douglas. *15 Minutes: General Curtis LeMay and the Countdown to Nuclear Annihilation.* New York: St. Martin's Press, 2011.

Kennedy, David M. *Freedom from Fear: The American People in Depression and War, 1929–1945.* New York: Oxford University Press, 1999.

Kiernan, Ben. *Blood and Soil: A World History of Genocide and Extermination from Sparta to Darfur.* New Haven: Yale University Press, 2007.

Klinkowitz, Jerome. *Yanks over Europe.* Lexington: University Press of Kentucky, 1996.

Koepple, Martin. *The Goerings 1845–1945.* August 2009 (Document updated)

Korda, Michael. *Ike: An American Hero.* New York: HarperCollins, 2008.

———. *With Wings Like Eagles: A History of the Battle of Britain.* New York: Harper-Collins, 2009.

Landry, Tom, with Gregg Lewis. *Tom Landry: An Autobiography.* New York: Harper-Collins, 1991.

Lebor, Adam, and Roger Boyes. *Seduced by Hitler. The Choices of a Nation and the Ethics of Survival.* Naperville, Ill.: Sourcebooks, 2004.

MacDonogh, Giles. *After the Reich: The Brutal History of the Allied Occupation.* New York: Basic, 2007.

Madley, Benjamin. "From Africa to Auschwitz: How German South West Africa Incubated Ideas Adopted and Developed by the Nazis in Eastern Europe." *European History Quarterly* 35, no. 3 (July 2005): 429–464.

Maiolo, Joseph. *How the Arms Race Drove the World to War, 1931–1941.* New York: Basic Books, 2010.

Malone, William A. WWII Air Combat Diary; www.303rdbg/journal.malone.html

Manvell, Roger, and Heinrich Fraenkel. *Goering.* London: Greenhill Books, 1962.

Markham, Beryl. *West with the Night.* New York: North Point Press, 2001.

Mazower, Mark. *Hitler's Empire: How the Nazis Ruled Europe.* New York: Penguin, 2008.

McCormick, John S. *Utah History Encyclopedia.* Salt Lake City: University of Utah Press, 1994.

McCullough, L., and S. Arora. "Diagnosis and Treatment of Hypothermia." *American Family Physician* 70, no. 12 (December 2004): 2325–2332.

Mendes, Sam, director. Steven Spielberg, producer. *Road to Perdition.* (Narration from director's cut.) DreamWorks, 2002.

Miller, Donald L. *Masters of the Air: America's Bomber Boys Who Fought the Air War Against Nazi Germany.* New York: Simon & Schuster, 2006.

Miller, Wayne G. *Providence,* November 19, 2006.

Moncur, Gary. "Hell's Angels: 303rd Bomb Group Combat Missions"; www
.303rdbg.com/missions.html

Moncur, Vern L. *Mission Journal,* p. 7; www.303rdbg.com/missions.html

Moody, Walton S. *Building a Strategic Air Force.* Washington, D.C.: Government Printing Office, 1996.

Morris, Rob. *Untold Valor: Forgotten Stories of American Bomber Crews over Europe in
WWII.* Sterling, Va.: Potomac, 2006.

Mosley, Leonard. *The Reich Marshal: A Biography of Hermann Goering.* New York:
Dell, 1974.

Nanney, James S. *The U.S. Army Air Forces in WWII: Army Air Forces Medical Services in
WWII:* Washington, D.C.: Air Force History and Museums, 1998. www.au.af
.mil/au/awc/awcgate/afhistory/aaf_medical_services_wwii.pdf

New World Encyclopedia, s.v. "Hermann Goering. www.newworldencyclopedia.org
/entry/Hermann_Goering?oldid=955093 (accessed November 18, 2011)

Nichol, John, and Tony Rennell. *Tail-End Charlies: The Last Battles of the Bomber War
1944–45.* London: Viking, 2004.

"Nuremberg Trial Proceedings, Vol. 9: Eightieth Day, Wednesday, 13 March 1946
Morning Session"; http://avalon.law.yale.edu/imt/03-13-46.asp.

O'Brien, Eugene J. "Memoirs from Molesworth, England." Hell's Angels: 303rd
Bomb Group; www.303rdbg.com/journal-obrien-eugene.pdf

Oliver, Michael J., and Derek Howard Aldcroft. *Economic Disasters of the Twentieth
Century.* Cheltenham, UK: Edward Elgar Publishing, Ltd., 2008.

O'Neill, Brian D. *Half a Wing, Three Engines, and a Prayer: B-17s over Germany.* New
York: McGraw Hill, 1999.

———. *303rd Bombardment Group.* Oxford, UK: Osprey Publishing, 2003.

Overy, Richard. *The Dictators: Hitler's Germany, Stalin's Russia.* London: Penguin,
2004.

———. *Interrogations: The Nazi Elite in Allied Hands.* New York: Viking Penguin,
2001.

Palmer, Allan. "Survey of Battle Casualties, Eighth Air Force, June, July, and August 1944." *Wound Ballistics.* Washington, D.C.: U.S. Army Medical Department, 1962; http://history.amedd.army.mil/booksdocs/wwii/woundblstcs
/chapter9.htm.

Pearson, Drew. "The Washington Merry-Go-Round." United Feature Syndicate.
Washington, D.C.: American University Library, Special Collections, 1942.

Persico, Joseph E. *Nuremberg.* New York: Penguin, 1994.

Read, Antony: *The Devil's Disciples: The Lives and Times of Hitler's Inner Circle*. New York: Norton, 2004.

Reese, Diane: Webmaster: www.457thbombgroup.com

Roberts, Andrew. *A History of the English-Speaking Peoples Since 1400*. New York: HarperCollins, 2007.

———. *The Storm of War: A New History of the Second World War*. New York: Harper-Collins, 2011.

Rooney, Andy. *My War*. New York: Public Affairs Books, 2002.

Rosenberg, David A. "The Origins of Overkill: Nuclear Weapons and American Strategy, 1945–1960." *International Security* 7, no. 4 (Spring 1983): 3–71; www .jstor.org/stable/2626731

Rosenblum, Jonathan D. *Copper Crucible: How the Arizona Miners' Strike of 1983 Recast Labor-Management Relations in America,* 2nd ed. Ithaca, N.Y.: ILR Press: 1998.

Satchell, Alistair. *Running the Gauntlet: How Three Giant Liners Carried a Million Men to War, 1942–1945*. London: Chatham, 2001.

Sereny, Gitta. *Albert Speer: His Battle with the Truth*. New York: Knopf, 1995.

Silvester, Jeremy, and Casper Erichsen. "Luderitz's Forgotten Concentration Camp"; www.namibian.org/travel/namibia/luderitzcc.html.

Sion, Edward M. *Through Blue Skies to Hell: America's "Bloody 100th" in the Air War over Germany*. Philadelphia: Casemate, 2007.

Smith, John M. *Airfield Focus 40: Molesworth*. Cambridgeshire, UK: GMS Enterprises, 2000.

Snyder, Timothy. *Bloodlands: Europe Between Hitler and Stalin*. New York: Basic Books, 2010.

Speer, Albert. *Inside the Third Reich*. New York: Macmillan, 1970.

St. Clair, Jeffrey. "The Case of the Missing H Bomb," Weekend Edition, May 15–17, 2009. *Counterpunch*.

Steinbeck, John. *Bombs Away: The Story of a Bomber Team*. New York: Viking, 1942.

Stenbuck, Jack, ed. *Typewriter Battalion: Dramatic Front-Line Dispatches from WWII*. New York: William Morrow, 1995.

Sterner, Douglas C. www.homeofheroes.com

Stiles, Bert. *Serenade to the Big Bird*. Atglen, Pa.: Schiffer Military History, 2001.

Strachen, Hew. *The First World War, Episode Ten:* "World Without End." Hamilton Film Partnership, London, 2003. www.imbd.com/title/tt1718038/.

Sundlun, Bruce G. "The Salamander" (unpublished autobiography).

Tiwari, Jaya, and Cleve J. Gray. *U.S. Nuclear Weapons Accidents*; www.sovrn.com /pdf/articles_u._s._nuclear_weapons_accidents.pdf.

Tobin, Jonathan. "The Most Unethical Act: Losing a War." *Commentary,* 2010; https://www.commentarymagazine.com/download/pdf-archive/1/?a= 15127.

U.S. Army Air Forces. "The Radio Operator." Second Air Force Training Aids Division, 1944; www.homeofheroes.com/wings/part2/13_vosler.html

U.S. Army Air Forces in WWII. "Aeromedical Challenges in Mounting an Attack from Great Britain"; www.usaaf.net/ww2/medical/mspg7.htm

U.S. Census Bureau. "S0201.Selected Population Profile in the United States," 2206–2008 data.

U.S. Strategic Bombing Survey. "Summary Report (European War)." Washington, D.C.: Secretary of War, September 30, 1945; www.anesi.com/ussbs02.htm.

USAAF. Casualties in European, North African and Mediterranean Theaters of Operation 1942–1946.

Von Lingen, Kerstin. "Conspiracy of Silence: How the 'Old Boys' of American Intelligence Shielded SS General Karl Wolff from Prosecution." *Holocaust and Genocide Studies* 22, no. 1 (Spring 2008): 74–109.

War Department, "Escape and Evasion Report." European Theater of Operations, U.S. Army Office of the Assistant Chief of Staff, G-2, Escape and Evasion Section. Administrative Branch (c. 1944, ca 1945).

Welty, Scott. *Oral History November 2007.* www.398th.org/History/Veterans/History/Welty/Interview-Welty-Merseburg.html.

Whipps, Heather. "Parachuting Dog Helped Win WWII." *Science on MSNBC;* www.msnbc.msn.com/id/24405578.

White, David, and Daniel P. Murphy. *WWII: The Roles of Women During the War.* "Women at Work." http://www.netplaces.com/world-war-ii/the-roles-of-women-during-the-war/woman-at-work.htm.

Wyllie, James. *The Warlord and the Renegade: The Story of Hermann and Albert Goering.* Gloucestershire, UK: Sutton, 2006.

NOTE FROM THE GOERING FAMILY

The Goering family's spiritual inspiration for *Hell Above Earth* comes from Romans 8:28–29, which states that we know that, in everything, God works for good to those who love Him and are called according to His purpose and that purpose is to be conformed to the image of His Son Jesus Christ; and from Romans 8:31, which asks if God is for us, who can be against us?

INDEX